Teaching Leadership

NEW HORIZONS IN LEADERSHIP STUDIES

Series Editor: Joanne B. Ciulla, *Academic Director, Institute for Ethical Leadership and Professor of Leadership Ethics, Department of Management and Global Business, Rutgers Business School, USA*

This important series is designed to make a significant contribution to the development of leadership studies. This field has expanded dramatically in recent years and the series provides an invaluable forum for the publication of high quality works of scholarship and shows the diversity of leadership issues and practices around the world.

The main emphasis of the series is on the development and application of new and original ideas in leadership studies. It pays particular attention to leadership in business, economics and public policy and incorporates the wide range of disciplines which are now part of the field. Global in its approach, it includes some of the best theoretical and empirical work with contributions to fundamental principles, rigorous evaluations of existing concepts and competing theories, historical surveys and future visions.

Titles in the series include:

Community as Leadership
Gareth Edwards

Madness and Leadership
From Antiquity to the New Common Era
Savvas Papacostas

The Leadership Imagination
An Introduction to Taxonomic Leadership Analysis
Donald R. LaMagdeleine

Thinking Differently about Leadership
A Critical History of Leadership Studies
Suze Wilson

Politics, Ethics and Change
The Legacy of James MacGregor Burns
Edited by George R. Goethals and Douglas Bradburn

Global Women Leaders
Breaking Boundaries
Regina Wentzel Wolfe and Patricia H. Werhane

Leadership, Popular Culture and Social Change
Edited by Kristin M.S. Bezio and Kimberly Yost

Leadership and the Unmasking of Authenticity
The Philosophy of Self-Knowledge and Deception
Edited by Brent Edwin Cusher and Mark A. Menaldo

Teaching Leadership
Bridging Theory and Practice
Gama Perruci and Sadhana Warty Hall

Teaching Leadership

Bridging Theory and Practice

Gama Perruci

Dean, The Bernard P. McDonough Center for Leadership and Business, Marietta College, USA

Sadhana Warty Hall

Deputy Director, The Nelson A. Rockefeller Center for Public Policy and the Social Sciences, Dartmouth College, USA

NEW HORIZONS IN LEADERSHIP STUDIES

Edward Elgar
PUBLISHING

Cheltenham, UK • Northampton, MA, USA

Published by
Edward Elgar Publishing Limited
The Lypiatts
15 Lansdown Road
Cheltenham
Glos GL50 2JA
UK

Edward Elgar Publishing, Inc.
William Pratt House
9 Dewey Court
Northampton
Massachusetts 01060
USA

A catalogue record for this book
is available from the British Library

Library of Congress Control Number: 2018932700

This book is available electronically in the **Elgar**online
Social and Political Science subject collection
DOI 10.4337/9781786432773

ISBN 978 1 78643 276 6 (cased)
ISBN 978 1 78897 517 9 (paperback)
ISBN 978 1 78643 277 3 (eBook)

Typeset by Servis Filmsetting Ltd, Stockport, Cheshire
Printed and bound in Great Britain by TJ International Ltd, Padstow

To my children – Caroline, Rebecca, and Alexander.
You taught me that parenting *is* leadership. *GP*

To my in-laws Dean and Henry Hall, my parents Kusum and Vasant
Warty, my sisters Gouri Seth and Daksha Warty, and my husband
Richard Hall.
You continue to inspire me to do my best every single day. *SWH*

Contents

Figures

Tables

Appendices

About the authors

Gama Perruci is the Dean of the McDonough Leadership Center and McCoy Professor of Leadership Studies at Marietta College in Ohio, USA. He also serves as a session facilitator for the Rockefeller Global Leadership Program (RGLP) and the Management and Leadership Development Program (MLDP) at Dartmouth College's Nelson A. Rockefeller Center for Public Policy and the Social Sciences, USA. He is the co-author of *Understanding Leadership: An Arts and Humanities Perspective* (Routledge, 2015) and is currently working on a new book, *Global Leadership: A Transnational Perspective* (Routledge, forthcoming). He serves as a consultant for *The New York Times*, focusing on the newspaper's educational programming for leadership students. In that role, he writes a weekly column ("Connecting Theory to Practice") for *The New York Times* on its Education website (nytimesineducation.com). He served as a member of the Ronald Reagan Presidential Library's Academic Advisory Council. He is the Past Chair of the International Leadership Association, Inc. (ILA) Board of Directors – a global nonprofit organization focused on the study and practice of leadership. He served as a member of the National Selection Committee (America's Best Leaders Project) convened by Harvard Kennedy School's Center for Public Leadership in collaboration with *U.S. News & World Report*. He has a Ph.D. in Political Science from the University of Florida, USA, and a Master's in International Journalism from Baylor University, USA.

Sadhana Warty Hall is the Deputy Director of the Nelson A. Rockefeller Center for Public Policy and the Social Sciences at Dartmouth College, USA, where she designs and oversees experiential learning programs for focusing on leadership, public policy, and civic engagement for undergraduate students. She is also a member of the Rockefeller Center's senior management team. In 2015, she received the Sheila Culbert Distinguished Employee Service Award from the President of Dartmouth College in recognition of the excellence she brings to the experiential learning programs that deepen students' knowledge and understanding of public policy and strengthen students' leadership skills at the Center and at Dartmouth College. Other highlights of her work include transforming the

Rockefeller Leadership Fellows Program, initiating the Management and Leadership Development Program in 2009, and launching the Rockefeller Global Leadership Program in 2012. Prior to her appointment at the Rockefeller Center, she worked for more than two decades in international development through Save the Children USA and directed global partnerships and conferences with the Global Health Council. Her experience has also included managing primary healthcare programs for the state of New Hampshire. She holds a B.S. from the University of Delhi, India, an M.A. from the University of Rajasthan, India, and an M.P.H. from the University of North Carolina at Chapel Hill's School of Public Health, USA.

Foreword: facilitating student learning

Susan R. Komives

If asked "Can leadership be taught?" (Parks, 2005), anyone reading this book should shout a resounding "Yes, of course!" and an even louder "*Yes*" to the profound parallel question "Can leadership be learned?" Yet, in reality, the gap between teaching and learning can seem insurmountable. In this book, Gama Perruci and Sadhana Warty Hall provide essential guidance to "inhabit the gap" between teaching leadership and learning leadership (Komives, 2000).

This book invites leadership educators, including teachers, faculty, student-affairs professionals, industry trainers, and supervisors in any sector – including education, for-profit and nonprofit sectors, and government agencies – to pause, and identify and reflect on their personal philosophy of the teaching and learning process. What do you believe about how teaching matters? How do you think students best learn? What environments and experiences can an educator create to best develop the capacity for leadership in individuals, as well as in groups or teams? What learning and developmental outcomes do you aim to address? How do you apply leadership theory to the practice of practice? And every leadership educator, employer, supervisor, and mentor should ask: "What does your own leadership teach through modeling?"

I retired in 2012. Writing this Foreword was a grand opportunity to reflect on lessons from 45 years in higher education focusing on college-student leadership. Some lessons are easy; for instance, every leadership educator must have or must develop a deep and pervasive belief that leadership is both learnable and teachable, and that the way they model leadership is a desirable pedagogical practice.

Some lessons are harder to implement, such as how to design and scaffold meaningful leadership learning experiences. In this book, Perruci and Hall present scaffolding for adding complexity from the study of leadership (education) to include building leadership competencies (training) and ultimately advancing personal leadership growth (development); indeed, they subtitle the book "Bridging Theory and Practice." Scaffolding is hard because it requires that both students and educators have a *growth mindset*

(Dweck, 2006), acknowledging they know they can learn leadership concepts and build effective leadership capacities. Developing a growth mindset and the motivation and readiness to dig deep and learn to apply leadership learning is a critical contribution of this book.

I applaud Perruci and Hall for taking a campus-wide approach to teaching and learning leadership. In 2004, when we wrote *Learning Reconsidered* (NASPA/ACPA, 2004), we reaffirmed that learning was a process that happens across the entirety of the student's experience – their families, jobs, sports teams, classrooms, residence halls, student organizations, friendship groups, religious groups, and service settings. Leadership is happening everywhere a student goes, including in cyberspace and social media. Becoming observers of leadership in action is a crucial step in students' awareness of leadership development.

The goals of learning and developing leadership capacity must include developing students' cognitive complexity, as well as their intrapersonal and interpersonal capacity. Fortunately, models and frameworks exist to guide educators in the design of experiences that promote learning and help educators "inhabit the gap." Baxter Magolda's (2004) Learning Partnership Model provides useful guidance in meeting students where they are, recognizing that they have meaningful experiences, validating them as knowers, and mutually constructing the meaning of new learning that challenges previously held assumptions and beliefs.

I remember a wonderful moment in my leadership classroom at Denison University circa 1975. My co-teacher (an economics faculty member) and I (an associate dean of students) were planning a unit on "power and leadership" for our next class. It was a beautiful spring day, and students clamored that our next class meet outside in a nearby grove of trees, as was often the campus spring tradition. Sharing the organization of content on my overhead transparencies (high tech in those days), I said it just wouldn't be possible; I had to use the overhead projector. Imagine my surprise to arrive to an empty classroom to find a message on the blackboard that said: "We are outside if you'd like to join us!" What a perfect exhibition of power and what a great class discussion jointly making meaning of how they claimed power in the context of the planned lesson!

The leadership development process has to start where students are in their own development, and it needs to attend to the development of two other critical processes addressed in this book: developing leadership self-efficacy and developing a leader identity. Leadership self-efficacy is critical to learning leadership and to engaging in leadership with others. Leadership self-efficacy is explored in this book as a central belief. This belief, in turn, contributes to the student's leader identity. In our leadership identity development research I found it enlightening to realize that one's view or philosophy of leadership is in dynamic reciprocity with how one views oneself as a leader (i.e., one's leader identity). If leadership is viewed only as what a person does when in a position of authority (e.g., the president of the organization), meaning only the leader does leadership, then someone does not believe they are a leader unless they have a title. Developing a more complex view or philosophy will expand students' access to seeing themselves as leaders without a title, and facilitators of the process of leadership when engaged with others working toward shared goals, even if not in a position of authority.

As a dean, I remember observing a student government association (SGA) meeting in which a quiet young woman was clearly following the whole discussion and said nothing until right before a key vote was to be taken. She raised her hand and said: "This has been a great discussion but sometimes confusing. Is it accurate that a 'yes' vote on this motion would mean . . . [and gave a summary] and a 'no' vote would mean . . . [and gave a summary]?" The group clarified further, summarized, and voted. After the meeting I told her: "That showed great leadership to intervene just at the right time and get the issues clarified. Good for you!" She sat up straighter and said: "I didn't realize that was leadership." I affirmed that she was indeed a good leader. Two years later she actually ran for president of the SGA and won. Once she had some language for leadership she started shifting her perspective of leaders and those doing leadership. She told me some months later that this affirmation contributed to her leadership self-efficacy and enhanced her leader identity.

Reading this book was a wonderful experience to affirm there is now a large body of research on *what* students should learn about leadership, as well as *how* students learn leadership. How students learn collaborative, relational leadership is the focus of our Multi-Institutional Study of Leadership (MSL; see leadershipstudy.net), which has over ten years of data studying nearly 500 000 students on 400 college campuses in the United States and several other countries. In this book, Perruci and Hall address several of the high-impact practices in MSL findings, including dialogue skills, mentoring, and community service.

This fine book draws from the liberal-arts experiences of the authors and their work at Dartmouth's Rockefeller Center and the McDonough Center at Marietta College to provide a comprehensive understanding of, for, and about leadership. Their years of experience are translated masterfully to examine the teaching role in exploring leadership training, education, and development of leadership students. Their focus on the roles of the leadership educator as teacher, mentor, curriculum designer, and leader peels away layers of complexity to challenge each educator to develop their own philosophy of leadership, understand their personal commitment to engaged scholarship, and, above all, commit to personal self-exploration to be aware of themselves as leaders.

Along with Perruci and Hall, I invite you to do the hard work to explore yourself, guide students to explore themselves, and together build an engaged learning environment (in the classroom and beyond) that meets students where they are, validates their growth mindsets and that they are knowers, and mutually makes meaning of how complex human beings can effectively work together in messy situations. This book is your support to try new pedagogies, take risks, and trust learners with exploring messy leadership topics with you and with each other. Leadership learning is a process that lasts a lifetime and, for many, it will start in your classroom.

REFERENCES

Baxter Magolda, M.B. (2004). Learning Partnerships Model: A Framework for Promoting Self-Authorship. In M.B. Baxter Magolda and P.M. King (Eds.), *Learning Partnerships: Theory and Models of Practice to Educate for Self-Authorship* (pp. 37–62). Sterling, VA: Stylus.

Dweck, C.S. (2006). *Mindset: The New Psychology of Success.* New York: Random House.

Komives, S.R. (2000). Inhabit the Gap. *About Campus: Enhancing the Student Learning Experience,* 5 (5), 31–2.

NASPA/ACPA. (2004). *Learning Reconsidered: A Campus-wide Focus on the Student Experience.* Washington, DC: National Association of Student Personnel Administrators and the American College Personnel Association.

Parks, S.D. (2005). *Leadership Can Be Taught: A Bold Approach for a Complex World.* Boston, MA: Harvard Business School Press.

Acknowledgments

This book is the result of consultation with many people and models the way in which we believe that leadership should be exercised in the 21st century. A good idea becomes a great idea when it has the input of many, because it combines many perspectives. Even though the process sometimes may feel messy and may take longer than anticipated, it creates a shared vision and even an innovative approach to the task, project, or problem at hand. It is impossible for us to thank all the people who have touched our lives, influenced us to become who we are today, and expanded what we believe about teaching leadership.

The idea for this book grew from an exchange that Alan Sturmer, Executive Editor, Edward Elgar Publishing, had with Joanne Ciulla, Professor Emerita, Jepson School of Leadership Studies, University of Richmond, who edits Edward Elgar Publishing's New Horizons in Leadership Studies series. Sturmer had published a book called *Teaching Entrepreneurship* that followed on a number of books Edward Elgar Publishing had done in different areas over the years that focus on how to teach (the first being 1999's *Teaching Economics to Undergraduates*). Sturmer was now looking to do a volume on *Teaching Leadership*. Ciulla suggested contacting Gama Perruci, who connected with Sadhana Warty Hall, and the rest of the "story" is found in the following chapters. Therefore, we are grateful to Sturmer and Ciulla for the vote of confidence in giving us this exciting project.

Once the project got underway, many key colleagues made significant contributions to its success. First and foremost, we acknowledge the Director of the Rockefeller Center, Andrew Samwick, who gave enthusiastic, unconditional, and unfailing support and encouragement for this project. He dedicated his time, resources, and thoughts to the production of this book. Our respective presidents, Phil Hanlon (Dartmouth College) and Bill Ruud (Marietta College), also played an important role in this project. Through their support, we were able to tap critical resources to bring this project to fruition. Dartmouth's Dean of the College, Rebecca Biron, who is currently developing a college-wide leadership program, contributed ideas for this project.

Our thanks to all the reviewers and contributors of thoughts and ideas to this book: Emily Anderson, Renata Baptista, Alicia Betsinger, Victoria

Blodgett, Tracy Brandenburg, Marc Brudzinki, Eleanor C. Bryan, Melody Burkins, Elizabeth Celtrick, Amanda Childress, Belinda Chiu, Marissa Curry, Lisa Davis, Barbara DeFelice, Hanadi Doleh, Tracy Dustin-Eichler, Francis Eberle, Kirk Eklund, Derek Epp, Gregg Fairbrothers, Courtney Feider, Nathaniel Fick, Robin Frye, Tatyana Gao, Richard Hall, Eric Janisch, Ashley Kehoe, Reese Kelly, Joshua Kim, Barbara Koll, Brian Kunz, Margaret Lawrence, Ying Liu, Tom Luxon, Vincent Mack, Loren Miller, Whit Mitchell, Haroon Moghul, Kristen Moss, John Mott, David Pack, Braden Pan, Ronald Price, Timothy Ruback, Lauren Russell, Belinda Russon, Ken Sharpe, Anne Sosin, Steven Spaulding, Lynn Spencer, John Steidl, Danielle Thompson, David Uejio, Samuel Williamson, Elizabeth Winslow, Amy Witzel, and Yanmin Zhang. From the McDonough Center, we are grateful to Amy Elliot, Christy Hockenberry, Rob McManus, Alexandra Perry, Tanya Judd Pucella, and Maribeth Saleem-Tanner for sharing their expertise in leadership program development. We thank Evan Hensel, Eric Wilken, and Mandee Young for their reflections as leaders in the EXCEL Workshop. We are also grateful to Matt Young from R.C. Brayshaw & Company for designing the figures and appendices in this book.

We owe gratitude to our student program assistants Rik Abels, Milla Anderson, Olivia Bewley, Lauren Bishop, Nicole Castillo, Peter Charalambous, Mark Daniels, Abhilasha Gokulan, Devyn Greenberg, Kristina Heggedal, Acacia Hoisington, Lillian Jin, Will Johnson, Alexander Kushen, Sydney Latimore, Vivian Lee, Meghana Mishra, Savannah Moss, and Sunpreet Singh who all helped with research in the limited hours they had in their busy academic schedules.

We thank alumni of both Centers who participated in a long survey and gave thoughtful responses. Also, thanks to the Rockefeller Center students and alumni who helped crystallize and edit our thoughts: Maura Cass, Esteban Castano, Lee Cooper, Kyle Dotterer, Daniel Fang, Whitey Flynn, Antonia Hoidal, Caitlin Keenan, Terren Klein, Dylan Landers-Nelson, Connor Lehan, Megan McIntire, Julia Marino, Ariel Murphy, Erica Ng, Taylor Ng, Barbara Olachea Lopez Portillo, Faith Rotich, Gustavo Ruiz, Krista Sande-Kerback, Joshua Schiefelbein, Daniel Shlien, Shoshana Silverstein, Iona Solomon, Nancy Vogele, Kate Vonderhaar, and Rui Zhang.

Our thanks to David Ager, Ella Bell, Jay Davis, Sydney Finkelstein, Linda Fowler, Susan Komives, Herschel Nachlis, Julie Owen, Eric Ramsey, Ron Riggio, Ronald Shaiko, Charles Wheelan, and Chris Hardy for reviewing the manuscript. Ben Campbell, Kathryn Guare, Joanne Needham, and Kathleen Perruci, thank you for helping to find the right voice and words. Thank you, Susan Komives, for your feedback and for writing the

Foreword! We also express our gratitude to the Board members of the Rockefeller and McDonough Centers. Here, we add a special thank-you to Fritz and Glenda Corrigan, Ron Schram, and Curt Welling. We truly appreciate their support and dedication to developing leadership programming at the Rockefeller Center!

Our heartfelt thanks to Kaitlin Gray and Erin McVicar for editorial and project management, Adrian Baggett for the cover design, and Helen Moss for the copy-editing. We appreciated their skill and collaborative approach in bringing this book to fruition.

Our families and family members supported us patiently through this project. Special thanks to Richard Hall, Gouri Seth, Daksha Warty, Shashank and Shubhangi Sarwate! Thank you, Kathleen Perruci, Caroline Perruci, Rebecca Perruci, and Alex Perruci.

Introduction

We sometimes hear from skeptical faculty, staff, students, parents, or employers this question: "Can you really *teach* leadership?" The emphasis of the question tends to fall on the word "teach." In a nutshell, the direct answer to this question is "Yes, you can."

But that is the simple answer. As in all matters of human phenomena, the real answer is much more complex and deserves a deeper investigation than simply those three words. And that is what has compelled us to write this book – to explain what we mean when we say "Yes, we can teach leadership."

In saying that we can teach leadership, we challenge faculty and staff as educators, as well as students, parents, or employers, to confront this question directly by addressing four other questions: What do we mean by teaching leadership? Why is it important to teach leadership? How do we teach leadership? And what impact does our leadership teaching have on our learners?

This book is written for educators in undergraduate and graduate-level leadership programs in universities, professional schools, technical institutes, and government institutions, as well as for those working in for-profit and not-for-profit organizations. These educators seek intellectual challenges, resources, and pedagogical tips to expand their instructional capabilities. While this book is written based on our personal experiences in developing and implementing programs in two liberal-arts institutions in the United States, we believe that concepts covered in the book also transcend national or cultural boundaries. We encourage readers to adopt, adapt or adjust this information to their particular situations and cultural contexts.

This book is written with a particular point of view about leadership. Challenging as it is, leaders must strive to make a positive difference in the lives of others and on our world. This requires empathy. Put simply, empathy is the ability to share and understand the feelings of others. In addition, we strongly believe that leaders should be elegant. This means they should have a leadership presence, inspire confidence in others, and use and choose words intentionally. They should be humble, honest, full of integrity, and transparent. Leaders should demonstrate empathy and other traits, all of which can be practiced, learned, and enhanced through training and deep reflection.

Leaders can be found or developed in formal and informal ways. Some are selected or elected to formally serve as "positional leaders." Others might serve as informal leaders within institutions and their communities. Regardless, as formal or informal leaders living and working at all levels within organizations and our global society, they should model behaviors that generate joy, hope, promise, and thoughtful engagements with others. Leadership by inciting fear or division is never a healthy option for society – domestically or globally.

The question "Can you teach leadership?" usually carries certain assumptions about the nature and value of leadership. The way this question is asked tends to reflect a biased view of nature versus nurture, which suggests that leaders are born and not made. We believe that leadership offers value, and we need good leadership to make a positive difference in the world. To achieve this, we need engaged leaders, along with followers who are concerned and engaged citizens. Our goal as educators should be to create the conditions in which we inspire leaders and engaged citizens alike.

At the programmatic level, we have to address questions related to methodology and expected outcomes: How do leadership programs add value? What are we doing well programmatically? What gaps do we need to address? What are some techniques that will enhance our teaching of leadership? We invite participants and educators in leadership programs to walk away with this understanding: it's all about you and not at all about you. It is about striking the delicate balance between focusing on yourself to become self-aware and working with others to make an impact on communities and causes that are larger than yourself.

Often, the students who choose to participate in leadership programs have been told from an early age that they were born to be leaders. Growing up, they were encouraged to take on leadership roles in school and in the community. For the students who did not grow up hearing that they were "natural" leaders, the idea of participating in a structured leadership program can be intimidating. Yet our programs are just as beneficial to these students as they are to the so-called "born leaders." The reality is that our methodologies should take into consideration that teaching leadership goes beyond the nature versus nurture debate. Our programs must offer personal and professional growth experiences that will challenge all of our students, both intellectually and developmentally.

Why is it important to teach leadership? While much of the pragmatic focus centers on the individual benefits that a leadership program may bring to the emerging leaders, leaders also provide an important social function. The empirical study of leadership may be only a hundred years old, but philosophers and political thinkers have written about and dealt with concepts and issues related to leadership for millennia, as far back as Plato's discussion of leadership in the *Republic* in 500 BCE.

Thus, this book is also written with the point of view that institutions and organizations in the for-profit, nonprofit, and public-service sectors need good and effective leaders. As educators in higher education, the more we do to prepare both positional and informal leaders to take on leading roles and strive to make a positive difference, the better off the world will be. This is not an idealistic proposition. It is grounded in realistic expectations that societies work best when they have highly educated leaders who are well versed in the complexities of leadership.

Teaching leadership matters because properly prepared leaders can make a hugely positive difference in our lives. The opposite is also true. We seem to willingly accept the idea that leaders do not need some basic education and training in order to perform satisfactorily, and yet we are sometimes surprised by the ineptitude of our leaders in action. The stakes, therefore, are high. As educators, we play a critical role in preparing the next generation of leaders not only to appreciate the complexities of leadership, but also to translate that knowledge into productive action, yielding substantive results.

Our focus on the connection between theory and practice springs from our concern that many aspiring leaders view themselves as "natural" leaders who are able to exercise leadership on the fly. They eagerly jump into action without having an understanding of how leadership works. To us, that is comparable to giving a piano to a child and expecting him or her to learn how to play simply by hitting the keys over and over again.

Yes, there are virtuoso players who quickly master the instrument and surpass the best of instructors. Those are rare cases. For most of us, the art and science of learning to play an instrument require long hours of focused practice – *and* proper instruction. One of the chief benefits of instruction, piano teachers tell us, is to avoid the development of bad habits, which keep a good player from becoming a great player.

And so it is with leadership. As an educator, you will help aspiring leaders to become aware of the theories and practices of leadership in a way that allows them to develop good habits. As learners master both the content and the experiential side of leadership, they will also discover their own voices. We should not teach leadership with a cookie-cutter approach. Each aspiring leader has his or her own personality. Your role as an educator is to help those leaders grow and become competent contributors to society.

This book is designed to give you an opportunity to engage in deep introspection. Throughout, we list reflection questions to help you become a more thoughtful educator of leaders. You can use these questions for personal reflection or as discussion questions with your colleagues. We encourage you to adapt them to meet your needs. We also hope that this process helps you and your learners to articulate your own philosophy of leadership and that this book will help you gain a deeper understanding of the impact that you have on future generations of leaders. "Teaching" leadership requires the educator to create and establish an environment in which it is at times difficult to pick out the educator and the participant. The end result is a platform upon which educators and students alike tread the path of lifelong learning.

The book is divided into three parts. In Part I, we explore teaching about leadership with a focus on the curricular side of leadership education. Aside from reviewing the empirical study of leadership, we suggest a leadership curriculum that takes into consideration the different components of leadership – leaders, followers, goals, context, and cultural norms or values – while at the same time recognizing that leadership draws its intellectual strength from a wide variety of fields.

In Part II, we focus on developing leadership competencies and capacities through co-curricular programming. We stress the importance of establishing a learning environment that promotes leadership competency and capacity. Through careful program conceptualization, we can establish powerful opportunities for our learners. Planning effective sessions can enhance the impact that our programs have on the participants. We appreciate the reality that some programs are more resource-intensive than others and that some schools or institutions are more fortunate than others to have resources directed toward leadership activities. But, regardless of resource intensity, the principles that make leadership programs great is being mindful, intentional, and organized in developing, implementing, and evaluating a program. When educators do all of this, they are likely to see results, which will create an effective argument for securing resources.

Part III builds on the other two components by searching for and exploring ways in which leaders can continue to grow and develop. As leaders in our world today, we face the daunting task of staying equipped to address challenges we face as the world around us changes rapidly. We suggest that understanding the complex facets of leadership and developing leadership skills and competencies prepare our students to grow even more after they graduate and can apply lessons learned in a workplace setting. This growth depends on: understanding the importance of mentoring and being mentored; recognizing that growing as leaders is a lifelong process; and developing the ability to practice "practical wisdom." As educators, we should create intellectually supportive environments in which our efforts continue to play a role beyond the campus walls.

The three separate parts of this book are not designed to build silos, and we recognize that leadership studies is a complex enterprise that does not necessarily fall into neat, separate categories. Rather, the three parts of the book provide an examination of the aspects that, once brought together, can have a powerful impact on our graduates and our world.

Curricular and co-curricular initiatives live in interconnected spaces that provide opportunities for integrated programming. "Curricular" in this context refers to courses that focus on leadership or incorporate leadership that are offered for academic credit. "Co-curricular" refers to activities, workshops, programs, or experiences that inform and complement subjects that students are learning through academic course work and can lead to leadership certificates or other credentials.

After reading this book and putting many of its suggestions into practice, you will be participating in an academic movement that goes beyond intellectual curiosity. The next time a skeptical educator, student, parent, or employer asks you if you can teach leadership, you will be ready to launch into an exhilarating discourse about the different ways this question can be answered – and how the answer informs the approach we take to addressing the urgent need to develop leaders for a complex and challenging world.

This book represents a collaboration between two academic centers at two different institutions and has been successful because we have similar missions as well as a similar understanding and approach to leadership education and development. As co-authors, we have been influenced by Paulo Freire's teachings and, in particular, his message in *Pedagogy of the Oppressed*. This influence has informed how experiential learning can be incorporated at our respective organizations.

This collaboration has enabled both institutions to reflect on their efforts and, we hope, add to the body of knowledge regarding leadership and teaching leadership. As co-authors, we also share common values and believe that having fun is an important part of co-creating a product. We are committed to continuously seeking to improve the quality of our curricular and co-curricular offerings and to try new, and potentially more effective, ways of presenting new information, and we encourage you to do the same.

This book represents several years of experimentation and rework to create programs that are responsive to our learners. At the time of this writing, programs we established have undergone many changes. For this, we thank all our colleagues and the speakers who, despite their busy schedules, have shown patience, enthusiasm, and dedication to making responsive and relevant programs for participants.

We also have received early indications that the approach and methodologies we have outlined in this book may be applicable in various settings.

For example, alumni participating in our leadership programs have used them in for-profit and not-for-profit settings. Finally, a leadership program for post-doctoral candidates is being conceptualized. So please use, adopt, adapt and adjust the information contained in this book to fit your own mission and vision. As you venture forth to teach leadership, we look forward to hearing from you about what works and what does not work in your particular context. We wish you success in implementing any of the lessons described in this book and from your independent exploration of this important topic.

PART I

Teaching about leadership

In Part I, we explore teaching about leadership with a focus on the curricular aspect of leadership education. In addition to reviewing the empirical study of leadership, we suggest a leadership curriculum that takes into consideration the different components of leadership – leaders, followers, goals, context, and cultural norms and values. At the same time, we recognize that leadership draws its intellectual strength from a wide variety of fields.

Leadership studies is a nascent discipline. After a century of empirical research in this area, leadership programs are gaining enough intellectual confidence to stake a claim in higher education. On many campuses, we see the establishment of leadership departments, centers, and schools. There are many disciplinary approaches to the study of leadership. In this part, we will introduce some of these examples and suggest a possible curriculum that seeks to capture the analyses found at the individual, team/community, organizational, and global levels in leadership education.

Through these chapters, we hope that you will explore leadership as a complex human phenomenon that goes beyond a study of individual traits of leaders. When teaching about leadership, let's help our learners gain a deeper understanding of the leader–follower relationship. While the trait approach continues to be the focus of many leadership programs, as educators let's challenge our learners to delve into the nuances of leadership as a relational process. We invite you to adopt, adapt, and adjust the contents of the chapters that follow.

1. Teaching leadership

When reviewing the promotional materials of most colleges and universities in the United States, we are hard pressed to find any without the use of the word "leader" or "leadership." Regardless of the size of the institution (from small liberal-arts to research institutions), leadership seems to be a prized commodity. Yet, when we delve deeper into their catalogues and websites, the numbers dwindle. Teaching leadership goes beyond thoughtfully articulated mission statements. An examination of history and context matters in teaching leadership, because it provides insights into how leadership is taught and conceived of in different institutions. It also requires careful attention to the way we build curricular and co-curricular initiatives that expand our learners' knowledge, competencies, and development in meaningful ways.

This chapter reviews the evolution of teaching leadership and its place in higher education. We approach the teaching of leadership as having three conceptual approaches – as an intellectual enterprise (the study of leadership), competency-building (leadership training), and the promotion of leadership development. We also frame the teaching of leadership through four levels of analysis – individual, team/community, organizational, and global. At the end of the chapter, we combine the three conceptual approaches and the four levels of analysis to create an overarching map of the different topics that are used in the teaching of leadership.

LEADERSHIP IS "IN"

When reviewing the mission statements of higher education institutions, we quickly spot the words "leader" and "leadership." Princeton University, for instance, includes as one of its "defining characteristics and aspirations" "a commitment to prepare students for lives of service, civic engagement, and ethical leadership."[1] Colorado College aspires to similar goals: "Drawing upon the adventurous spirit of the Rocky Mountain West, we challenge students, one course at a time, to develop those habits of intellect and imagination that will prepare them for learning and leadership throughout their lives."[2]

Our respective institutions show the same high level of interest in preparing undergraduate students for leadership. Marietta College has as its stated mission to provide "a strong foundation for a lifetime of leadership, critical thinking, and problem solving."[3] Dartmouth College conveys a similar desire and expresses it as preparing students for "a lifetime of learning and of responsible leadership."[4]

What is particularly striking about all of these mission statements is the connection made between leadership preparation and the commitment to a lifetime of leadership. However, many institutions do not take into consideration the level of intentionality needed when teaching leadership. To some, this preparation is offered as an indirect by-product of a traditional college or university education. This book, however, challenges educators to think more deeply about teaching leadership – as an intentional endeavor of higher education. Because the stakes are so high today, we can no longer leave "teaching leadership" to serendipity. Our programs and initiatives need to be carefully designed to produce deep impact.

A Brief History of "Teaching Leadership"

The history of "teaching leadership" at the undergraduate level in the United States has at its roots the great socioeconomic transformations that took place in American society in the 1960s. The social upheaval brought about by the various movements of this decade was expressed on campuses through a growing emphasis on civics education – how to prepare citizen-leaders to become engaged in the life of a pluralistic democracy. This movement took place at student life offices in the 1970s, and residence halls and campus organizations became the "test lab" for new ideas related to leadership. Concepts such as civic engagement, conflict resolution, democratic decision-making, and empowerment found avid takers on campuses whose administrations were eager to develop a more communitarian language of leadership.

In 1976, the American College Personnel Association (ACPA) convened a Task Force (Commission IV Committee on Leadership), which was designed "to explore what was happening in leadership development through student affairs offices."[5] The Task Force encouraged the sharing of best practices among the ACPA members as a way to develop a comprehensive view of leadership development initiatives in higher education (Roberts, 1981). This publication eventually served as the basis for the development of the CAS Student Leadership Program Standards in the early 1980s under the direction of Susan Komives, Denny Roberts, and Tracey Tyree (Wells, 2015). Community service, volunteerism, and service learning emerged as new tools to advance leadership training (competency-building) on college campuses. These formal leadership programs were open to students from all majors.

Leadership scholars and practitioners spoke in the 1970s of a "crisis of leadership." Everywhere we turned, it seemed that our leaders had let us down. John Gardner challenged the notion that we needed "better" leaders. Instead, he argued for "more" leaders – the concept of *dispersed leadership* (Gardner, 1993). This argument became a powerful one on college campuses, as higher education came to be seen as fertile ground for leadership training.

By the 1980s, many colleges and universities had begun to introduce for-credit courses dealing with leadership studies. These curricular offerings sought to bridge leadership education and leadership training. In many cases, faculties were hostile to the notion that leadership could be taught as an academic discipline. In 1986, for instance, Marietta College, a small liberal-arts institution in Ohio, received a substantial gift from the McDonough Foundation and family to establish a curricular-based undergraduate leadership program. This gift divided the faculty into three factions: one that was excited about the opportunity to develop an innovative initiative that would make the college distinct; another that was more pragmatic, willing to take the money, even if it meant going against its commitment to liberal-arts "purity;" and a third that was downright hostile to the idea that teaching leadership had any business in a pure liberal-arts classroom.

The first two factions banded together and supported the Trustees' decision to accept the gift. The "winners" were given the resources to establish the first comprehensive, liberal-arts-based, undergraduate leadership program in the country. What was particularly fascinating about that debate in the 1980s was the notion that leadership education and the liberal arts were somehow antithetical. Yet some of the first liberal-arts-based leadership program institutions, including the University of Richmond's Jepson School of Leadership Studies (founded in 1993 as the first academic school – as opposed to a program – of leadership studies in the world), argued effectively that many of the values traditionally associated with the liberal arts (e.g., critical thinking, problem-solving, intellectual curiosity) were associated with the competencies of successful leaders in the late 20th century.

Teaching Leadership under Globalization

By the 1990s, leadership was really "in" – just in time, as a fourth factor drove the popularity of the field: globalization. Just as in the 1970s, the last decade of the 20th century saw economic turmoil and political upheavals. Events such as the demise of the Soviet Union, the end of the Cold War, the rise of China as an economic power, the relative economic decline of the United States, and the technological revolution in communication and transportation made for a very turbulent decade. Leaders on the political, social, and economic sides seemed ill-prepared to handle this onslaught of events.

These developments in the 1990s gave rise to the popularity of global leadership as a distinct field of research and education, compared to the "traditional" study of leadership (Mendenhall, 2013). Aspiring leaders were asked to learn about leadership not only as a human phenomenon but also as part of a cultural context. It was not enough to talk about leadership as the relationship between leaders and followers pursuing a goal. Now, leaders also had to take into consideration the cultural norms and values that guided this relationship. We could no longer assume that leaders and followers would be using the same cultural language. In the age of globalization, leaders and followers could be from different cultures, thus rendering the relationship much more complex than previously acknowledged.

By the beginning of the new millennium there was an emerging consensus in higher education that leadership had a place on campus. Note that we did not include the word "legitimate" next to "place." To some faculty members and staff, the jury is still out about the legitimacy of leadership as an academic field of study. We will discuss this issue further in Chapter 3. For now, we can say that there is a general consensus that leadership is "in."

"Drinking from the proverbial fire hose" became the apt metaphor to describe the incessant spewing of new information, crises, ethical challenges, and constant change in the new century. Somehow our leaders were supposed to thrive in this new environment. It became very clear that more attention needed to be paid to the ways in which our leaders were educated.

Today, there is a certain urgency to the task of developing leaders for the new millennium (Conger and Benjamin, 1999).[6] While colleges and universities continue to incorporate civic engagement into the language of leadership development, there is a new interest in the pragmatic side of leadership education. As the cost of higher education continues to increase, parents are asking hard questions about the return on investment.

There is also an interesting convergence between the evolution of leadership and globalization. As the global marketplace has become increasingly competitive, students (and their parents) are turning to market differentiators on their resumes. Leadership studies is now viewed as a "value-added" benefit of a college education. Many of our alumni are quick to point out that having the word "leadership" on their resume made them more noticeable in job interviews. The high cost of a college education is driving students to take a more "utilitarian" perspective on leadership – "How will this program help me get a better job?"

Yet a general overview of the field shows that the preponderance of undergraduate programs in the United States still emphasize the importance of civic engagement and service learning as the core value of leadership development. We are not arguing here for abandoning this emphasis and embracing a more competency-based approach. We are pointing out that there is, on many campuses, a convergence between the civic-engagement narrative (e.g., developing citizen-leaders) and the new millennium's pragmatic focus on leadership competency-building as a "value-added" strategy.

In reality, the two sides are not exclusive. Gardner's argument for dispersed leadership in the 1970s still resonates with our college students today. They see civil society deeply divided by economic inequality, race, religion, and ethnicity; and they wonder how leaders are making a positive difference.

Surveys of the Millennial and Z generations show a strong interest on their part in communitarian issues. They are engaged in community service and see themselves as contributors to the success of their communities. However, they also worry about finding a job after graduation.

Another aspect of the increasing emphasis on "value-added" education is found at the graduate level. While throughout the second half of the 20th century the focus of graduate-level leadership education was on research – the creation of knowledge that can be directly applied to the marketplace – there has been a proliferation in the past two decades of graduate programs focused on individual leadership development. The Internet has become a critical platform for online adult education in this area. Professionals are able to secure a graduate degree in leadership while still keeping a full-time job. A graduate degree is viewed as an opportunity to enhance one's existing career – again, a "value-added" proposition.

THE "BRANCHES" OF LEADERSHIP

While a book about "teaching leadership" may seem to fall naturally under the leadership education rubric, the field of leadership studies actually has three branches (Roberts, 1981). Therefore, teaching leadership has different dimensions that need to be considered when developing programs. In other words, teaching leadership can be approached through three different lenses.

Teaching "about" Leadership

The first branch, leadership education, deals with leadership as an intellectual field of study. There is a body of knowledge related to this topic that we pass on to our students in the classrooms, as Chapter 3 will introduce. This body of knowledge has dramatically expanded in the past three decades and forms what we call the "leadership canon." While we recognize that some scholars are not quite ready to call leadership a discipline – the same way that we talk about political science, biology, and economics – we contend that we are a lot closer to that level than we imagine (Harvey and Riggio, 2011).

In an insightful article for *The Atlantic* magazine, Tara Isabella Burton denounced what she called the American "obsession" with leadership. As she argues, "The implicit message behind the rhetoric of leadership is that learning for learning's sake is not enough" (Burton, 2014). There is an emphasis in our college admissions process that puts the spotlight on the impact that our students will have on campus and beyond: "A desirable student is expected to do more than merely learn effectively, to further the transmission of knowledge from professor to student. They're expected to go further."

Burton highlights an important point – the satisfaction that can be derived from the acquisition of knowledge. Our leadership programs should provide an environment in which our aspiring leaders can be free to test out ideas. This intellectual dimension has a value in and of itself – allowing our students to sharpen their critical thinking and communication skills. These skills, in turn, open up the space through which we can teach "for" leadership.

Teaching "for" Leadership

Most of our leadership students do not join leadership programs because of the intellectual side of the field, although we suspect that with time that number will grow. They seek these programs because of the second branch – leadership competency-building. They are interested in acquiring the necessary competencies to become better leaders. This branch suggests a different approach to "teaching leadership."

Our students expect us, instead of teaching about leadership, to teach "for" leadership. They want us to show the practical side of leadership, meaning that they associate teaching leadership with competency-building. Despite our deeper understanding of leadership at the scholarly level, the popular conception of leadership remains stuck in a simplistic formulation – the field of leadership should be connected to direct application of what a leader needs to be successful in an organization.

We should not necessarily assign a value hierarchy to the first two branches – as if leadership education is superior or inferior to leadership competency-building. In reality, they are deeply interconnected. When Marietta College was first established in 1835, its charter called for a quality education in the "various branches of useful knowledge" (McGrew, 1994). The term "useful knowledge" can be interpreted as a combination of the intellectual and experiential dimensions – the way we connect knowledge to action.

Teaching "Practical Wisdom"

If leadership education deals with teaching "about" leadership and leadership competency-building refers to teaching "for" leadership, what can we say about leadership development? The third branch, leadership development, is the result of the first two: knowledge plus experience leads to wisdom (Wei and Yip, 2008).

Can we teach leadership wisdom? In this book, we focus on "practical wisdom." Through our programs – as Part III of the book will show – we allow our students to reflect on experiences and make connections between failure or success and the current state of knowledge of a field. This reiterative process allows the aspiring leader to grow not only in knowledge but also in wisdom. It is no accident that many societies value the wisdom of the elderly (Silverman and Siegel, 2018). They have seen more, experienced more, and hopefully derived life lessons that can be passed on from generation to generation.

We want to pass on not only leadership knowledge and competencies but also the wisdom that goes with the responsibility of being leaders and followers in complex organizations and societies. We want our students to reflect on their experiences and make connections between the canon and the real world; and that is how they will grow.

An important message that we often tell our students is that, once they graduate and receive their diploma, they are not done as leaders. In other words, leadership development deals with the process by which people become leaders, a topic that will be further explored in Part III of this book. From this perspective, leadership development represents teaching "to live" leadership.

Much attention in the Western leadership literature has been placed on defining leadership, as if we could all agree on a single definition. Joseph Rost (1993) cleverly argued that, if we put a group of scholars in a room, we would get as many different definitions of leadership as there were scholars. We do not flatter ourselves that we could offer the definitive definition. However, we think that a more productive intellectual direction in this debate might be to ask our learners if they have a "philosophy of leadership," as opposed to having their own definition. By philosophy, we mean the value proposition that is an articulation of who you are as a leader.

We can view development as the acquisition of knowledge through education – the way that a political-science student could strive to become a political scientist by acquiring the knowledge of the field. Or we can approach development as the command of the tools through competency-building – the way that an aspiring political scientist would master statistical analysis and survey techniques in order to practice the craft.

Leadership development, however, calls for a much deeper understanding of the philosophy behind the process of becoming a leader. Leadership refers to "a way of being" in which leaders develop the principles and values that guide their behavior regardless of the context. The old saying "Character is how you behave when no one is looking" is particularly applicable in this case. Under leadership development, aspiring leaders tend to the nurturing of principles and values that will emerge as their philosophy of leadership.

UNITS OF ANALYSIS

In the previous section, we framed "teaching leadership" in terms of three separate branches. Another way to look at this area is to explore the organizing principles used in the teaching of leadership. We can organize these principles around four levels – individual, team, organizational, and global. Once we bring both the branches and the units of analysis together, the resulting three-by-four table allows us to explore how teaching leadership can take many programmatic forms. Each cell in this table represents a different focus an educator can take to teach leadership (Table 1.1). The multiplicity of areas demonstrates the many ways in which educators can guide aspiring leaders to combine knowledge and experience to develop leadership wisdom.

Teaching at the Individual Level

The "leader" still serves as an important organizing principle of leadership studies. For many educators, the teaching of leadership has to focus on the leaders and followers as individual contributors to the leadership process. That is the essence of leadership.

Many theories and models continue to emphasize the centrality of the leader in leadership (e.g., Conger, 1989; Kirkpatrick and Locke, 1991). Therefore, a leadership curriculum may pay attention to topics such as authentic leadership, servant leadership, and charismatic leadership. In

Table 1.1   *Interconnected dimensions*

	Leadership education *Intellectual dimension*	Leadership training *Experiential dimension*	Leadership development *Growth dimension*
Individual level	Understanding the individual role of leaders and followers (leadership styles)	Competency-building experiences that enhance the leadership toolbox	Developing a personal philosophy of leadership
Team/ community level	Understanding the leader–follower relationship	Knowing how to lead effective teams (group dynamics)	Developing high-performance teams
Organizational level	Mastering the field of organizational leadership	Knowing how to lead effective organizations (situational awareness)	Developing high-performance organizations
Global level	Mastering the field of global leadership	Acquiring global competencies (leading across cultures)	Becoming a global leader (transnational norms and values)

leadership education, this emphasis on the leader translates into a curricular focus on the theories and models that highlight the study of leaders' traits. What are the ideal traits of effective leaders?

Aspiring leaders also can benefit from leadership competency-building. The leadership literature is filled with "how-to" books that offer ways that leaders can expand their skill-sets (e.g., McClatchy, 2014; Heyck-Merlin, 2016). These sources can be incorporated into a leadership studies curriculum through workshops, leadership practicum courses, and exercises. They often offer quick steps to competency-building.

A third way of approaching leadership at the individual level is to focus on leadership development. In the previous section of this chapter, we introduced the notion of "practical wisdom" through the development of a personal philosophy of leadership. Leaders not only know leadership concepts and are able to apply leadership competencies, but also reflect on their experiences and use those insights to develop their own approach to leadership (Conant, 2011).

Teaching at the Team Level

The next level in our understanding of teaching leadership is to bring the individual components (leaders and followers) together and see how they relate to one another. There is a growing segment of the leadership literature that examines the leader–follower relationship within the context of teams (e.g., Cobb, 2012; Wheelan, 2013). Our students can benefit from these studies and begin to formulate general principles related to group dynamics.

The experiential dimension of teams allows our students to put those principles into practice and experience first-hand how to lead effective teams. Through team projects, students quickly see the importance of "stepping up" (for the introverts) and "stepping back" (for the extroverts). They learn how to delegate and how to hold all members accountable for the success of the project.

The knowledge of different theories of group dynamics and the acquisition of team-related competencies ultimately provide our aspiring leaders with the insights that allow them to develop high-performance teams. One of the most often-cited researchers on team development is Bruce Tuckman, whose research in the 1960s uncovered four "stages" in the process (Tuckman, 1995; Tuckman and Jensen, 2001). He labeled each phase with a specific dynamic. When the team members come together, he characterized that stage as *forming*. This is the time when the participants become aware of the challenges they face, including the task and resources available and the different abilities each member brings to the team. Next, the team moves to the *storming* stage – the time when the team members wrestle with their different styles, strengths, and personalities. If teams successfully pass through this stage, they move to the *norming* phase – when the team members accept their differences and begin to work together to achieve the task. Once that is achieved, the team moves to the fourth stage – *performing*.[7]

With leadership development (the growth dimension), we want our students to develop the wisdom that comes from knowing how individuals relate to one another in productive ways. Once they are able to practice Tuckman's model and derive leadership lessons from their experiences, our students gain a deeper understanding of how to put together high-performance teams.

Teaching at the Organizational Level

The third level deals with the organizational context of leadership. Many of the how-to books tend to treat the leader–follower relationship as if it takes place in a contextual vacuum. In reality, we cannot separate this relationship from the surrounding environment.

Leadership education involves the study of organizational leadership as a separate field within leadership studies. This intellectual dimension allows aspiring leaders to learn how organizations work in different settings. There is a robust literature dealing specifically with organizational leadership, which can be offered in our leadership programs as a separate academic area.

Research at the organizational level also has yielded many insights that can be applied to leadership training. Many organizations spend millions of dollars every year to optimize team performance. Learning how to work collaboratively in organizations is indeed a growth industry in itself.

Ultimately, we want our aspiring leaders to combine the two dimensions (intellectual and experiential) to develop high-performance organizations (Cavaleri and Fearon, 1996). It is not enough to know intellectually the qualities of organizations that perform at a high level. We want aspiring leaders to take this knowledge and apply it to different contexts and, in the process, gain a deeper understanding of how organizations work.

Teaching at the Global Level

The global level has become particularly relevant in recent decades because of globalization. In fact, many leadership programs have added a global component to their curriculum in response to these changes at the global level. Many scholars now recognize that "global leadership" is a field of study in its own right (Mendenhall, 2013). When teaching about leadership, we now feel compelled to expose our students to this growing literature. They have to understand the historical forces that brought us to this point.

We make a distinction between "international" and "global." While the former refers to the system of nation-states, the latter draws our attention to the forces that transcend national borders. Global leadership, therefore, is a topic that takes us beyond the study of leaders who operate at the international level – relations among the nation-states. Instead, it focuses on leaders who operate as the transnational level (Henson, 2016).

Multinational corporations contributed in the 20th century to this transnational perspective (Cohen, 2007). Globetrotting business executives participated in the building of an interdependent marketplace. More recently, with new communication technologies and lowering transportation costs, ordinary individuals have become a part of this increasingly interconnected world.

Now, global leaders deal with challenges that require global competencies – intercultural communication, conflict resolution, and global mindset, to name a few (Cabrera and Unruh, 2012). Study-abroad programs have become an excellent opportunity for our students to gain many of these global competencies. However, our programs can also offer on-campus, competency-building exercises that allow our aspiring students to have inter-cultural experiences. Our campuses serve as a "global lab," with an increasing number of students traveling to other parts of the world for an education.

As globalization takes hold, we see more and more the rise of "global leaders" as a separate category – beyond local, national, and international. Local leadership has always been the reality of social groups through millennia. National and international leadership are by-products of the "international system" created in Europe since the 1600s, in which borders and statehood defined the line separating domestic and foreign affairs. The term "international leaders" refers to those individuals who represent their nation-state in its relations with other nation-states. Global leadership deals with issues that transcend the individual nation-states and create transnational challenges.

Many of our students will operate at this transnational level and will take on the "global leader" role. It is incumbent upon us – as educators – to create the environment in which they will understand the historical processes that brought us to the realities of the 21st century (intellectual dimension), to help them develop the global competencies required to be effective con-tributors to global organizations (experiential dimension), and ultimately to guide them as they take their first steps to becoming "global leaders."

As we have seen in this chapter, teaching leadership is a complex tapestry of different branches and units of analysis. All these branches and units of analysis require an understanding of citizenship, the "process whereby the individual and the collaborative group become responsibly connected to the community and the society through the leadership development activity."[8] The ultimate goal is to achieve positive change and societal good (Komives et al., 2009).

In the next chapter, we will introduce another layer of complexity, as we explore the interdisciplinary roots of leadership studies. The teaching of leadership can take place in many different disciplinary settings, each contributing to our understanding of this human phenomenon.

REFLECTION QUESTIONS

1. Does your institution use the words "leader" and "leadership" in its promotional literature and website?
2. If the answer to the previous question is "yes," do these references reflect an intentional strategy to promote leadership development?

3. If the answer to the first question is "no," is that omission intentional? How does "leadership" fit in the institutional mission?
4. How does leadership studies add "value" to a college education?
5. Looking at Table 1.1, assess your institution's strengths and challenges within each cell of the table. For instance, how does your institution address the students' educational needs in the area of global leadership?

NOTES

1. As stated on its website (http://www.princeton.edu/main/about/mission/). Accessed December 22, 2016.
2. See its website (https://www.coloradocollege.edu/basics/welcome/mission/). Accessed February 21, 2017.
3. See its website (http://www.marietta.edu/mission-core-values). Accessed February 19, 2017.
4. See its website (http://dartmouth.edu/mission-statement). Accessed February 19, 2017.
5. As quoted on http://thestamp.umd.edu/leadership_community_service-learning/about_lcsl/history/leadership_program_history. Accessed February 19, 2017.
6. Conger and Benjamin (1999) call this the "new imperative."
7. Tuckman amended this cycle in the 1970s to include a fifth stage – *adjourning* (once the task is completed and the team is dissolved; or when the team stops performing and breaks up).
8. Astin et al. (1996, p. 23). Astin et al. describe their approach to leadership development in *A Social Change Model of Leadership Development: Guidebook*. The model examines leadership development at the individual, group, and community/society level to effect positive change.

REFERENCES

Astin, H.S., Astin, H., Boatsman, K., Bonous-Hammarth, M., Chambers, T., and Goldberg, S. (1996). *A Social Change Model of Leadership Development: Guidebook*, Version III. Los Angeles, CA: Higher Education Research Institute, University of California. Website (http://www.heri.ucla.edu/PDFs/pubs/ASocialChangeModelofLeadershipDevelopment.pdf). Accessed March 12, 2018.

Burton, T.I. (2014). Why Are American Colleges Obsessed with "Leadership"? *The Atlantic*. January 22. Website (http://www.theatlantic.com/education/archive/2014/01/why-are-american-colleges-obsessed-with-leadership/283253/). Accessed December 27, 2016.

Cabrera, A. and Unruh, G. (2012). *Being Global: How to Think, Act, and Lead in a Transformed World*. Boston, MA: Harvard Business Review Press.

Cavaleri, S. and Fearon, D. (Eds.). (1996). *Managing in Organizations That Learn*. Cambridge, MA: Blackwell.

Cobb, A. (2012). *Leading Project Teams: The Basics of Project Management and Team Leadership*, Second Edition. Thousand Oaks, CA: SAGE.

Cohen, S. (2007). *Multinational Corporations and Foreign Direct Investment: Avoiding Simplicity, Embracing Complexity*. New York: Oxford University Press.

Conant, D. (2011). *Touchpoints: Creating Powerful Leadership Connections in the Smallest of Moments*. San Francisco, CA: Jossey-Bass.

Conger, J. (1989). *The Charismatic Leader: Behind the Mystique of Exceptional Leadership*. San Francisco, CA: Jossey-Bass.

Conger, J. and Benjamin, B. (1999). The New Imperative: Building Effective Leaders throughout the Company. In *Building Leaders: How Successful Companies Develop the Next Generation* (pp. 1–24). San Francisco, CA: Jossey-Bass.

Gardner, J. (1993). *On Leadership*. New York: Free Press.

Harvey, M. and Riggio, R. (Eds.). (2011). *Leadership Studies: The Dialogue of Disciplines*. Cheltenham, UK and Northampton, MA, USA: Edward Elgar Publishing.

Henson, R. (2016). *Successful Global Leadership: Frameworks for Cross-cultural Managers and Organizations*. New York: Palgrave Macmillan.

Heyck-Merlin, M. (2016). *The Together Leader: Get Organized for Your Success – and Sanity!* San Francisco, CA: Jossey-Bass.

Kirkpatrick, S. and Locke, E. (1991). Leadership: Do Traits Matter? *Academy of Management Executive*, 5 (2), 48–60.

Komives, S., Wagner, W., and Associates (2009). *Leadership for a Better World: Understanding the Social Change Model of Leadership Development*. San Francisco, CA: Jossey-Bass.

McClatchy, S. (2014). *Decide: Work Smarter, Reduce Your Stress, and Lead by Example*. Hoboken, NJ: Wiley.

McGrew, V. (1994). *In the Various Branches of Useful Knowledge*. Marietta, OH: Marietta College.

Mendenhall, M. (2013). Leadership and the Birth of Global Leadership. In M. Mendenhall, J. Osland, A. Bird, G. Oddou, M. Maznevski, M. Stevens, and G. Stahl (Eds.), *Global Leadership: Research, Practice, and Development*, Second Edition (pp. 1–20). New York: Routledge.

Roberts, D. (1981). *Student Leadership Programs in Higher Education*. Carbondale: ACPA Media, Southern Illinois University Press.

Rost, J. (1993). *Leadership for the Twenty-First Century*. Westport, CT: Praeger.

Silverman, I. and Siegel, E. (Eds.). (2018). *Aging Wisely . . . Wisdom of Our Elders*. Burlington, MA: Jones & Bartlett Learning.

Tuckman, B. (1995). Developmental Sequence in Small Groups. In J.T. Wren (Ed.), *The Leader's Companion: Insights on Leadership through the Ages* (pp. 355–9). New York: Free Press.

Tuckman, B. and Jensen, M. (2001). Stages of Small-Group Development. In W. Natemeyer and J.T. McMahon (Eds.), *Classics of Organizational Behavior* (pp. 241–8). Prospect Heights, IL: Waveland Press.

Wei, R.R. and Yip, J. (2008). *Leadership Wisdom: Discovering the Lessons of Experience*. Greensboro, NC: Center for Creative Leadership.

Wells, J. (Ed.). (2015). *CAS Professional Standards for Higher Education*, Ninth Edition. Washington, DC: Council for the Advancement of Standards in Higher Education.

Wheelan, S. (2013). *Creating Effective Teams: A Guide for Members and Leaders*, Fourth Edition. Los Angeles, CA: SAGE.

2. The interdisciplinary nature of leadership education

Over the decades, scholars have borrowed heavily from different disciplines to study leadership (Harvey and Riggio, 2011). When teaching about leadership, educators often build on this tradition and connect leadership to a wide variety of academic areas of study (Komives et al., 2011). It seems natural, therefore, to see leadership studies as an interdisciplinary endeavor.

This chapter is designed to introduce educators to the interdisciplinary connections that have given rise to leadership studies. While many leadership programs trace their roots to student affairs offices, the current academic study of leadership is often housed in various academic departments. The first part of this chapter engages the reader in a question about the interdisciplinary teaching of leadership: Is it a dialogue of disciplines or a pedagogical tool for understanding human relations? The chapter next reviews the different approaches that educators have taken to advance the teaching of leadership – including pre-professional, liberal-arts, and topic-based programs. The chapter ends with a discussion about the dynamic of finding an academic home for leadership studies.

THE KALEIDOSCOPE EFFECT

Back in the 1970s, as the world shifted away from its post-World War II stability, many scholars observed the growing scarcity of great leaders. Amid this sense of a "crisis" in leadership, James MacGregor Burns (1978) posited that the crisis was not in the way we prepared our youth for leadership; the real crisis was intellectual in nature – the standards we used to assess leadership. He contended that we certainly knew much about our leaders, but very little about leadership. For Burns, the lack of a general theory of leadership was a sign of intellectual mediocrity.

Since the 1970s, we have seen a dramatic explosion of academic programs focused on leadership. For many scholars and educators, the variety of leadership approaches is in fact a sign of intellectual vitality. While the next chapter will focus on the "disciplinary" nature of leadership studies, this chapter will explore leadership as an interdisciplinary endeavor. Proponents of the interdisciplinary approach often use the kaleidoscope metaphor (Bennett, 2016). The mystery in a kaleidoscope is found in the unexpected combination of images that reflect different patterns that evoke ambiguity, complexity, and (best of all) beauty.

Using the kaleidoscope as a leadership metaphor, disciplines contribute individual elements to the overall picture. Manfred Kets de Vries and his colleagues applied this metaphor by painting a multi-faceted picture of leadership through the prism of an integrative, psychodynamic approach to leadership development (Kets de Vries et al., 2010). In an age of increasing globalization and interdependence, it seems counterintuitive to see leadership studies as falling under a single disciplinary category. After all, as new disciplinary elements are added to the kaleidoscope, new surprising patterns emerge with their complexity.

This interdisciplinary view of leadership is consistent with our increasing understanding of leadership as involving, in Larraine Matusak's words, an appreciation of the "kaleidoscope of views" (Matusak, 1997). Leadership cannot be easily put in a box and labeled as a discipline. Rather, emerging leaders are asked to find "their voice" when learning to lead. Not surprisingly, this entrepreneurial approach has also been reflected in the intellectual underpinnings of the field.

The "downside" of the kaleidoscope metaphor is that it looks increasingly like an art, as opposed to a science. We put the word in quotation marks on purpose. As an art, the teaching of leadership is subject to individual interpretation. For those scholars seeking the certainty of theories, models, and the scientific method, the ambiguity of leadership – between art and science – is intellectually discouraging. What passes for "creativity" can simply be the development of yet another copyrighted model designed to advance someone's professional career.

Barbara Kellerman, in her provocative book *The End of Leadership*, has questioned the value of the "leadership industry" itself (Kellerman, 2012). Is the teaching of leadership yielding the expected results? Are we developing effective leaders *and* followers? As leaders have grown increasingly in disrepute, Kellerman calls for new ways of teaching leadership that account for changes in the new millennium related to the balance of power between leaders and followers. Kellerman's words serve as a cautionary tale that our focus on developing leaders – as a path to power – oversimplifies the study and practice of leadership. Her real target, therefore, is the "leadership industry" itself – our simplistic models that advance individual professional careers, but do little to deepen our understanding of how leadership works in the 21st century.

THE INTERDISCIPLINARY NEXUS

There are two ways of looking at the interdisciplinary nature of leadership education (Figure 2.1). First, we can see it as having a direct application to a particular field of study. In other words, leadership can be studied within a specific academic context, such as agricultural leadership or engineering leadership. Our understanding of leadership, therefore, informs how the leader–follower relationship takes place within a certain profession. We call this connection the "pre-professional approach."

Second, we can reverse the perspective and see how academic disciplines can contribute to our understanding of leadership. This perspective, which we call the "liberal-arts approach," takes into consideration the multi-faceted nature of leadership as a complicated human phenomenon. This approach requires us to borrow insights from different disciplines in order to inform our understanding of leadership itself.

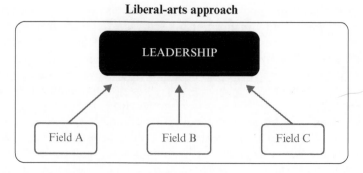

Figure 2.1   Approaches to leadership education

The Pre-professional Approach

Leadership education under this approach serves as a way to encourage the learner to see the application of leadership principles to a specific field of study. The "pre-professional" approach allows the educator to draw connections between leadership and the professional context that the learner is intending to enter upon graduation.

Nowadays, leadership is being applied to many, many professional fields, and it is not possible for us to cover all of them in this book. Rather, we will single out some of the most popular in higher education. As you consider your own institutional context, you can then evaluate whether this is the appropriate approach to take as you develop a leadership education program within your institution.

Business leadership

This pre-professional approach has long paid attention to the importance of leadership in both for-profit and nonprofit organizations. Scholars in business schools have made significant contributions to our understanding of leadership (Gallos, 2008). This scholarship, such as Daniel Goleman's emotional intelligence and Bill George's authentic leadership, is used in many leadership programs, regardless of their approach (George, 2003; Goleman, 2014).

Business leadership has long been the realm of graduate programs and executive education, offering leadership skill-building opportunities for business leaders. However, we cannot discount the contribution that business programs are making to the development of an undergraduate leadership curriculum. The Mason School of Business at the College of William & Mary, for instance, offers concentrations for its undergraduate students, which can be combined with a major. One of its concentrations is "Management and Organizational Leadership."[1] In another example, the University of Kansas's School of Business offers a Bachelor of Science in Business (B.S.B.) in "Management and Leadership." The program is designed to help participants develop "the perspective, skills and knowledge that you will need to manage and lead the modern organization more effectively."[2]

Aside from the contribution to the study of leadership, business schools also have recognized the importance of ethics in leadership education (Doyle et al., 2013; Campbell, 2017). An ethical component in a business leadership program is considered a must (Garsten and Hernes, 2009; Arnold et al., 2013). Its absence seriously affects the conceptual credibility of a program. The Katz Graduate School of Business at the University of Pittsburgh, for instance, offers an undergraduate-level Certificate Program in Leadership and Ethics (CPLE). The CPLE curriculum is based on the assumption that "an emphasis on leadership, without proper consideration of ethics, will not generate leaders who approach their roles with a sense of responsibility and accountability."[3]

Engineering leadership

Many of today's engineering schools have embraced the notion that the combination of "hard" and "soft" skills can be a powerful preparation for the world of work, particularly in areas that involve technology in a rapidly changing environment. Engineering students know that they will acquire the "hard" skills (the technical knowledge associated with the discipline, e.g., data analysis, mathematics, computer skills). The engineering work environment, however, will demand the "soft" skills associated with project management and supervisory roles (e.g., problem-solving, critical thinking, teamwork, collaboration, communication, and willingness to learn). There is a growing literature in this area, which has helped shape academic initiatives (Morrison and Ericsson, 2003; Kock, 2009).[4]

Engineering leadership has been promoted particularly through professional and distance-education programs. MIT's Professional Education Office, for instance, offers a five-day summer course on engineering leadership "designed to equip you with the skills and perspectives needed to lead yourself and others in today's engineering and technology environments."[5] The Ohio State University's College of Engineering offers the Global Engineering Leadership (GEL) certificate program. The completely online program is designed "specifically for working engineers to help them learn real-world management skills, how to apply them within their industry, and how to grow as a leader within their organization."[6] Faculty teaching in this interdisciplinary program are drawn from the College of Engineering, the John Glenn College of Public Affairs, and the Fisher College of Business.

At the undergraduate level, students will find a good variety of programs that offer minors and certificates that can be combined with an engineering degree. Penn State University's College of Engineering, for instance, offers a minor in Engineering Leadership Development (ELD), which includes courses that provide participants with "the understanding of individual, team, and organizational leadership; multicultural awareness and sensitivity; and innovation and management."[7] The Engineering Leadership minor at Purdue University offers concentration areas in communication, creativity and innovation, global and societal impact, and ethics.[8]

Teacher leadership

K–12 education and leadership are natural allies in higher education. The traditional view of educational leadership has been focused on the movement of teachers into administrative positions (e.g., becoming a principal) within the school system. To become a leader within this framework is to leave the classroom and take on an administrative position. Since the 1990s, there has been an increasing interest in empowering teachers to play a leadership role in their schools – without the need to leave the classroom (Froyen, 1993; Bolman and Deal, 1994; Collay, 2011).

Higher education has responded to this new development by offering graduate programs in the area of teacher leadership. Topics of particular interest revolve around accountability, working with stakeholders across boundaries and borders, approaches to change, and becoming a strategic leader (Crawford, 2014). Walden University, for instance, offers a Graduate Certificate in Teacher Leadership, which helps participants

> discover your leadership strengths and learn to apply them to key educational challenges, such as increasing student achievement levels and fostering parent involvement. Build your skills as a teacher leader as you advance your knowledge of subject matter and curriculum goals and explore how to implement effective teaching models, strategies, and practices. Use the latest research to guide your decisions and help you lead with greater confidence.[9]

Institutions also offer full master's degrees focused on teacher leadership. Quinnipiac University offers a completely online graduate program, which is designed to build "advanced knowledge in areas of leadership, learning motivation, shaping school culture and more."[10] As the Teacher Leadership Program at Brandeis University asserts, "the most important change agents in education are our classroom teachers. Teachers change lives day after day, and the influence of many extends beyond their classrooms, schools, and communities."[11] Brandeis offers a hybrid program that brings together cohorts of like-minded gifted teachers to learn skills essential to becoming an effective teacher leader.

In recent years, the teacher leader field has begun to include undergraduate students in the leadership development process. Marietta College's McDonough Leadership Center, for instance, offers a Teacher Leadership Certificate for undergraduate students majoring in education. In close collaboration with the College's Education Department, the Center has put together a curriculum that stresses the shift from "teacher to leader," as well as leadership skill development.

Healthcare leadership

The marriage of technical skills with leadership is particularly salient in the healthcare field (Dye, 2010; Ledlow, 2018). We all expect our healthcare providers to be technically competent to deliver critical care, particularly in time-sensitive situations. Increasingly, the field has paid attention to an important question: How is this critical care delivered? And that involves elements of leadership (e.g., working in teams, changing strategies amid uncertainty, "bedside manner").

Healthcare leadership involves all levels of healthcare organizations. Traditionally, we think of executives in this field as the leaders and followers. However, the literature has increasingly involved other key players, including doctors and nurses. After all, they also work in an environment that demands leadership skills. Preparing healthcare providers to take on leadership roles in their organizations is a critical task. They deal with life-and-death situations.

The "leadership industry," to use Kellerman's (2012) terminology, is filled with short-term executive-education programs for healthcare administrators. Harvard University's T.H. Chan School of Public Health, for instance, offers a short-term (ten days long) initiative, the Physician Leadership Development Program, which provides "focused training in management and leadership, ensuring participants are prepared to lead effectively and improve organizational performance."[12]

Cornell University offers a number of online certificates (e.g., Executive Leadership for Healthcare Professionals), which are designed to give participants "the leadership skills you need to navigate today's evolving healthcare landscape in courses that combine top research with real-world insights."[13] The Amy V. Cockcroft Nursing Leadership Development Program in the College of Nursing at the University of South Carolina prepares "nurse executive leaders to meet the increasingly urgent demands of today's health care organizations."[14]

Healthcare leadership is framed in terms of healthcare administration – applying insights from business leadership to the healthcare sector. Vanderbilt University's Owen School of Management, for instance, offers a Master of Management in Health Care, which includes a Leadership Development Program, designed to develop "the leadership skills to manage and motivate teams, influence stakeholders and execute change."[15]

Graduate programs in this field assume that successful clinical expertise eventually leads to administrative demands. As the Harvard program mentioned above indicates, "Physicians are often selected for senior leadership positions based on clinical expertise. These expanded roles require knowledge of critical business skills and leadership practices for which most physicians have rarely received training."[16]

A number of online programs cater to professionals who are making the transition from the lab to the executive suite. Capella University, for example, offers a "professionally aligned education," with several online options: Bachelor of Science (B.S.) in Healthcare Administration in Leadership; Master of Health Administration (M.H.A.) in Healthcare Leadership; Doctor of Health Administration (D.H.A.) in Healthcare Leadership. Capella's courses are designed around "real-world application to ensure you gain the skills and knowledge needed to be successful in the health care industry."[17]

Agricultural leadership

Another highly successful marriage is the combination of agricultural education and leadership development (Jordan et al., 2013). Agricultural leadership has a long history in American higher education, particularly at the undergraduate level (Moore et al., 2013). Not surprisingly, land-grant institutions have led the way in curricular development at both under-graduate and graduate levels in the United States. Texas A&M University's College of Agriculture and Life Sciences offers an undergraduate degree in agricultural leadership and development (ALED). This multidisciplinary degree is designed to "develop students for leadership positions in local, state, regional, and national organizations and agencies involved in the agriculture industry."[18]

The University of Illinois at Urbana-Champaign's College of Agricultural, Consumer, and Environmental Sciences sees "agricultural leadership education" as preparing students for "professional careers in ag-related industries, nonprofit organizations, and government agencies. Career paths include organizational development, education and training, human resources, sales, advocacy, and Extension."[19]

The Department of Agricultural Communication, Education, and Leadership at the Ohio State University's College of Food, Agricultural, and Environmental Sciences offers a Bachelor of Science in Agriculture Community Leadership, which includes courses such as agricultural communication, ethics, human resources management, public service/ civic engagement, leadership in teams, and community organizations. The department curricular offerings are designed to educate students "with skills and through real world experiences that will develop them into well-rounded agricultural professionals."[20]

The Department of Agricultural Education and Communication at the University of Florida's Institute of Food and Agricultural Sciences offers an undergraduate degree in Communication and Leadership Development. This major prepares students for entry into "agribusiness and communica-tion positions related to human resource development, corporate training, political interests and agricultural literacy. Course work focuses on a core of leadership and communication courses that includes digital media, campaign strategies, interpersonal skills and presentation development."[21] Students participating in this major are also eligible to enroll in the University's minor in Leadership.

The Liberal-Arts Approach

In the previous section, we explored how leadership finds its way to diverse fields as part of a pre-professional approach. Now, we can reverse the direction of the arrow (Figure 2.1) and take a look at the way programs use different disciplines to analyze leadership itself. Leadership programs at liberal-arts institutions have been particularly interested in this approach (Wren et al., 2009).

We see two ways that institutions have used the liberal-arts approach to build their leadership programs. First, they can use the arts and the humanities as sources (artifacts) to help students understand how leadership works. That can be done through the readings students use in leadership courses (e.g., Plato, Aristotle). Marietta College's McDonough Leadership Program uses this approach. The program's "Foundations of Leadership" course, more fully discussed in the following chapter, is based on Robert McManus and Gama Perruci's *Understanding Leadership: An Arts and Humanities Perspective* (McManus and Perruci, 2015). We will explain the history of this program in more detail later in this chapter.

Second, the University of Richmond's Jepson School of Leadership Studies has intentionally used disciplines from the liberal arts as the basis for understanding different aspects of leadership. The school has a "multidisciplinary faculty" (e.g., philosophy, history, ethics, politics, economics, law) dedicated to "the pursuit of new insights into the complexities and challenges of leadership and to teaching undergraduates what they know."[22] While the Jepson faculty carry the title of Assistant/Associate/Professor of Leadership Studies, they are hired on the basis of their traditional disciplinary identity. Aside from teaching the foundational courses one would expect in a leadership curriculum, as we will discuss in the next chapter, they also contribute discipline-based courses (e.g., political thought, history, political economy) that leadership students can take in order to deepen their understanding of leadership from a liberal-arts perspective.

TOPIC-BASED CURRICULAR APPROACH

The interdisciplinary nature of leadership education also reaches across topical areas. In particular, we can point out two: gender and leadership, and global leadership. Dramatic changes in the marketplace in recent decades are driving these topics to the forefront of leadership education. Colleges and universities are increasingly engaging their students in gender-related curricula, and they are establishing a connection between leadership education and globalization as well.

Women in Leadership

As more women have entered the labor force since the 1960s, leadership education has increasingly paid attention to gender issues in the workplace (Belasen, 2012; Décosterd, 2013; Liautaud, 2016). Some institutions now have leadership programs specifically dedicated to women's leadership development. Other institutions also offer executive-education programs for women in leadership positions. These graduate-level programs have proven to be particularly lucrative.[23]

Since the 1990s, more institutions have focused on undergraduate leadership development initiatives for women. The gender revolution in the workforce does not simply refer to women working outside the home. It also involves leadership roles within organizations. Words such as "empowerment," "advancement," "realizing potential," "cooperation," and "role models" are frequently used in women's leadership programs.

The Women's Leadership Program at Bentley University's Center for Women and Business (CWB), for example, "empowers young women to lead." CWB Leaders gain "essential skills and experiences that enhance their potential to advance into leadership roles across all areas of business."[24] The Somers Women's Leadership Program at George Washington University examines "different configurations of leadership as they appear in society and culture, thinking about how leadership depends not only on more traditional notions of a single, strong, inspirational figure, but also on a whole set of relationships that encompass creativity, co-operation, and consent."[25]

Teaching about leadership in this context involves the development of skills, knowledge, and competencies that allow women to see how gender impacts the leader–follower relationships in organizations. The curriculum, therefore, reflects certain topics and context-specific realities that women will encounter in the workforce.

Global Leadership Programs

Another important topic that shapes the curricular nature of a leadership program is the impact that globalization is having on the leader–follower relationship (Nirenberg, 2002; Harvey and Barbour, 2009; Gundling et al., 2011). Institutions, in general, have responded to the increasing interdependence at the global level by emphasizing courses and academic programs that prepare students for a global workforce. As we will discuss in the next chapter, leadership programs have been sensitive to this new reality by enhancing their curricular focus on new issues, such as diversity, intercultural communication, and the challenges of cross-cultural teamwork.

Some institutions have gone a step further and developed leadership programs specifically dedicated to the study and practice of global leadership. Similar to the women's leadership programs, a wide variety of lucrative executive-education programs exist for already established leaders.[26] Since the 1990s, the number of undergraduate-level global leadership programs has increased. Key words that we see in those programs include "community," "connection," "inspirational," and "boosting potential."

The University of Southern California's Marshall School of Business, for instance, offers a Global Leadership Program for incoming freshmen and includes "community" and "connection" as two of its stated programmatic goals.[27] Marietta College's McDonough Center offers an International Leadership Studies major, which combines both the academic field of international studies and global leadership development.[28]

THE ROCKEFELLER AND MCDONOUGH EXPERIENCES

So far, we have made reference to many different programs as a way to illustrate the variety of approaches to the study and practice of leadership. In this section, we focus on our own institutions in order to provide a deeper perspective on the interdisciplinary nature of leadership education. We recognize that each institution has its own contextual dynamic that shapes this developmental process. These two cases, therefore, serve an illustrative purpose from which educators can derive insights into their particular institutional contexts.

The Rockefeller Center

The Rockefeller Center's commitment to leadership began in 1999 with a two-day leadership conference. Former Director of the Center Professor Linda Fowler recalls that the event was organized for and by women faculty, staff, and students who were active at the Center during that time.

Back then, the percentage of female students was about 38%, and women were
saying to me: "Dartmouth says we are here to be leaders, but wherever we look
we see only men." They were taking issue with the assumption that because
Dartmouth had admitted them, they would inevitably become leaders. I was,
at the time, one of the most visible females on campus as director of Rocky
[Rockefeller Center], and as a graduate of a women's college, I was quite aware
of the different challenges women face. We did the women's conferences for
several years, but then [in 2001] the men said that they felt the need of coaching,
too. That was when the Thursday night Rockefeller Leadership Group started.
At the time, I ran each session. Many of the guests were board members or
people I knew.[29]

The program continued to be offered after Professor Andrew Samwick
was appointed Director in 2004, and by 2007 it was firmly established as
a year-long program for seniors. Popularly known as "RLF" (Rockefeller
Leadership Fellows Program), the program attracted seniors from different
departments and majors throughout the college and had evolved to include
a fall and winter retreat, weekly leadership sessions offered by faculty,
staff, and practitioners during the fall and winter terms, and peer teaching
through student-directed sessions. As a key feature of the program, each
cohort of Fellows practiced their learned management and leadership
skills by selecting their successors. Demand grew as the program gained
visibility and popularity. Eventually, for every 25 seniors accommodated in
the program, the Center was turning away more than 50 applicants.

Although there was some discussion of expansion, the Center's administrators believed a larger program would change the group dynamics, which
could adversely impact the deep learning taking place within each cohort.
They also feared it would dilute the sense of camaraderie created among
a diverse group of students from different academic backgrounds and the
strong support network that continued after its completion. Further, an
expanded number of participants would change the perception of the program as a Fellowship program that required a high level of commitment.

Meanwhile, a parallel development was taking place on the curricular
side of the Rockefeller Center in 2007 – the redesign of the Public Policy
minor and the development of the Policy Research Shop. The Center
offered the popular Civic Skills Training Program three times a year in
Washington, DC for students with approved internships focused on preparing students (typically for sophomores, juniors, and seniors). The purpose
of this program was to help students become successful in their internship
responsibilities and learn about managing themselves and leadership concepts. This program, however, was resource-intensive, and it led the Center's
administrators to begin thinking about how a similar program could be
offered on campus to benefit a large number of students. This observation
resulted in delinking the Civic Skills Training Program from internships.

The First-Year Fellows Program was then molded together with curricular courses (introduction to public policy and a statistical methods course) and co-curricular programs (civic skills training and internship placements) to create a robust experience in and out of the classroom, on and off campus, for up to 25 students. The First-Year Fellows Program, as well as the Rockefeller Leadership Fellows Program, now formed the "bookends" for a student's four-year experience and left a gaping hole for the Center to address. Students needed a program on campus that fulfilled their needs to develop their management and leadership competencies through a program similar to Civic Skills Training.

Committed to addressing this unmet need for a larger cohort of students, the Center's Director approved the development of a new program that would be based on open enrollment, capped at 95 students per term, and open to all sophomores, juniors, and seniors who applied. With a donor generously supporting its development and implementation, a pilot offering of the Management and Leadership Development Program was offered in the fall term of 2009 and made its debut as a full-fledged program in the winter term of 2010.

With the addition of this program to the existing First-Year Fellows Program and the Rockefeller Leadership Fellows Program, the Center had moved toward the establishment of a continuum of co-curricular leadership programs for the four-year undergraduate experience on campus, but a gap still existed. While the Center offered several programs targeting students of different ages and maturity levels at the individual or collegiate level, it did not yet offer a program with an in-depth look at the concepts and capacities required for leadership in a global context. Leaders today face additional challenges when operating in unfamiliar environments and cultures, and they often find themselves managing multinational team members with expectations and attitudes different from their own. Additionally, given the College's mission to prepare global leaders, the Rockefeller Global Leadership Program was born out of this identified gap, and its pilot offering took place in the spring term of 2012.

As programs continued to develop and mature, the administrators and educators at the Center monitored and evaluated curricular and co-curricular offerings based on the perceived need for programs and budget availability. The criteria for program evaluation included student learning outcomes, participation, and effectiveness and efficiency; programs were added, revised, or dropped according to the results of these reviews.[30]

Rounding out the Center's continuum of leadership offerings was the Dartmouth Leadership Attitudes and Behaviors Program, added in 2014. This program was included to enable first-year students to examine their personal values, their relationship to behaviors they have identified, and the impact of individual and group behavior on community. The Rockefeller Center faculty and staff believed it appropriate to introduce this program in the first year of student life on campus because of the high level of professionalism they sought from students engaged in the First-Year Fellows Program, given the competitive work environment in which they are placed for internships. This level of professionalism had its roots embedded in helping students to examine their values and to align them with their behaviors. Other considerations included the need for introducing civility and respect in dialogue, as well as the need for these topics to be introduced early in the Rockefeller Center leadership development experience. As a result, Dartmouth Leadership Attitudes and Behaviors has become one of the three prerequisites for students to participate in the First-Year Fellows Program. It is offered in collaboration with Dartmouth's Office of Student Life to broaden the reach of the program. Recently, it was expanded again through Dartmouth's newly established house system as a pilot program in an effort to make it a campus-wide offering.[31]

The McDonough Center

Whereas the Rockefeller Center's approach was to pull together or create programs to meet a need, the Marietta College Leadership Program followed a unique path to development inspired by receiving funding. Normally in higher education, educators have a great idea first, and then they go out and find the funding to support its implementation. For Marietta, this process was reversed. In 1985, following the passing of Bernard P. McDonough, the family wanted to do something to recognize the accomplishments of this successful industrialist and community leader. From humble beginnings, Mr. McDonough built a highly successful enterprise with a global reach. The family – supported by the McDonough Foundation – offered the College $5.7 million to start an undergraduate leadership program grounded in the liberal arts.

At the time, the College had no plans to start an undergraduate leadership program. The gift was actually controversial among the faculty. The faculty became split into three factions. First, there were the "pragmatists" – those who were not ready to turn down what at the time was the largest gift the College had ever received. They were willing to go along with the process. Second, there were the "entrepreneurs" – those who were excited about the opportunity to use this gift to develop a program that could break new ground in a liberal-arts institution. That proposition upset the third faction, the "purists" – those who viewed a leadership program as belonging to pre-professional institutions (e.g., business schools), the military (e.g., West Point's leadership development curriculum), and research universities (e.g., The Ohio State University's ground-breaking research on leadership in the 1950s).

During a contentious faculty meeting in 1986, from which a non-binding vote would be taken on whether the faculty would endorse the acceptance of the gift by the College, one purist stood up and shouted "Give back the gift; we don't do leadership here." The faculty voted, and the first two factions (pragmatists and entrepreneurs) combined forces and carried the vote to accept the gift. Eventually the Trustees did accept the gift, and the College was faced with the exciting (and daunting) task of building a brand-new leadership program from the ground up. There were no models out there for a comprehensive undergraduate leadership program grounded in the liberal arts.

The founding Dean cleverly took the purist's statement ("Give back the gift") and made that the mission of the McDonough Center. The students brought their gifts and talents to the program. The Center's role, therefore, became to develop those gifts and give them back to the community. Right from the start, the Center's mission became closely connected to the students' ability to make a difference in the community.

Initially, the Center offered a Certificate in Leadership Studies. In 1987, the Center welcomed its first cohort (21 McDonough Scholars) to campus. The program drew students from all majors. Through a liberal-arts curriculum (e.g., the students read Plato, Aristotle, and Machiavelli as part of their leadership course work), the participants expanded their knowledge of how leadership works (leadership education). The Center focused on four leadership competencies: critical thinking, teamwork, problem-solving, and communication (written and oral). Through the use of a cohort format, students went through the program together and received a lot of individual attention.

Eventually, the Center added four more academic tracks (in chronological order – minor in Leadership Studies, International Leadership Studies major, Teacher Leadership Certificate, and Engineering Leadership Certificate). In addition, the Center added the Office of Civic Engagement to coordinate co-curricular programming, particularly in the areas of service learning, community-based projects, alternative-break programs, and capacity-building initiatives for local nonprofit organizations. The Center also added other co-curricular initiatives, such as the EXCEL (Experience Civic Engagement and Leadership) Workshop (a five-day, student-driven welcome week for the new McDonough Scholars starting their participation in the Leadership Program), the Fitzgerald Executive-in-Residence Program, the Schwartz Leader-in-Residence Program, and the NextGen Program (e.g., board-leadership development for traditional college-age leaders).

FINDING A "HOME"

All of the approaches discussed in the previous sections have one challenge in common – they have to be housed somewhere in the higher education institution. Each program has its unique story that explains its location on campus. While student life has a long history of providing co-curricular programming in the area of leadership, on the curricular side at the undergraduate level there are two organizational models: department and school.

Teaching about leadership takes place at many levels – from the single course that a faculty member may develop because of his or her interest in the field to the development of a "school of leadership" with undergraduate degrees and full-time faculty in leadership studies. For the purpose of this section, we will not discuss the first level of the lone faculty teaching a course or two about leadership and focus instead on the department and school levels in which leadership programs are located.

The Departmental Model

There are two ways to approach this model. First, we can house a leadership academic program within an existing department. This model works particularly well for a minor/certificate program, which draws its intellectual inspiration from its home discipline. Despite its disciplinary home, the program can still be interdisciplinary. The Department of Psychology at Texas Christian University, for instance, offers an interdisciplinary Psychology of Leadership Minor Program using a behavioral science approach.[32] The Department of Communication at the University of Colorado-Colorado Springs offers an interdisciplinary minor in Leadership Studies. Aside from communication courses, the program also draws from courses in philosophy, psychology, and sociology.

The second approach related to this model is to develop a stand-alone departmental unit. Fort Hayes State University, for instance, has a very successful Department of Leadership Studies with over 1000 students. The department identifies itself as a "flexible interdisciplinary program" providing its students with "the knowledge and skills necessary for a broad range of organizational and supervisory positions."[33] Aside from a certificate and minor in Leadership Studies, the department also offers a Bachelor of Science/Bachelor of Arts in Organizational Leadership – with on-campus and online options.

Another excellent example of this model is found at Christopher Newport University's Department of Leadership and American Studies. This department "immerses students in the study of American life, history and culture from an interdisciplinary perspective, and helps you develop the knowledge, skills and attitude to participate meaningfully in leadership and apply this knowledge in thoughtful ways in and out of the classroom."[34]

The School/Center/Institute Model

Moving beyond the departmental model, some institutions choose to house their leadership program using a school/center/institute model. There are two ways of approaching this model. First, the leadership curricular offering can be housed within an existing school. Dartmouth College's Rockefeller Center, for instance, houses both curricular and co-curricular leadership programs. Chapter 3 will go into more detail of curricular offerings, while Part II of this book will present a more in-depth look at co-curricular programs.

A second approach is to have a stand-alone school/center/institute. We mentioned in the previous section the liberal-arts approach of Marietta College's McDonough Center and the University of Richmond's Jepson School of Leadership Studies. They fall under this model. Other examples include Claremont McKenna College's Kravis Leadership Institute (KLI) and Kansas State University's Staley School of Leadership Studies. KLI offers the Leadership Studies Sequence – a multidisciplinary curricular program designed for "students interested in pursuing a career involving the scholarly study and/or practice of leadership."[35] The Staley School offers a Graduate Student Leadership Development Program (GSLDP), as well as undergraduate programs (minor in Leadership Studies and Certificate in Community-Engaged Leadership) designed to develop "knowledgeable, ethical, caring, inclusive leaders for a diverse and changing world."[36]

The growing number of undergraduate and graduate leadership programs, coupled with a century-old "leadership canon," has caused some scholars and educators to ponder whether we are witnessing the emergence of leadership studies as a discipline, separate from other academic fields. While borrowing from different disciplines certainly gives programs a multi-faceted view of leadership, a leadership curriculum can offer its own set of intellectual questions that help build a distinct and compelling programmatic architecture. The next chapter explores this area of leadership education by suggesting that maybe the field has matured enough over the past decades to merit its own designation as a discipline.

REFLECTION QUESTIONS

1. How do disciplines contribute to our understanding of leadership?
2. How does the study of leadership contribute to our understanding of disciplines?
3. Which of the two approaches discussed in this chapter ("pre-professional" and "liberal-arts") would best suit your institutional context? Why?
4. Aside from women in leadership and global leadership, what other topical areas would you see as being of particular interest to your institutional context? Why?
5. What are the similarities and differences between the Rockefeller and McDonough experiences and your own institutional context?

NOTES

1.   As quoted on its website (http://mason.wm.edu/programs/undergraduate/academic/index.php). Accessed April 23, 2017.
2.   As quoted on its website (https://business.ku.edu/degrees). Accessed April 23, 2017.
3.   As quoted on its website (http://www.business.pitt.edu/katz/berg/programs/cple.php). Accessed April 23, 2017.
4.   See, for instance, the quarterly journal *Leadership and Management in Engineering*, published since 2001 by the American Society of Civil Engineers.
5.   As quoted on its website (http://professional.mit.edu/programs/short-programs/engineering-leadership-emerging-leaders). Accessed April 19, 2017.
6.   As quoted on its website (https://professionals.engineering.osu.edu/global-engineering-leadership-certificate). Accessed April 19, 2017.
7.   As quoted on its website (http://www.sedtapp.psu.edu/eld/). Accessed April 19, 2017.
8.   As quoted on its website (http://catalog.purdue.edu/preview_program.php?catoid=7&poid=6423). Accessed April 19, 2017.
9.   As quoted on its website (https://www.waldenu.edu/certificates/teacher-leadership). Accessed April 19, 2017.
10. As quoted on its website (https://quonline.quinnipiac.edu/campaign/landing/mstl02.php). Accessed April 19, 2017.
11. As quoted on its website (http://www.brandeis.edu/programs/education/leadership/). Accessed April 19, 2017.
12. As quoted on its website (https://www.hsph.harvard.edu/ecpe/programs/the-international-leadership-development-program-for-physicians/). Accessed April 23, 2017.
13. As quoted on its website (http://info.ecornell.com/healthcare). Accessed April 23, 2017.
14. As quoted on its website (https://www.sc.edu/study/colleges_schools/nursing/centers_institutes/center_nursing_leadership/cockcroft_program/). Accessed April 23, 2017.
15. As quoted on its website (http://www.owen.vanderbilt.edu/programs/mm-health-care/curriculum/leadership-development.cfm). Accessed April 23, 2017.
16. As quoted on its website (https://www.hsph.harvard.edu/ecpe/programs/the-international-leadership-development-program-for-physicians/). Accessed April 23, 2017.
17. As quoted on its website (https://www.capella.edu/lp/healthcare/). Accessed April 23, 2017.
18. As quoted on its website (https://alec.tamu.edu/academics/undergraduate/afleadershippaled/). Accessed April 23, 2017.

19. As quoted on its website (http://aged.illinois.edu/concentration/agricultural-leadership-education). Accessed April 23, 2017.
20. As quoted on its website (https://acel.osu.edu/undergraduate). Accessed April 23, 2017.
21. As quoted on its website (http://aec.ifas.ufl.edu/undergraduate/communication--leadership-development/#d.en.298222). Accessed April 23, 2017.
22. As quoted on its website (http://jepson.richmond.edu/). Accessed April 23, 2017.
23. Northwestern University's Kellogg School of Management, for instance, charges $10 200 for a three-day executive education seminar, the Women's Director Development Program. As quoted on its website (http://www.kellogg.northwestern.edu/executive-education/take-action/ps/women-wslead/2016-10-women-wslead-01/). Accessed April 24, 2017.
24. As quoted on its website (http://www.bentley.edu/centers/center-for-women-and-business/womens-leadership-program). Accessed April 24, 2017.
25. As quoted on its website (https://wlp.gwu.edu/leadership). Accessed April 24, 2017.
26. The Harvard Business School, for instance, offers a five-day Leading Global Businesses seminar for $15 500. As quoted on its website (https://www.exed.hbs.edu/programs/gel/pages/default.aspx). Accessed April 24, 2017.
27. As quoted on its website (http://students.marshall.usc.edu/undergrad/international-programs/glp/). Accessed April 24, 2017.
28. For more information about this major, please visit its website (https://webapps.marietta.edu/~lead/?q=ILS%20Major). Accessed April 24, 2017.
29. Electronic communication with Linda Fowler, Former Director of the Rockefeller Center; Professor of Government, Frank J. Reagan Chair in Policy Studies, Emerita.
30. As Komives et al. (2011) discuss in *The Handbook for Student Leadership Development*, programs must be evaluated based on institutional and staffing considerations with regard to the feasibility of the program.
31. Website (https://students.dartmouth.edu/residential-life/house-communities/about-house-system). Accessed May 24, 2017.
32. For more information about this program, you can visit its website (https://psychology.tcu.edu/current-undergraduate-students/psychology-of-leadership-minor/). Accessed April 24, 2017.
33. As quoted on its website (https://www.fhsu.edu/leadership/). Accessed April 23, 2017.
34. As quoted on its website (http://cnu.edu/academics/departments/lams/). Accessed April 23, 2017.
35. As quoted on its website (http://kravisleadershipinstitute.org/leadership/leadership-studies/). Accessed April 23, 2017.
36. As quoted on its website (http://www.k-state.edu/leadership/about/ourmission.html). Accessed April 23, 2017.

REFERENCES

Arnold, D.G., Beauchamp, T.L., and Bowie, N.E. (Eds.). (2013). *Ethical Theory and Business*, Ninth Edition. Boston, MA: Pearson Education.

Belasen, A. (2012). *Developing Women Leaders in Corporate America: Balancing Competing Demands, Transcending Traditional Boundaries*. Santa Barbara, CA: Praeger.

Bennett, R.J. (2016). The Kaleidoscope Called Leadership. *Industrial and Commercial Training*, 48 (2), 86–8.

Bolman, L.G. and Deal, T.E. (1994). *Becoming a Teacher Leader: From Isolation to Collaboration*. Thousand Oaks, CA: Corwin Press.

Burns, J.M. (1978). *Leadership*. New York: Harper & Row.

Campbell, K.P. (2017). Business Ethics in Undergraduate Education. American

Association of Colleges and Universities. Website (https://www.aacu.org/public ations-research/periodicals/business-ethics-undergraduate-education). Accessed April 23, 2017.

Collay, M. (2011). *Everyday Teacher Leadership: Taking Action Where You Are*. San Francisco, CA: Jossey-Bass.

Crawford, M. (2014). *Developing as an Educational Leader and Manager*. Los Angeles, CA: SAGE.

Décosterd, M. (2013). *How Women Are Transforming Leadership: Four Key Traits Powering Success*. Santa Barbara, CA: Praeger.

Doyle, E., Buckley, P., and Carroll, C. (Eds.). (2013). *Innovative Business School Teaching: Engaging the Millennial Generation*. New York: Routledge.

Dye, C.F. (2010). *Leadership in Healthcare: Essential Values and Skills*, Second Edition. Chicago, IL: Health Administration Press.

Froyen, L.A. (1993). *Classroom Management: The Reflective Teacher-Leader*. New York: Maxwell Macmillan International.

Gallos, J.V. (Ed.). (2008). *Business Leadership: A Jossey-Bass Reader*, Second Edition. San Francisco. CA: Jossey-Bass.

Garsten, C. and Hernes, T. (Eds.). (2009). *Ethical Dilemmas in Management*. New York: Routledge.

George, B. (2003). *Authentic Leadership: Rediscovering the Secrets to Creating Lasting Value*. San Francisco, CA: Jossey-Bass.

Goleman, D. (2014). *What Makes a Leader: Why Emotional Intelligence Matters*. Florence, MA: More Than Sound.

Gundling, E., Hogan, T., and Cvitkovich, K. (2011). *What Is Global Leadership? 10 Key Behaviors That Define Great Global Leaders*. Boston, MA: Intercultural Press/Nicholas Brealey Publishing.

Harvey, M. and Barbour, J.D. (2009). *Global Leadership: Portraits of the Past, Visions for the Future*. College Park: James MacGregor Burns Academy of Leadership, University of Maryland.

Harvey, M. and Riggio, R. (2011). *Leadership Studies: The Dialogue of Disciplines*. Cheltenham, UK and Northampton, MA, USA: Edward Elgar Publishing.

Jordan, J.P., Buchanan, G.A., Clarke, N., and Jordan, K.C. (2013). *Leadership in Agriculture: Case Studies for a New Generation*. College Station: Texas A&M University Press.

Kellerman, B. (2012). *The End of Leadership*. New York: HarperCollins Publishers.

Kets de Vries, M., Guillén, L., Korotov, K., and Florent-Treacy, E. (Eds.). (2010). *The Coaching Kaleidoscope: Insights from the Inside*. New York: Palgrave Macmillan.

Kock, N. (Ed.). (2009). *Virtual Team Leadership and Collaborative Engineering Advancements: Contemporary Issues and Implications*. Hershey, PA: Information Science Reference.

Komives, S.R., Dugan, J.P., and Owen, J.E. (2011). *The Handbook for Student Leadership Development*, Second Edition. San Francisco, CA: John Wiley & Sons.

Ledlow, G.R. (2018). *Leadership for Health Professionals: Theory, Skills, and Applications*, Third Edition. Burlington, MA: Jones & Bartlett Learning.

Liautaud, M. (2016). *Breaking Through*. Hoboken, NJ: Wiley.

McManus, R. and Perruci, G. (2015). *Understanding Leadership: An Arts and Humanities Perspective*. New York: Routledge.

Matusak, L. (1997). *Finding Your Voice: Learning to Lead – Anywhere You Want to Make a Difference*. San Francisco, CA: Jossey-Bass.

Moore, L.L., Odom, S.F., and Moore, K.T. (2013). What a Degree in Agricultural Leadership Really Means: Exploring Student Conceptualizations. *Journal of Agricultural Education*, 54 (4), 1–12.

Morrison, R. and Ericsson, C. (2003). *Developing Effective Engineering Leadership*. London: Institution of Electrical Engineers.

Nirenberg, J. (2002). *Global Leadership*. Oxford: Capstone.

Wren, J.T., Riggio, R., and Genovese, M. (Eds.). (2009). *Leadership and the Liberal Arts: Achieving the Promise of a Liberal Education*. New York: Palgrave Macmillan.

3.   Developing a leadership curriculum

The wide variety of disciplines incorporating leadership components into their curricula seem to suggest that leadership studies is inherently an interdisciplinary enterprise, as discussed in the previous chapter. However, the study of leadership has become increasingly sophisticated, to the point that it has developed its own canon and its own academic niche in higher education.

In this chapter, we explore this intellectual development as a way to suggest different paths that educators may take in developing a leadership curriculum. Leadership education, as an intellectual endeavor, not only provides our students with an entry point into the scholarship traditions of the field, but is also a way to show how our own thinking about leadership has evolved over time.

IS LEADERSHIP A DISCIPLINE?

The empirical study of leadership is a little over a century old. From the great man theory of the late 19th century, to the use of chaos theory to explain organizational behavior in the 21st century, scholars have grappled with an increasing level of complexity in the field. With so many theories and models explaining minute elements of this human phenomenon, can leadership studies claim that it is a discipline? The search for legitimacy goes beyond the politics of academic halls. It also forces us to ask deep questions about the nature of the intellectual space that leadership studies occupies in higher education.

Defining a Discipline

As we mentioned in Chapter 1, some faculty and staff wonder whether leadership is an academic field of study. Is leadership a discipline? It really depends on how we define what we mean by the word "discipline" (Perruci and McManus, 2012). In the previous chapter, we traced the influence of many disciplines on the study and practice of leadership. Therefore, it seems natural to view leadership in terms of an interdisciplinary approach.

After all, how can we understand leadership without also understanding history, psychology, politics, economics, philosophy, and biology (neuroscience), to name just a few?

And yet, Ronald Riggio argues, "leadership studies is a distinct discipline, albeit a discipline that is 'emerging.' I have every expectation that a generation from now leadership studies will be a recognized discipline and universities that do not have departments of leadership studies (or at least programs devoted to leadership) will be in the minority" (Riggio, 2011, p. 9). This is a bold statement, but it is from a highly respected scholar in the field. In fact, the book in which this statement was made is part of Edward Elgar Publishing's New Horizons in Leadership Studies, edited by Joanne B. Ciulla, another well-respected scholar in the field.

Despite this bold assertion, Riggio readily admits that there are other scholars who vehemently disagree with the notion that leadership is a discipline. For the dissenters, this is simply a topical area, which allows scholars from different disciplines to explore leadership from their disciplinary lenses. In this at times visceral debate, the language of religion is sometimes invoked. Riggio himself states in the same chapter that he is a "true believer" in the distinction of leadership as a discipline. "James MacGregor Burns also professed his allegiance" (2011, p. 9). Riggio also admits that this debate is far from settled. Instead, he offers an operational definition of a discipline under which:

> [F]aculty share a common disciplinary identity and are classified and housed in the same unit [school or department] on campus. Faculty teach a distinct content area; courses are labeled with the disciplinary title ["leadership" or "leadership studies"]. There are a number of academic journals dedicated to research in the discipline. There are national and/or international organizations that are devoted to the academic discipline, and those disciplinary organizations play a key role in defining and promoting a discipline. (2011, p. 14)[1]

From this operational definition, it is easy to see that we are moving toward a "critical mass" or a "tipping point," whichever metaphor you may want to use, to describe how the field is coalescing and developing its own identity in higher education. If there is a litmus test for leadership studies, Riggio adds, it may simply come down to "when (and if) a majority, or a significant percentage, of universities have departments of leadership studies, the discipline most likely will have fully emerged" (2011, p. 10).

Legitimacy as Currency

This disciplinary debate may seem trivial, but in higher education the acceptance of a field of study as a discipline can potentially confer it with three types of high rewards (Trowler et al., 2012). First, disciplinary status provides the field with the legitimacy to gain a seat at the table – literally. In some institutions, departmental meetings are defined in terms of disciplinary recognition. In those meetings, critical issues related to the allocation of resources are discussed. If leadership does not have a seat, it has to rely on surrogates to argue its case.

Second, disciplinary status elevates its position with regard to university fundraising initiatives. The presence of a leadership department may attract potential donors who are interested in funding scholarships and experiential education endowments that are directly linked to a departmental structure. The institution's strategic plan also takes cues from the priorities that are often established at the disciplinary level (e.g., new labs for the sciences, a new building for the fine arts, endowed faculty chairs for the humanities).

Third, disciplinary status not only attracts dedicated faculty who feel that they have a home, but also draws undergraduate and graduate students who develop a sense of identity and intellectual community. Physical space is golden currency on a college or university campus. When a leadership school, department, or center acquires its own building, that infrastructure becomes a physical representation that the leadership discipline exists, and it serves as an official recognition of leadership's presence on campus.

The reasons above supporting the importance of disciplinary legitimacy can also be used as an argument against it. Many critics of the leadership-as-a-discipline position argue that its emergence also can lead to a silo effect, thus impoverishing the field intellectually. What makes the field so vibrant, they argue, is the fact that many different disciplines contribute to its theory-building. In their search for academic legitimacy, leadership departments may starve the very intellectual dynamism that led to its emergence in the first place.

THE LEADERSHIP CANON

The rise in popularity of leadership studies in the 1970s carried in its foundation the fear that leadership itself was in crisis. Leaders were not living up to our expectations. During the same decade, James MacGregor Burns (1978) noted that the true crisis was intellectual. While we knew so much about our leaders' personal habits and even their pets, we knew very little about leadership as a human phenomenon.

Burns drew our attention to the fact that the field of leadership remained too grounded in a cult of personality as opposed to the building of a strong theoretical foundation. He suggested that this was similar to the way that social scientists seek to develop theories and models to explain observable reality. Intellectual mediocrity inevitably leads to a shallow perspective on leadership as a field of study. Since Burns issued his call for a deeper understanding of leadership, the field has actually exploded into a wide variety of theories, models, and approaches. Barbara Kellerman (2010) explains that there is now a "leadership canon," or a body of knowledge that can be taught in the classroom.

The Empirical Study of Leadership

While debates about leadership have been going on for millennia, the empirical study of leadership in the West is only a century old. John Dugan's (2017) work entitled *Leadership Theory: Cultivating Critical Perspectives* examines different narratives that help us think about the leadership canon from a critical-analysis perspective. He recommends that we need to examine how these theories shape power and privilege. The dominant narrative in this century of theory-building is often divided into five historical periods:

- *The trait approach*: At the turn of the 19th century and the beginning of the 20th century, leadership was studied as the great feats of male leaders (the great man theory). This approach, focused on famous historical figures who seemed to have superior traits to be studied and emulated, equated leader with leadership (e.g., Ferris, 1889). This bias is still present today in many leadership studies. We often hear students refer to leadership as traits of great leaders (e.g., courage, charisma, fearlessness).[2]

- *The behavioral approach*: As it became increasingly obvious that scholars could not agree on a definitive list of the best traits for great leadership, studies shifted in the 1940s to the most appropriate behavior of leaders. This approach began to take into consideration the followers, because they were part of the leader's responsibility to reach certain goals. Empirical studies revealed two approaches that leaders could take: task orientation, which involved focus on the goal, versus relational orientation, which involved putting the leader–follower relationship above the goal (e.g., Stogdill and Coons, 1957).

- *The contingency approach*: By the 1960s, scholars had expanded the view of leadership to consider the organizational and environmental context.[3] The situation under which the leader–follower relationship took place became a critical variable in our understanding of leadership. Scholars such as Ken Blanchard and Paul Hersey (Hersey et al., 2013) developed the situational leadership model, which is still used today by consultants in organizations.

- *The relational approach*: By the 1970s, scholars had begun to pay attention to the quality of the leader–follower relationship in different contexts (Reitz, 2015). Burns's *Leadership* (1978) provided an intellectual breakthrough in this area. In Burns's "transforming leadership," leaders and followers became partners in the relationship. By the 1980s and into the 1990s, followers had gained increasing attention by scholars (e.g., Kelley, 1992). In fact, followership has come to have its own designation in the leadership canon (Kellerman, 2008; Chaleff, 2009; Hurwitz and Hurwitz, 2015; Schindler, 2015), although the bias continues to be on the development of leaders, as opposed to both leaders and followers. We are yet to see the founding of a followership studies school in higher education.

- *The cultural approach*: The 1990s experienced an explosion of theories and models, as the canon became a complex tapestry. One of the critical components to receive particular attention was cultural values and norms (e.g., Joynt and Warner, 1996). As globalization deeply impacted organizations, both locally and internationally, scholars paid increasing attention to the influence of cultural norms in the leader–follower relationship (Minkov, 2013). Global leadership emerged as a separate field of studies (Mendenhall et al., 2013). Many leadership programs today recognize this new dynamic and include separate courses and programmatic initiatives dealing with global leadership. Scholars such as Gert Hofstede, who developed the cultural dimensions theory, and Robert House, who implemented the GLOBE Study, have made significant contributions to our understanding of how cultures influence the behavior of leaders and followers (Hofstede, 1992; Chhokar et al., 2007).

With the evolution of the canon described above, each phase added a new component to an understanding of leadership, ranging from the simplest perspective of leadership (leader as synonymous with leadership – the first phase) to the most complex (cultural norms shaping the leader–follower relationship – the fifth phase). Each subsequent phase did not mean the disappearance of the previous one. After a century of leadership scholarship, for instance, scholars still pay attention to the trait approach (Kirkpatrick and Locke, 1991). As new components are continually added to new theories and models, our view of leadership has become more nuanced and complex.

The Five Components of Leadership

Before we delve into examples of leadership curricula, we need to examine more closely the constituent components of leadership. These components can be excellent building blocks for the development of a leadership curriculum. This examination will suggest possible ways to weave different curricular paths.

The first phase focused exclusively on the leader (the trait approach). As the focus turned to the behavioral approach, the follower was added to the mix – finding ways for the leader to motivate followers to move toward the goal. This new configuration suggested three basic components of leadership: leader, follower, and goals. Many programs build their curricula around these three components and see leadership as the manner in which leaders motivate their followers toward a goal.

If leadership took place in a vacuum, that would be enough. However, the leader–follower relationship exists within a societal or organizational context. In the leadership canon, we see that the contingency approach (situational leadership) supplanted the behavioral approach in the 1960s. Many leadership programs add an organizational leadership component to their curriculum as a way to capture the importance of contextual analysis.

In the 1970s, transformational leadership was added to the canon. What made this perspective particularly revolutionary was the treatment of leaders and followers as partners in the study and practice of leadership. The concept of followership emerged as a viable analytical variable. Leadership was no longer simply about the leader. The follower was incorporated into the process, and scholars studied the ways that power played a role in the leader–follower relationship.

This relationship can take two extremes – one based on the leader "in charge" (the command-and-control approach) and another based on the followers being the main focus of attention (with the leader as a facilitator). In between these two extremes lies a continuum that captures the distribution of power between leaders and their followers (McManus and Perruci, 2015). A leadership curriculum can be built around this power continuum, stressing the different facets of the leader–follower relationship, as they seek to accomplish their goals.

By the 1990s, the literature had added a fifth component to the study of leadership – the cultural norms and values that shape the behavior of leaders and followers. This cultural dimension opened scholarship to the importance of culture in shaping the way leaders view themselves. The emerging global leadership literature compared cultural perspectives on leadership, explored the skill-set of global leaders, and even assessed the impact that globalization was having on global leadership.

Today, these five components (leader, follower, goal, context, and cultural norms or values) constitute the main elements of theories and models designed to explain how leadership works. While we may not be close to achieving a general theory of leadership, the multiple variety of approaches have created a robust selection from which educators can draw when developing a leadership curriculum.

THE MCDONOUGH AND ROCKEFELLER EXPERIENCES

Most educators interested in leadership have been exposed to some of the five components discussed above. The purpose of this book is not to examine the merits of each theory and model. We will leave that to the canon builders. Rather, we invite educators to be thoughtful and intentional when developing a leadership curriculum. In this section, we offer two experiences. The first one integrates the five components model (McManus and Perruci, 2015) into a core curriculum in a leadership program. In the other, leadership themes are incorporated into an existing curriculum within a specific area of study (in this case, public policy).

The McDonough Leadership Curriculum

The McDonough Center uses the five components of leadership model to build its core curriculum (McManus and Perruci, 2015).

Foundations course

This Leadership 101 introduction provides students with a common language related to leadership. Students come to our institutions with a wide variety of perspectives on what leadership is. While most of them tend to equate leader with leadership (traits approach), it becomes the instructor's challenge to move them away from this simplistic view and introduce them to a more complex understanding of leadership. This foundations course also introduces students to ethical dilemmas in the power continuum. Using a critical thinking approach, this course exposes students to the leader–follower relationship – giving equal billing to both leaders (leadership) and followers (followership).

At McDonough, we begin this introductory course with an excerpt from John Gardner's *On Leadership*, in which he presents the concept of dispersed leadership (Gardner, 1993). This reading sets the stage for a deep discussion about the responsibility of stepping up and responding to the call to lead. It also creates a space to introduce a way of viewing the leader–follower relationship as a continuum, ranging from an all-powerful leader on the one hand (leader-centric approach; individualism) to the primacy of the group (follower-centric; collectivism) on the other. This continuum allows us to engage the learners in a meaningful discussion about their "comfort zones."

Once exposed to the continuum, they begin to expand their leadership language. What does it mean to be a servant leader in this continuum? Or a transformational leader who is intent on transforming not only himself or herself but also the followers? Here, we introduce them to Burns's distinction between transactional and transforming leadership. Again, these concepts allow the learners to begin to develop a deeper understanding of the field of leadership studies.

We then ask our students to consider the extreme of each side of the continuum. They read Karl Marx's *The Communist Manifesto* and Ayn Rand's *Anthem* – representing the extremes of collectivism and individualism, respectively. As a pedagogical method, through the introduction of the extremes, students examine their own conceptions of what it means to lead with the leader (individualism) and the group (collectivism) in mind.

Using a liberal-arts model, as mentioned in the previous chapter, we also introduce them to Plato's philosopher-king concept in *The Republic* (the celebration of leadership as the realm of the elite) and Aristotle's idea of leadership as a life cycle in *A Treatise on Government* (generations taking turns to lead). This contrast allows the students to examine their own assumptions about human nature. Plato's argument is that if leadership is left to the collective, it quickly degenerates into mobocracy. Therefore, the educated few are given the responsibility of leading. Enlightened leaders supposedly are capable of leading with the group interests in mind. Students quickly point out that Plato's idealism is fraught with red flags: Will the philosopher-king only take the group's interests into consideration? Are we to expect that enlightened leaders will set aside their individual interests for the sake of the group? Students know that real life tells us a different story.

Then learners are invited to contrast that view with Aristotle's argument that, if everyone is educated, then everyone can take turns leading. Again, that shows a degree of idealism: Can everyone be educated to the point that they can effectively take turns leading? In reality, do some people show little interest in becoming well versed in the art of leading? If so, then what are we to do?

Somewhere between Plato's philosopher-king and Aristotle's direct democracy lies the perspective that the leader–follower relationship is filled with tension, self-interest, and messy power dynamics. It falls to the educator to facilitate a deep discussion concerning learners' assumptions about human nature. If the assumption is that human beings are selfish and self-interested, then transactional leadership is the best we can hope for; however, there is always Burns telling us – in Aristotelian fashion – that we are capable of rising above self-interest to look after the interests of the collective.

The McDonough faculty members use this power dynamic as an opportunity to introduce the role of the follower in leadership. The students always find this a bit jarring. Few of our students have heard the term "followership." Yet they can readily see that followers are also part of the equation. Models such as Robert Kelley's (1992), Ira Chaleff's (2009), and Barbara Kellerman's (2008) provide their theoretical entry point into the language of followership.

However, we do not stop at the theoretical level. We push our learners to consider the degree to which followers are willing to submit to authority. Why is it that research shows that followers are easily swayed to conform to authority? Students are left with the uncomfortable feeling that they too could be guilty of atrocities by not questioning misguided leaders' orders.

The introduction of the two key players, leaders and followers, provides the students with an opportunity to examine the role of teamwork. Further, they examine how leaders and followers work together and share power. At this point in the course, the McDonough Center actually makes use of service learning as a pedagogical tool. We divide the class into teams, introduce them to different models of teamwork, and then give them a community-service project. At the end of the semester, they present their project to the rest of the class and draw insights into the challenges of working in teams.

Once the roles of both the leaders and the followers have been thoroughly examined individually and in teams, the students are ready to consider the third component of the McDonough Center's definition of leadership – the goal. Most students assume that the leader is in charge of defining the goal. As a result, they find it fascinating when we pose the concept of an "invisible leader" – when a goal drives the actions of leaders and followers (Hickman and Sorenson, 2014).

At this point, McDonough faculty introduce ethical considerations leaders and followers think about as they journey toward the goal (Ciulla et al., 2005; Ciulla, 2014). Niccolò Machiavelli is always a favorite when the concept of an amoral perspective is discussed. Invariably, the instructors find a student who is willing to stake his or her campus reputation on the notion that Machiavelli had it right. Most students embrace the ethical dimensions of leadership. However, agreement breaks down once we contrast Immanuel Kant's categorical imperative, which suggests that once a position is considered unethical it should always be so, regardless of the circumstance, to British utilitarianism under John Stuart Mill, who believed in the greatest good for the greatest number of people. Students discuss questions such as: Is the killing of noncombatant civilians – especially children – always unethical? If so, how does one justify a leader's decision to use nuclear weapons, as in the U.S. case in World War II?

These three components – leader, follower, and goal – serve as the foundation for expanding the students' language of leadership. The seminar format allows for ample discussion and sharing of different points of view, providing students with an opportunity to develop their critical-thinking skills. The purpose of this course is not necessarily to dictate what conclusions they should derive from the course content. In most cases, the students leave the course feeling that their previous simplistic assumptions are not enough. They need to learn more. When they reach this point in their reflection, they are ready to dig deeper into the study of leadership. This is provided through the next course in the core curriculum, organizational leadership.

Organizational leadership course

Following the discussion of the "units of analysis" in Chapter 1, the next level in a leadership curriculum is a course on organizational leadership with a focus on context. After all, the leader–follower relationship does not take place in a vacuum. It exists within an environmental context that shapes the behavior of both leaders and followers.

The field of organizational leadership is well established enough that McDonough faculty can find textbooks that provide a general overview of the main theories and concepts related to this area. However, in the same liberal-arts spirit that is used in the foundations course, this course allows the students to question old assumptions and challenges their views of leadership within an organizational context.

McDonough's course uses two main textbooks, the first by Gil Hickman (2016) and the second by Barbara Kellerman (2010). The course is divided into six units. The first unit highlights the thinking about organizational leadership. This unit provides students with a general overview of the field, including global demographic trends that are influencing organizational leadership. Drawing from Gareth Morgan's *Images of Organization* (2006), students also explore the use of metaphors to explain organizational behavior in this unit. In particular, the class contrasts two images – organizations as machines and organizations as organisms.

The second unit of the course focuses on leader-centric approaches to organizational leadership. In particular, students are exposed to liberal-arts-based literature, such as the typology found in Max Weber's *The Theory of Social and Economic Organization* (1969), as well as traditional theories such as charismatic leadership, emotional intelligence, and servant leadership. In this unit, the goal is to get students to think of how leaders impact their organizations through their leadership styles.

The third unit switches the focus to the follower-centric approaches related to organizational leadership. While students were introduced to followership theory in the foundations course, this unit allows students to dive deeper into the connection between followership and the organizational context. Topics such as situational leadership democracy in the workplace, women and leadership, generational differences in workplace behavior, and group psychology provide students with more challenging issues to debate and process.

In the fourth unit, we explore goals in the context of organizational leadership. The organizational environment helps students to understand the context of goal development and implementation. In particular, they grapple with the challenges of promoting organizational change. There is a solid body of literature in this area, including the work done by John Kotter with his change model (Kotter, 2012; Kotter and Cohen, 2012).

The fifth and sixth units put theoretical approaches into practice by exploring two organizational challenges – establishing an ethical organizational culture, and leading through organizational social responsibility. Students are able to draw from current events to discuss these two topics more intensively.

Theories and models course
Once students have mastered the fundamentals (the leader–follower relationship and organizational leadership), they are ready to tackle heavier materials – an in-depth review of the empirical study of leadership. The five phases in the empirical study of leadership can be organized into a semester-/quarter-long course that provides a comprehensive overview of the leadership canon.

At McDonough, we use Peter Northouse's *Theory and Practice* (2015) for this course as the standard textbook most associated with this area. The course's stated objective is to introduce students to the major streams of thought within historical and contemporary contexts, and to provide students with the opportunity to begin developing their own philosophy of leadership.

While the course covers all of the five phases of the empirical study of leadership, it ends with a discussion of chaos theory and its application to our understanding of leadership. The course also includes other emerging approaches, including current research connecting leadership behavior and neuroscience.

Aside from the heavy theoretical content, the course includes a poster project. Students are asked to select a particular theory or model and then apply it to a historical figure. They then develop an actual poster summarizing their findings and present their poster as part of a three-day poster conference. The students present their posters formally before an audience composed of first-year students who are taking the foundations course and judges who include McDonough faculty, staff, or affiliated faculty. Each night of the conference, the judges work together to select the best poster. The three posters then are framed and displayed in the McDonough Gallery during the following academic year.

Global leadership course

The last core course in the McDonough curriculum focuses on global leadership. For many scholars, global leadership in the past two decades has emerged as a separate field of study. Students are introduced to this field and its subcomponents as the fourth and final core course in the curriculum. The subcomponents include: comparative leadership studies, or the study of how different cultures view leadership; the impact of globalization, or the sources of collaboration and competition on the global stage; and the competencies of a global leader.

The course begins with the introduction of the growing global leadership literature. Similar to organizational leadership, the field of global leadership has received more attention lately as a separate field of study. Explaining the historical context is critically important at this stage in the course because few students have the historical understanding of the global events of the past four centuries.

Students are introduced to the 1648 Peace of Westphalia as the entry point into the modern state system. The treaty that ended the Thirty Years War is used to make students aware of the main characteristics of a nation-state. Students discuss issues related to sovereignty and territorial claim, as well as the distinction between domestic and international affairs. Intuitively, students know these concepts because they grew up under them.

A basic understanding of the modern state system allows students to explore the concept of globalization as a challenge to the Westphalian world order. Up to this point, students have recognized the existence of leaders at the local, national, and international levels. The fourth type of leader, or global leader, as a result of globalization, now emerges in the discussion. Students learn that many of them will inherit or embrace this transnational leadership perspective and see the whole world as their domain – irrespective of national borders.

Students struggle with this transnational leadership perspective because they see the backlash it generates in the form of ultra-nationalism. The current tug-of-war between nationalism and globalism is a new revelation to many students. In their minds, the world has always embraced Western values as the symbol of globalization. In this course, they realize how some American leaders are rejecting globalization.

Once students gain familiarity about the current historical processes that are shaping global leadership, they are ready to investigate different cultural perspectives on leadership. This comparative study begins with a general view of the Western context. Leadership is viewed as a "prize" in which individuals compete for the top spot in the organizational hierarchy. This individualist perspective shows preference for the leader as opposed to the follower. We remind our students of the saying, particularly in the United States, "Be a leader, not a follower."

Starting from the Western perspective, the course now moves to Latin America, which for some historians is considered a Mediterranean vision of Western civilization. Latin America's ultra-individualism is compared to the collectivist perspectives of Islam, which treats leadership as a trust. Students study the concept of leadership through Ubuntu in the continent of Africa, and they learn about leadership as being a personal journey through a study of Buddhism. Finally, they explore the concept of leadership as service through a study of Confucianism and Taoism in East Asia.[4]

The global leadership course seeks to bridge theory and practice by next exploring the global competencies that leaders will need in order to thrive under globalization and the individual cultural perspectives. Globalization is bringing cultures around the world into close contact, so leaders and followers may not share similar norms and values even though they work for the same organization. The past expectation that followers had to conform to the leaders' norms may not necessarily be the case. Followers are now empowered through advanced education, information technology, and open communication platforms that allow them to share, mobilize, and advocate.

In the global competencies section of the course, students discover some key skills that global leaders should seek to master. Scholarship in this area has uncovered too many competencies to adequately review in a single course. As a result, the course focuses on developing a global mindset or transnationalism, dealing with diversity, conflict resolution, team-building, intercultural communication, and adapting to change. It is clearly not an exhaustive list, but the students are able to get a sense of the complexity of global leadership in the new millennium.

Infusing Leadership into the Rockefeller Curriculum

At the Rockefeller Center, the leadership courses are embedded within Dartmouth's Public Policy curriculum. The introduction to public policy research, for instance, provides the foundation from which students are able to participate in the Public Policy Research Shop, which is a faculty-mentored research enterprise that allows students to engage directly in the public policy-making processes in Vermont and New Hampshire. Students participating in the Policy Research Shop provide "valuable, non-partisan research to state legislative committees, statewide commissions, and executive agencies on critical issues facing each state."[5]

The global policy leadership practicum is another course offered by the Rockefeller Center, which serves as the capstone experience for the Public Policy minor. The course gives students an opportunity to implement civil society programming at the global level. Most recently, students focused on Ukraine and studied the methodologies employed by the United States Agency for International Development (USAID). Students then traveled to Ukraine and conducted a democracy and government assessment for USAID. In the process of completing this client-driven exercise, students developed "a full and comprehensive understanding of what civil society entails in democratic societies and the roles that civil society organizations (CSOs) play in linking citizens to government, both in general and in the specific context of contemporary Ukraine."[6]

The Rockefeller Center also offers leadership electives, which students may take as part of the public policy curriculum. The Leadership in Civil Society course, for instance, focuses on three key social and political concepts – leadership, social capital, and civil society. Through this course, students explore "the broad literature on nonprofit leadership as well as the more targeted literatures that address grassroots mobilization, religious (lay/servant) leadership, interest group influence, organizational maintenance and political representation, and the leadership problems associated with collective action."[7] We mention these examples from our respective centers as a way to show different approaches to curriculum development.

There is no single formula for developing a rigorous curriculum that can expand students' knowledge of how leadership works. Academic strengths of educators as well as an institution's traditions may influence the types of courses that are integrated into a leadership program. These choices must give students an exposure to the concepts and literary contributions that give students a deeper understanding of the leadership canon.

Every leadership program obviously will have a different history and reality that will shape the curricular choices that are made. The key to a vibrant leadership curriculum is to be purposeful in curricular development. It has to make sense as a value proposition for the learners. This high level of intentionality expressed in the development of the curriculum will also appear in the way educators structure their own teaching environment, a topic that we turn to in the next chapter.

REFLECTION QUESTIONS

1. Is leadership studies viewed by the faculty as a legitimate discipline at your institution? Why or why not?
2. What are the conceptual and administrative differences between a department and a program? Do these distinctions matter at your institution?
3. Where is your leadership department or program located on campus? What does this location say about the legitimacy of the department or program?
4. How does your leadership curriculum reflect an intentional commitment to a certain intellectual tradition found in the "leadership canon"?
5. How can leadership theories and models be infused into your institution's existing curriculum?

NOTES

1. Bracketed text added by the authors.
2. See, for instance, Micha Kaufman (2014), 10 Traits of Great Business Leaders, *Forbes. com*, February 5. Website (http://www.forbes.com/sites/michakaufman/2014/09/05/10-traits-of-great-business-leaders/#6b99067668b2). Accessed February 18, 2017.
3. Fred Fiedler (1967), one of the best-known contingency theorists, argued that there is no single best leadership style, as proposed by the trait approach. Rather, effective leaders are able to adapt their style according to different situations.
4. The purpose of this section of the chapter is not to review all of the cultural perspectives in-depth, because it would make this chapter too long. For the sake of brevity, we will simply mention the other cultural perspectives that we cover in the course, and you can find their individual content in Part II of McManus and Perruci (2015).
5. As quoted in http://rockefeller.dartmouth.edu/public-policy/class-1964-policy-research-shop. Accessed May 22, 2017. Every year, about 50 students are involved in the Policy Research Shop, resulting in the development of 15 projects. Interview with Ronald G. Shaiko, Senior Fellow and Associate Director of the Rockefeller Center, April 11, 2017.
6. As quoted in the course syllabus; accessed during interview with Shaiko, April 11, 2017.
7. As quoted in the course syllabus; accessed during interview with Shaiko, April 11, 2017.

REFERENCES

Burns, J.M. (1978). *Leadership*. New York: Harper & Row.
Chaleff, I. (2009). *The Courageous Follower: Standing Up To and For Our Leaders*, Third Edition. San Francisco, CA: Berrett-Koehler.
Chhokar, J., Brodbek, F., and House, R. (2007). *Culture and Leadership across the World: The GLOBE Book of In-Depth Studies of 25 Societies*. Mahwah, NJ: Lawrence Erlbaum Associates.
Ciulla, J. (Ed.). (2014). *Ethics, the Heart of Leadership*, Third Edition. Santa Barbara, CA: Praeger.

Ciulla, J., Price, T., and Murphy, S. (Eds.). (2005). *The Quest for Moral Leaders: Essays on Leadership Ethics.* Cheltenham, UK and Northampton, MA, USA: Edward Elgar Publishing.

Dugan, J.P. (2017). *Leadership Theory: Cultivating Critical Perspectives.* San Francisco, CA: Jossey-Bass.

Ferris, G.T. (1889). *Great Leaders: Historic Portraits from the Great Historians.* New York: D. Appleton & Company.

Fiedler, F. (1967). *A Theory of Leadership Effectiveness.* New York: McGraw-Hill.

Gardner, J. (1993). *On Leadership.* New York: Free Press.

Hersey, P., Blanchard, K.H., and Johnson, D.E. (2013). *Management of Organizational Behavior: Leading Human Resources*, Tenth Edition. Boston, MA: Pearson.

Hickman, G. (2016). *Leading Organizations: Perspective for a New Era*, Third Edition. Los Angeles, CA: SAGE.

Hickman, G. and Sorenson, G. (2014). *The Power of Invisible Leadership: How a Compelling Common Purpose Inspires Exceptional Leadership.* Thousand Oaks, CA: SAGE.

Hofstede, G. (1992). Cultural Dimensions in People Management: The Socialization Perspective. In V. Pucik, N. Tichy, and C. Barnett (Eds.), *Globalizing Management: Creating and Leading the Competitive Organization* (pp. 139–58). New York: Wiley.

Hurwitz, M. and Hurwitz, S. (2015). *Leadership Is Half the Story: A Fresh Look at Followership, Leadership, and Collaboration.* Toronto: University of Toronto Press.

Joynt, P. and Warner, M. (1996). *Managing across Cultures: Issues and Perspectives.* Boston, MA: International Thomson Business Press.

Kellerman, B. (2008). *Followership: How Followers Are Creating Change and Changing Leaders.* Boston, MA: Harvard Business School Press.

Kellerman, B. (2010). *Leadership: Essential Selections on Power, Authority and Influence.* New York: McGraw-Hill.

Kelley, R. (1992). *The Power of Followership: How to Create Leaders People Want to Follow, and Followers Who Lead Themselves.* New York: Doubleday/Currency.

Kirkpatrick, S. and Locke, E. (1991). Leadership: Do Traits Matter? *Academy of Management Executive*, 5 (2), 48–60.

Kotter, J. (2012). *Leading Change.* Boston, MA: Harvard Business Review Press.

Kotter, J. and Cohen, D. (2012). *The Heart of Change: Real-Life Stories of How People Change Their Organizations.* Boston, MA: Harvard Business Review Press.

McManus, R. and Perruci, G. (2015). *Understanding Leadership: An Arts and Humanities Perspective.* New York: Routledge.

Mendenhall, M., Osland, J., Bird, A., Oddou, G., Maznevski, M., Stevens, M., and Stahl, G. (2013). *Global Leadership: Research, Practice, and Development.* New York: Routledge.

Minkov, M. (2013). *Cross-cultural Analysis: The Science and Art of Comparing the World's Modern Societies and Their Cultures.* Thousand Oaks, CA: SAGE.

Morgan, G. (2006). *Images of Organization.* Thousand Oaks, CA: SAGE.

Northouse, P. (2015). *Theory and Practice*, Seventh Edition. Los Angeles, CA: SAGE.

Perruci, G. and McManus, R. (2012). The State of Leadership Studies. *Journal of Leadership Studies*, 6 (3), 49–54.

Reitz, M. (2015). *Dialogue in Organizations: Developing Relational Leadership*. New York: Palgrave Macmillan.

Riggio, R. (2011). Is Leadership Studies a Discipline? In M. Harvey and R. Riggio (Eds.), *Leadership Studies: The Dialogue of Disciplines* (pp. 9–19). Cheltenham, UK and Northampton, MA, USA: Edward Elgar Publishing.

Schindler, J.H. (2015). *Followership: What It Takes to Lead*. New York: Business Expert Press.

Stogdill, R. and Coons, A.E. (Eds.). (1957). *Leader Behavior: Its Description and Measurement*. Columbus: Bureau of Business Research, College of Commerce and Administration, Ohio State University.

Trowler, P., Saunders, M., and Bamber, V. (Eds.). (2012). *Tribes and Territories in the 21st Century: Rethinking the Significance of Disciplines in Higher Education*. New York: Routledge.

Weber, M. (1969). *The Theory of Social and Economic Organization*. Transl. by A.M. Henderson and T. Parsons. New York: Free Press.

4.   The "smart" classroom

One of the questions that we often get asked about "teaching about leadership" is: How do you teach leadership? While Part II of this book will deal with some of the co-curricular tools that we can use to teach leadership, we thought it would be helpful at this point in the book to reflect on the classroom setting in which we teach about leadership.

Much has been written about the use of technology in the classroom (Lloyd, 1997; McKamey, 2008; Blink, 2016). In fact, the term "smart" has become associated with a technology-enhanced classroom that gives an instructor access to the latest bells and whistles. The assumption seems to be that the more technology you use in the classroom, the more effective you will become in reaching your educational mission. In this chapter, we offer a different take on the term "'smart' classroom" – one in which the educator and the learners alike engage in a transformative process and one which enables them to grow. Technology may be part of that process, but it is not an end in itself.

In the first section of the chapter, we examine the assumptions we make about the term "'smart' classroom." The second section of the chapter will introduce strategies that educators can use to increase engagement in the classroom (e.g., the Socratic method, use of artifacts, case studies). We do not discount the use of technology in the classroom, because we believe that it can be a useful tool when teaching about leadership. The chapter closes with an examination of "nontraditional" approaches to leadership pedagogy; for example, service-learning projects, simulations, the flipped classroom, and the "mobile" classroom.

WHAT MAKES A CLASSROOM "SMART"

The rapid expansion of technology use in the classroom has left us with the increasing expectation that educators should be well versed in using the latest gadgets and applications. In our age of rapid technological change, we are eager to incorporate all the bells and whistles that we can find. However, consider the pointed question: What makes a classroom "smart"? In leadership education, we believe that the "smart" quality of a classroom experience is found not in technology per se, but in the way our learners become engaged and contribute to the success of leadership education.

When Technology Replaces/Complements Pedagogy

Technology has always been a part of the learning process (Carr-Chellman and Rowland, 2017). It comes in many forms and shapes. The blackboard and chalk are themselves technological innovations that provide the educator with an effective tool for delivering course content. When words and shapes are written on a blackboard, the learners are drawn to them in a way that enhances the visual experience. The introduction of whiteboards with markers has further expanded visual learning through the use of different colors.

In recent decades, we have seen new technology brought into the classroom through the use of computers, projectors, WiFi access to the Internet, and ultimately "smartboards" – whiteboards that have become interactive. At the risk of sounding slightly nostalgic, it sometimes feels as though technology has invaded our classrooms, now populated by students who are "digital natives" (Prensky, 2012; Blink, 2016).

The advent of computers and projectors revolutionized the classroom by giving the teacher greater access to visual content. Back in the early 1990s, when one of the co-authors began his teaching career in political science, he dreamed of the ability to build lectures that could include photographs of political leaders, thus breaking the monotony of the blackboard. Later in the decade, PowerPoint and the Internet entered the picture, which made that "dream" possible (Knoblauch, 2013). From blackboard, we moved to the whiteboard; next, we dabbled with the smartboard, only to settle on the PowerPoint screen that sidelined the "boards." In a way, the screen became the new board with pre-fabricated content.

The advent of online learning has further mixed technology and pedagogy (Kearsley, 2000; Poritz and Rees, 2017). Leadership education has become adept in the use of online technology, particularly at the graduate level. Online teaching can be effective in promoting group discussion, the delivery of packaged course content (e.g., PowerPoint slides), and ancillaries (e.g., multimedia clips) for full-time working professionals.

The "Smart" Classroom

We acknowledge the power of technology to make knowledge more accessible to a growing number of professionals who use online education as a way to expand their grasp of complex issues in a marketplace that demands continuous professional development (Lloyd, 2005; Tomei, 2008). Our contention, however, is that undergraduate leadership education requires a different approach.

At the undergraduate level, we can identify two general objectives of a classroom experience. First, the classroom setting can be the environment through which knowledge about the academic field of leadership is transmitted from educators to learner. That is the traditional view of a classroom – the place where educators speak, students take notes, and, later on, an exam is given in order to test whether the students have mastered the material. Many disciplines use this classroom structure effectively. In a way, teaching the leadership canon can follow the same approach, particularly in a course focused on "theories and models of leadership."

However, the traditional classroom experience does not necessarily mean a rote type of delivery that often frustrates students. Joan Marques, Satinder Dhiman, and Jerry Biberman (2012), for instance, encourage leadership educators to consider using humor as a pedagogical tool in the classroom. There are different pedagogical tools, as the next section of this chapter will suggest, that a teacher should consider to "spice things up" in the classroom. We believe that the traditional lecture style, so popular in many disciplines, does not work well for teaching leadership.

We invite you to consider the second objective of a leadership education classroom experience – the classroom as the setting in which critical thinking takes place. Most leadership programs identify critical thinking as one of their leadership competencies. We want our emerging leaders to gain an appreciation for critical thinking, as an important tool in both leading and following. The classroom can be the perfect setting for bridging theory and practice – the environment in which students learn the canon, while at the same time developing the engagement skills that will serve them well in the workplace.

That is the true potential of a "smart" classroom – one in which theory and practice are connected in meaningful ways. What makes the classroom truly "smart" is its ability to make connections between theory and practice. The key word that links the two is *engagement*. We do not necessarily mean student participation in the form of answering questions posed by the educators. Instead, by engagement we mean the students being present (fully committed to the classroom experience), listening to their peers' comments, making a meaningful contribution to the classroom discussion, challenging one another's assumptions, and intellectually growing in the process.

The Classroom as a Metaphor

The "smart" classroom can be used as a metaphor for the growth component that we expect in our leadership programs. As you recall from Chapter 1, we structured "teaching leadership" around three components: leadership education; leadership competency-building; and leadership development. The classroom is a perfect environment for an emerging leader's development to take place.

We often treat our classrooms as great examples of transactional leadership. Students see themselves as consumers whose tuition fee "buys" knowledge. In turn, the instructors are paid wages in order to deliver the content expected within the curriculum. This relationship is short-lived. Once the exchange is completed, each side moves on to other tasks – and new transactional opportunities. After all, the semester or quarter has a time limitation.

The "smart" classroom in our leadership programs should intentionally create an environment in which transformational leadership takes place. One of the most common shortcomings of some leadership programs is to focus mainly on competency-building as a transactional enterprise. Leadership programs that truly stand out tend to approach teaching leadership as a transformative opportunity that connects theory and practice in a way that leads to leadership development at the individual learners' level.

Human-Centered Design

As a student of community development many years ago, one of the co-authors learned from a thoughtful professor that people are capable of solving, and willing to solve, problems they themselves identify. Further, given the appropriate resources, they will find appropriate solutions for these problems. At the heart of these two statements lies the user of any product or service.

The co-author, in her experience in several countries, observed that any community project that actively involves users of an intervention in its design, implementation, and evaluation often meets with positive and desired results. In recent years, the field of design thinking, user-centered design, or human-centered design has further substantiated this. Human-centered design is based on the fundamental idea that the most innovative and constructive solution to a problem can only be found if the underlying human need is properly and precisely identified. It is a creative multilayered process and methodology that invites collaboration among people who have gathered together to address an identified problem. Done thoughtfully under the guidance of trained facilitators, it sparks energy and optimism to find thoughtful, interdisciplinary, and creative solutions to complex problems. Most importantly, these solutions are developed with the user in mind and with the involvement of the user.

Within the context of our discussion in this book, design thinking helps educators approach their curricular and co-curricular offerings and careers with a sense of creative purpose, and it helps them pass this sense on to their students. As a methodology, it helps to develop a spirit of innovation among learners because they are driven to explore new ideas, which are different from their own. The step-by-step process of "guided mastery" helps learners to build, test, and retest ideas or "prototypes" with different stakeholders until one of these emerges as a possibly viable solution to an identified problem. It presents possibilities, which can expand and contract after every step. The pathway to the solution starts with an exhaustive effort to deeply understand the user and the need. The first idea is almost never the right one, and every subsequent proposal is tested against the core beliefs carefully developed at the beginning of the process.

The process of continuous experimentation, though hard and sometimes even taxing, builds grit and determination to "get it right." The step-by-step approach, and the small successes achieved as a result of such a process, builds confidence in the learner, or "self-efficacy," as Albert Bandura (1997) calls it. The process also encourages learners to recognize their own potential and capability to address problems with compassion.[1] The entire methodology is infused with the practice of empathy, which is a learner's capability to understand and share the feelings of his or her team members as well as those of the people for whom a solution is being designed. Authentic listening is critical to demonstrating authentic empathy! The viable solution in the end generates joy and a feeling of accomplishment. It instills creative confidence within the learners to tackle the next problem with the same enthusiasm and anticipation. It also helps to build a "growth" mindset, as Carol Dweck (2006) would say, and helps learners to practice working as a team toward a common goal.

Although there are several examples of how human-centered design methodology has been used in different fields such as health, agriculture, and education, we are highlighting one example from the health field. A group of Stanford students was tasked to reconstruct a typical incubator to address the issue of infant mortality in premature and low-birthweight babies in developing countries. After careful research and dedicated work, their first prototype was still too expensive and difficult to use. This prototype required access to electricity or assistance from a medical facility. Only after a visit to Nepal, in which one of the team members truly felt the desperation of the mothers she spoke to, did the team really understand the human need. It drove them to a complete conceptual reframing of their solution's criteria and purpose. The resulting innovation, the Embrace incubator, is a low-cost polymer blanket which helps regulate infants' body temperature, giving them a better chance to survive.[2] Priced at around $25, the blanket is portable, safe, and reusable, and requires only intermittent access to electricity.[3] The key takeaway here is that such an unconventional yet life-changing solution was only possible when the team took the time to gain real insight into the problem by talking to mothers and really understanding their perspectives on the problem.

We conclude our thoughts about human-centered design by suggesting that, without knowing the user and the need, our preconceived notions, however well educated, need to be tested and retested. Claudia Kotchka, IDEO Fellow, who successfully led an innovation culture transformation at Procter & Gamble, says:

> The most important thing a design thinking leader needs to do is ask the right broad question. This question is the type that allows a team to brainstorm an infinite amount of possible solutions. The next thing a leader needs to know is that you stifle innovation if you ask your team to prove it works. Instead, ask them, "What are your consumer insights?" or "Show me your prototypes." The key is to always keep the team customer-focused.[4]

The true meaning of empathy in human-centered design is to resist the urge to find a solution by looking inward and instead practice the patience needed to test assumptions, reflect meaningfully, and absorb key insights from the users themselves. We urge educators to avail themselves of the resources design thinking opens up for them in their curricular or co-curricular offerings.

STRATEGIES FOR INCREASING ENGAGEMENT

In the previous section, we focused on the leadership classroom as the place where all three components come together in powerful ways – leadership education, leadership competency-building, and leadership development. The key word linking all of these components is "engagement." Leadership students come to classrooms not only open to expanding their knowledge of leadership, but also with an engagement mindset. They need to be ready to use critical thinking in a way that will challenge the educator and themselves to achieve deep learning.

How can educators promote this type of engaging environment? While we recognize that the responsibility does not solely fall on the educators, strategies that allow learners to participate in a transformative experience can be used.

Start with the "Why"

Simon Sinek offers an insightful perspective on product development that he calls the "Golden Circle."[5] Organizations operate on three levels – who, how, and what. Imagine the levels as concentric circles, with "who" occupying the core, "how" being the middle circle, and "what" being the outer circle. Sinek suggests that many organizations fail because they mainly focus on the "what" – e.g., manufacturing computers – and then work their way in to the other circles.

Instead, Sinek says that true innovators tend to start with the "why": Why do you do what you do? What do you believe in? He offers the example of Apple. Rather than focusing on the "what" (e.g., "We sell computers. Do you want to buy one?"), Apple focuses first on the "why" (e.g., "We believe in challenging the status quo"). This perspective allows Apple to go beyond computers and innovate in many related fields (e.g., phones, music players). Sinek makes the argument that people do not buy "what" you do; rather, they focus on "why" you do what you do.

"Smart" leadership classroom strategies should begin with the "why" and seek to answer the question: Why have a leadership program in the first place? If educators can clearly articulate why they believe a leadership program is necessary for their learners, everything else follows. If they start with the "what," they are most likely inviting learners to take on a transactional leadership approach.

We fully recognize that most of our learners initially approach our leadership programs from a "what" perspective. They demonstrate a transactional mindset and want to be credentialed in leadership because it will look good on their resume. Admissions offices often encourage this perspective because it easily translates into marketing materials. Prospective students can quickly identify with the success stories that our graduates offer.

There is nothing wrong per se with that initial inclination. Students interested in going to law school, for instance, may choose to major in political science because they know that this particular major will sharpen their analytical skills and will improve their writing and critical-thinking skills. This skills-building strategy is an excellent path toward a successful career in the legal profession. However, leadership programs often use a "bait and switch" approach (hooking our students on the "what" and then later on trying to sell the "why"). That often causes a disconnect between the students' transactional expectations and the transformational core of our leadership programs.

The "smart" leadership classroom offers a deeper level of engagement. We want our learners to be well versed in the latest leadership theories and models and exhibit strong leadership competencies (e.g., communication, problem-solving). However, the "why" demands a profound articulation of the ethical grounding of leadership development. Our emerging leaders should be questioning their own values as they seek to grow in our classrooms.

Next: The "How"

Once educators have clearly articulated the "why" of their leadership program, they can next focus on the "how." Many different strategies can be used in the classroom to promote engagement. In this subsection, we focus specifically on three that we have found particularly helpful in a "smart" leadership classroom.

The Socratic method

Students attending law school are introduced to this teaching method from the very beginning. This tool is also common in medical residency programs and in M.B.A. programs. The Socratic method refers to a discussion in which the instructor engages the learner in a continual dialogue that contributes to intellectual discovery. The ancient Greek philosopher Socrates (470–399 BC) pioneered this style as a way to get his students to engage in meaningful thinking about deeply held assumptions. While we tend to associate this pedagogical method with classroom discussion, this tool actually has a deeper meaning in Socratic questioning (Seeskin, 1987; Dillon, 2016).

We are all familiar with instructors who love "cold calls" that strike fear in the hearts of students. The Socratic method works at this most basic level – everyone should be prepared to contribute meaningfully to a class discussion (Shadel, 2013). In order to participate in the discussion, learners must be prepared by completing their assignments and mastering the basic elements of the topics to be covered in the classroom.

Next, the Socratic method takes the learners outside their comfort zone. It is not enough to understand the basics. The purpose of this method is to engage the learners in a higher level of thinking. As the Critical Thinking Community mentions on its website,

> The Socratic questioner acts as the logical equivalent of the inner critical voice which the mind develops when it develops critical thinking abilities. The contributions from the members of the class are like so many thoughts in the mind. All of the thoughts must be dealt with and they must be dealt with carefully and fairly. By following up all answers with further questions, and by selecting questions which advance the discussion, the Socratic questioner forces the class to think in a disciplined, intellectually responsible manner, while yet continually aiding the students by posing facilitating questions.[6]

The Socratic method is designed to lead students in an exploration of their own values. When teaching leadership with the goal of connecting knowledge, action, and growth, instructors can use the Socratic method to explore the canon, sharpen critical-thinking skills, and promote leadership development.

Similar to many highly regarded law schools, educators have the opportunity to build their whole undergraduate leadership studies curriculum around the Socratic method. This strategy will not only move leadership students beyond the traditional lecture format, but also align with some of the educator's leadership competency-building objectives, for example critical thinking, oral communication, and problem-solving. Its deeper value lies in the way that learners will critically evaluate theoretical assumptions in the leadership literature, while at the same time developing their own philosophy of leadership.

The use of artifacts

While the Socratic method should be appealing to leadership programs that emphasize oral communication as a learning objective, the use of artifacts such as paintings, novels, sculptures, and movies as pedagogical tools can be very effective. These artifacts allow the learners to engage in "textual analysis." McManus and Perruci define "textual analysis" as a methodology that allows the learner to read and interpret "the themes found in the artifacts and the context in which the artifact was originally produced" (McManus and Perruci, 2015, p. 7). Textual analysis uses an inductive approach, drawing insights about certain leadership themes such as power or ethics through the study of artifacts.

Artifacts in the classroom are particularly applicable to leadership studies programs that use a liberal-arts approach – as discussed in Chapter 2. Artifacts from the arts and humanities easily lend themselves to textual analysis. That serves as a method to engage students in deep analytical thinking. Many students by the time they reach college have read Niccolò Machiavelli's *The Prince*. However, very few will have read that book with the purpose of extracting insights about the nature of leadership from a Western perspective. A textual analysis of *The Prince* will yield important lessons about Machiavelli's thinking related to the ideal leader–follower relationship.

Similar to the Socratic method, the use of artifacts invites an opportunity for the learners to assess their own value system. When they read Machiavelli's assertion that the ends justify the means, the instructor can then invite the learners to assess whether they agree or disagree with this statement. Once a learner responds, the instructor has an additional opportunity to invite agreement or disagreement among the student's peers.

The resulting dialogue allows the participants to test ideas that otherwise might go unchecked. It is essential that the instructor create an open environment that allows students to feel comfortable to challenge one another. The spirit of this dialogue should not be to put others down in order to elevate one's position. Rather, as in an orchestra, the instructor works as a conductor, inviting point and counterpoint in order to create a flow of ideas.

Case study pedagogy
The use of case studies in the classroom is well documented (e.g., Herreid, 2007; Scarpaci, 2007; Teays, 2015). This method provides the learners with opportunities that include three points of engagement. First, the learners must be able to articulate the essence of the case – its main players, the key issues, and options to be considered. In leadership development, this is an essential skill. Quite often, our learners are eager to offer an opinion on a case only to find out that they completely missed the main points.

A second consideration in the use of case studies in the leadership classroom is the application of creative thinking when brainstorming possible solutions. Leadership requires innovation and diversity of thoughts. The case study pedagogy invites learners to wrestle with different perspectives and difficult choices. Educators should consider using case studies that connect leadership to ethics.

Leaders often confront ethical dilemmas that test their values. Case studies allow them to consider different options in an intellectually supportive and non-judgmental environment. This consideration applies not only to learners individually, but also to teams. In fact, we would recommend that the case studies be used as a team assignment in order to give the students an opportunity to test their views in the context of group consensus-building.

The third valuable use of case studies deals with how learners in teams are able to present their solutions. It is not enough for instructors to say that the teams should make a presentation. They should give the teams a clear prompt of what is expected. Oral communication is a critical skill in leadership development. We encourage educators to expect teams to present their final positions to the whole class in order to practice public speaking with supporting visual aids. Visual tools could include a PowerPoint slide deck accompanying a presentation, or a poster supporting a presentation.

One recommendation is for the educators to set aside a whole class period and simulate a formal presentation. Learners in this instance are required to dress professionally and are evaluated and receive feedback from faculty and community members who serve as judges. The presentation instructions should include the rubric (e.g., delivery, content, body language) that will be used to evaluate the presentations.

The "Good Side" of Technology

Many of us had, at some point in our childhood, an educator who threaded the movie projector or popped the VHS tape in, hit play, and sat at his or her desk passively waiting for the classroom period to end. Obviously, in this case, technology was simply used as "filler," with very limited educational value. This type of technology use has no place in the leadership classroom.

Used properly, technology can play a significant role in the leadership classroom and assist in further engaging learners to thrive as critical thinkers and problem-solvers (Moore, 2012). We suggest at least three strategies for the incorporation of technology into your pedagogy. First, please consider the use of a presentation through TED Talks or the use of video clips to spark conversations about a particular topic. Tailor the piece to an issue that involves leadership challenges. Educators can move beyond the topic by asking the learners to analyze the presentation itself. The way that the TED Talk presenter delivers his or her message serves as a learning opportunity in itself.

A second common use of technology in the leadership classroom involves movie clips. Students can access those movie clips outside of class and then come prepared to discuss them. The entire class time can then be dedicated to discuss the clips, which become useful in connecting theory to practice. While the movie clips have an entertainment value of breaking the class routine, they are also valuable connectors. Used as artifacts, these clips should be followed by specific questions that educators would like learners to address. Answers to those questions can serve as a tool for critical thinking and self-evaluation – the ultimate goals of a "smart" leadership classroom activity.

A third common use of technology in the classroom deals with the incredible possibilities that platforms such as Skype have created for educators to virtually invite guests into their classrooms. As we mentioned in Chapter 3, McDonough leadership students take a sophomore-level course focusing on global leadership. Several of them then decide to study outside the United States during their junior year. While abroad, they write blogs and Skype with the sophomores taking the course. The students studying abroad are able to frame their experiences within the context of the global leadership issues discussed in class. For the students taking the course, this opportunity to engage in conversation with a peer who is abroad serves as another valuable bridge between theory and practice.

These three examples are designed to spark thinking about how to incorporate technology into a "smart" classroom. Regardless of how technology is used, the goal is to be intentional and thoughtful in considering how this technology engages learners to enhance critical thinking, problem-solving, communication, and self-reflection.

"CREATIVE DEVIANCE"

Despite incredible changes in the world in recent decades, we continue to approach the classroom in very traditional ways. The classroom has individual chairs facing a board on a wall, with the instructor standing and facing the chairs. The overall set-up screams passivity. The instructor lectures, students take notes, and at a later date students take individual tests to evaluate their mastery of the course content. For many students, that arrangement constitutes their comfort zone. This predictable environment allows students to become passive consumers of knowledge.

That conceptualization of education does not fit the general spirit of the "smart" leadership classroom that we are proposing in this chapter. After all, leadership educators strive to take students outside their comfort zones in order to promote growth and development. Ronald Heifetz (1994), in his celebrated *Leadership without Easy Answers*, introduces the concept of "adaptive leadership," which serves as an excellent metaphor for the very notion of leadership development. Heifetz suggests that leaders, when confronted with a challenge, may use different approaches. They can treat the challenge as a technical issue, requiring clear solutions. For instance, if the light bulb in the classroom burns out, it is difficult to teach in the dark. This challenge requires a technical solution – change the light bulb.

Heifetz is not particularly interested in technical challenges. He suggests that many challenges in life require complex solutions, which involve adaptation and changes in values. The civil rights movement, for instance, did not involve a technical solution. Calculated "creative deviance," such as sit-ins, marches, and boycotts, forced society to confront the absurdity of segregation and discrimination in general. Civil rights leaders challenged society to adapt. Heifetz advises leaders to engage in "creative deviance" as a way to apply pressure on followers and opponents to change their values.

On a smaller scale, our leadership classrooms offer the same type of "creative deviance" opportunities for our aspiring leaders. The classroom should be a dynamic and intellectually supportive environment that challenges students to apply critical-thinking and problem-solving skills. Sometimes even a simple reconfiguration of the classroom physical space (e.g., sitting in a circle or moving desks into pods for smaller classroom discussions) can promote higher levels of engagement. Educators should compassionately take their learners outside their comfort zones and challenge them to engage in adaptive learning. In this section, we suggest some of the strategies that have worked well at both the Rockefeller and McDonough centers.

Service Learning and Group Projects

Leadership programs have long made a connection between community service and leadership education (Wagner and Pigza, 2016; Gardinier, 2017; Shumer, 2017). Aside from making connections between the campus and the local community, service learning has been used to introduce our learners to the global community (Larsen, 2016). In the previous chapter, we introduced a course (Foundations of Leadership) in the McDonough leadership curriculum that uses service learning as an educational method. In this subsection, we can elaborate further on this method. The distinction between service learning and voluntarism is critical to our understanding of a "smart" leadership classroom. While the latter stresses the use of service to meet community needs, the former connects service to specific learning objectives.

In order for service to be truly a "learning" tool, it should have three components. First, a service-learning course should include a "preflection" – the opportunity for the learners to first talk about the service project in terms of the "why" and the "how." A service project allows the educator to connect the activity to specific leadership concepts, for example power, teamwork, the leader–follower relationship, and goal setting. The service-learning project, therefore, becomes the laboratory through which the learners gain insights about these concepts.

The planning of a project to address a community need provides an important learning opportunity while students are in college. It pays rich dividends for students after they graduate, and many become involved in project planning and implementation in their professional lives. Recently, the leadership literature has stressed the growing use of teamwork in the workplace. Group projects allow our learners to gain a deeper understanding of group dynamics, styles of team members, and conflict resolution.

Second, service-learning projects involve implementation. Our learners leave the classroom and become direct participants in the life of their communities. All the planning is now put into action, which allows our learners to translate theory into action. The strength of the "preflection" exercise becomes apparent during the implementation phase.

The third component of service learning is reflection (Jacoby, 2015). This final phase is where deep learning takes place. Through a carefully designed debriefing session, the instructor is able to engage the learners in thinking about the connections between the concepts introduced in the preflection and the implementation of the project. Through the debriefing process, the learners can extract valuable leadership lessons that will stay with them for a lifetime. In particular, our students can learn the value of failure whenever the service-learning project does not go well (Gail, 2016).

The reflection component of service learning also serves as an introduction to the habit of using critical thinking to assess lessons learned from experiential education. The use of reflection will be applicable to students' professional lives beyond college. In other words, service learning can provide lifelong learning skills.

The Use of Simulations

Students are always looking for ways to break the routine in the natural flow of a traditional classroom (Letson, 1981). The use of simulations is an excellent means to model "creative deviance" and is an effective tool for creating a "smart" classroom environment. By simulations, we mean the use of role-playing that gives students the opportunity to consider the implications of decisions under specific conditions. There are two types of simulations – passive and active. In the former, students are given a scenario that calls for steps to be taken. The students can run the simulation and offer an analysis of the possible outcomes. The passive type is very similar to the case study pedagogy. The advent of powerful computer processors and, more recently, artificial intelligence now allows instructors to design computer simulations that provide students with opportunities to run complex scenarios with multiple variables. This format is particularly applicable to graduate leadership programs that draw students with more life and professional experience.

For undergraduate leadership programs, consider using the active type of simulations, which get students out of their chairs and moving around. Students are always interested in activities that are fun and thought-provoking, and it is the educator's responsibility to connect such activities to conceptual lessons. Active simulations, as a "creative deviance" tool, have three components. First, educators can introduce the conceptual framework to ground the activity in a particular theory or model. For this introduction, educators need to ensure that students fully grasp the theory or model.

The second component of the activity is the actual running of the simulation. Short simulations are always popular because they keep the students focused. The longer the simulation, the higher the risk of students losing interest or, worse, turning the activity into an entertainment exercise, with diminishing educational value.

The third component is probably the most critical of all. The debriefing of a simulation should be done in two stages – description and interpretation. In the description stage, students should be asked simply to describe what took place. At this point, learners should be encouraged to avoid jumping right into the interpretative stage and be given an opportunity to practice their observational skills. The second stage, interpretation, involves the intentional connection between theory and practice in such a way that participants derive "lessons" from the experience.

Every leadership class should have at least one simulation during a semester or a quarter. When done right, they leave powerful imprints on learners' minds that extend beyond their college days. We still receive notes from our students recalling lessons from certain simulations and showing delight in the applicability that they are finding to their personal and professional lives, years after they participated in a simulation.

The Flipped Classroom

We began this chapter offering a word of caution regarding the use of technology in our undergraduate leadership classrooms. Technology certainly has a role in the logistical side of our leadership classes; for example, grading, keeping a calendar, and assignment prompts. On the pedagogical side, we have highlighted useful ways to incorporate technology into the classroom; for example, short movie clips and TED Talks.

More recently, instructors have embraced the use of "flipped classrooms" as a productive way to engage students in meaningful discussions (Green, 2017). The traditional classroom in higher education involves three steps. First, students read the assignments. Next, they come to class, and the instructor explains the concepts. Finally, the students are tested on the material in order to assess how much they have retained and understood the content. This format leaves very little room for discussions, which allow much more student engagement than traditional lecturing.

Recent studies are showing that engaged students not only retain the material better, but are also able to gain a deeper understanding of it (Waldrop and Bowdon, 2016). Therefore, it makes more sense to get the lecturing part "out of the way," so students can discuss the material. But time is limited during class, and that is when technology plays a critical role. Instructors can deliver their lectures electronically *before* class meets. For traditional students, that format is truly an exercise in "creative deviance." The traditionalists see devoting the entire class period to discussion to be a waste of time. Creative deviants see this strategy as the creation of real learning.

The flipped classroom strategy seems perfect for undergraduate leadership programs whose objectives include the fostering of critical thinking and oral communication. Students are asked to articulate (and, sometimes, defend) their positions regarding the readings and lectures. They have to come prepared for the give-and-take of a marketplace of ideas, modeling the Socratic method discussed earlier in this chapter.

In order for the flipped classroom format to truly work, several elements must be in place. First, instructors have to record the lecture material, and that takes time. It is not enough to turn the video camera on. Students are sophisticated consumers of screen material, and they expect a professional-quality presentation (e.g., the use of visual aids, smooth transitions, high-quality sound) – and, again, that takes time to prepare and upload.

Second, students also need to do their part, which includes completing assignments for a class before it takes place. Assignments can range from readings, to watching videos, to analyzing a case. One effective technique that many educators have embraced is to administer a quick online quiz to ensure that students have understood the material before coming to class. Another useful technique is to ask students to prepare a set of discussion questions for a given topic that the instructor may focus on during class.

Third, students should come prepared to discuss the material in a meaningful way. Leadership students do not normally shy away from expressing their opinions about anything. However, if they are not prepared to contribute, the discussion can quickly degenerate into a superficial exchange. Our students often use expressions such as "I feel" and "I believe" prefacing their opinions about issues. There is a prevailing acceptance among their peers that, once their statements are prefaced by these words, their opinions are to be respected and considered of equal value to all the others. While we understand that respect and civility are essential elements in a higher education environment, educators should facilitate discussions in which learners are forced to articulate arguments grounded in facts and thoughtful considerations.

Fourth, in a "smart" leadership classroom setting, instructors may use the flipped classroom as a great opportunity to engage in leadership competency-building. For example, by assigning a different student every class period to lead the discussions, the students also gain valuable skills in the area of facilitation and deliberation. Through an intentional strategy to promote individual leadership development, course syllabi can include the information that the flipped classroom pedagogy is designed to promote the development of facilitation skills. An educator's responsibility, however, does not end with including this statement in the syllabi. If that is a stated learning objective, the educator should provide resources on facilitation that the students can review beforehand and, when it is their turn to facilitate a discussion, they can practice in the classroom. Educators may also want to facilitate some of the first class discussions as a way to model the use of facilitation skills.

The Mobile Classroom

We often think of the classroom experience as involving four walls, chairs, and a board of some kind. In reality, this traditional view of the classroom has been changing dramatically in the past decades as technology reshapes the nature of learning (Crompton and Traxler, 2016). Online education has certainly challenged this notion of the traditional classroom. For this final section of the chapter, we would like educators to take a further step and focus on the articulated student learning goals. If learning can take place in a wide range of spaces, leadership educators have a lot more flexibility than they may realize. As an exercise in "creative deviance," we invited educators to explore different spaces that may contribute to higher levels of learning. One such space is the mobile classroom.

In reality, the idea of a mobile classroom is not new. Socrates himself was known to use any public encounters as an opportunity to engage learners in a question-and-answer session. Driven by a deep desire to find truth and promote human development, Socrates can be characterized as the "first leadership teacher" in the Western world. That got him in trouble, particularly when young people began questioning authority and imitating his quest for truth. Socrates certainly took "creative deviance" to the extreme and eventually paid a steep price for it.

A key lesson that can be derived from Socrates' experience is that the instructor–learner relationship can be nurtured anywhere. The leadership educator should be prepared to engage in leadership education any time a learner shows eagerness to learn and grow as a leader. In our 21st-century, chaotic, hyper-connected, technology-driven world, it seems rather daunting to carve out impromptu time for reflection and deep learning. In a way, the traditional classroom setting offers an intellectual and luxurious respite through which the mind can be quieted and focused.

The mobile classroom provides a "smart" alternative that connects key learning objectives to visual experiences. For instance, an instructor at the McDonough Center, when exploring different metaphors to describe organizations, takes his students to the College's greenhouse – a perfect environment to discuss "organizations as organisms." As students explore the interconnectedness of units within an organization, all they need to do is look around to see the metaphor come alive (no pun intended). That is a powerful visual cue that will stay with them throughout their lives.

The greenhouse example serves as a way to drive an important point as we close Part I of this book. Teaching leadership does not solely belong to the traditional classroom. It can take place in a variety of settings. The key in leadership education is the purposeful and intentional ways that we can use our pedagogical tools and course content to promote leadership development.

We chose to end Part I of the book with this discussion of pedagogy because it serves as a bridge between the curricular and co-curricular side. In our leadership programs we often make a clear distinction between "teaching about leadership" and "teaching for leadership." In reality, we have seen in this chapter that this distinction is often fuzzy. As Part II will show, teaching leadership takes place at all levels – curricular and co-curricular. As we develop our leadership programs, we need to be aware that our activities in and out of the classroom must be carefully examined in order to have the desired impact.

REFLECTION QUESTIONS

1. How have you used technology to enhance your students' learning in a leadership classroom?
2. Consider the proposition that the leadership classroom can be used as a metaphor for "transforming leadership," using James MacGregor Burns's perspective introduced in Chapter 3. How would that differ from a classroom based on "transactional leadership"?
3. How can human-centered design help shape the way leadership is taught in the classroom?
4. In this chapter, we suggested the use of several methods to promote an engaged classroom, for example the Socratic method, artifacts, case studies, and TED Talks. Which of these strategies have you found particularly effective for your students? Why are they effective?
5. In this chapter, we introduced Ronald Heifetz's concept of "creative deviance" – carefully designed ways to disrupt existing structures. As an exercise in "creative deviance," we challenged you to explore different spaces that might contribute to higher levels of learning. What are some possible spaces in your particular institutional context?

NOTES

1. Kelley and Kelley (2013) refer to this as "creative confidence."
2. Website (https://www.embraceinnovations.com). Accessed August 24, 2017.
3. Lisa Sibley (2008), Stanford Startup's $25 "Sleeping Bag" Could Save Newborns, *Silicon Valley Business Journal*, April 18. Website (https://www.bizjournals.com/sanjose/stories/2008/04/21/story10.html?b=1208750400%255E1622061&surround=etf). Accessed August 24, 2017.
4. Quote from Claudia Kotchka received via email on August 29, 2017.
5. See his presentation of the model in "Start with Why – How Great Leaders Inspire Action," TEDxPugetSound (https://www.youtube.com/watch?v=u4ZoJKF_VuA). Accessed August 24, 2017.

6. As quoted on https://www.criticalthinking.org/pages/socratic-teaching/606. Accessed May 19, 2017.

REFERENCES

Bandura, A. (1997). *Self-Efficacy: The Exercise of Control*. New York: W.H. Freeman.

Blink, R. (2016). *Leading Learning for Digital Natives: Combining Data and Technology in the Classroom*. New York: Routledge.

Carr-Chellman, A. and Rowland, G. (2017). *Issues in Technology, Learning, and Instructional Design: Classic and Contemporary Dialogues*. New York: Routledge.

Crompton, H. and Traxler, J. (Eds.). (2016). *Mobile Learning and STEM: Case Studies in Practice*. New York: Routledge.

Dillon, J. (2016). *Teaching Psychology and the Socratic Method: Real Knowledge in a Virtual Age*. New York: Palgrave Macmillan.

Dweck, C. (2006). *Mindset: The New Psychology of Success*. New York: Random House.

Gail, M. (Ed.). (2016). *Reflecting on Service-Learning in Higher Education: Contemporary Issues and Perspectives*. Lanham, MD: Lexington Books.

Gardinier, L. (Ed.). (2017). *Service-Learning through Community Engagement: What Community Partners and Members Gain, Lose, and Learn from Campus Collaborations*. New York: Springer.

Green, L.S. (2017). *The Flipped College Classroom: Conceptualized and Re-conceptualized*. New York: Springer.

Heifetz, R. (1994). *Leadership without Easy Answers*. Cambridge, MA: Belknap Press of Harvard University Press.

Herreid, C. (Ed.). (2007). *Start with a Story: The Case Study Method of Teaching College Science*. Arlington, VA: NSTA Press.

Jacoby, B. (2015). *Service-Learning Essentials: Questions, Answers, and Lessons Learned*. San Francisco, CA: Wiley.

Kearsley, G. (2000). *Online Education: Learning and Teaching in Cyberspace*. Belmont, CA: Wadsworth Thomson Learning.

Kelley, D. and Kelley, T. (2013). *Creative Confidence: Unleashing the Creative Potential within Us All*. New York: Crown Business.

Knoblauch, H. (2013). *PowerPoint, Communication, and the Knowledge Society*. Cambridge: Cambridge University Press.

Larsen, M. (Ed.). (2016). *International Service Learning: Engaging Host Communities*. New York: Routledge.

Letson, R. (1981). *Simulation and Gaming Activities in the Classroom*. Tucson: University of Arizona.

Lloyd, L. (Ed.). (1997). *Technology and Teaching*. Medford, NJ: Information Today.

Lloyd, L. (Ed.). (2005). *Best Technology Practices in Higher Education*. Medford, NJ: Information Today.

McKamey, J. (2008). *Smart Classroom Technology: Instructional Effectiveness and Faculty and Student Satisfaction*. Fort Lauderdale–Davie, FL: Nova Southeastern University.

McManus, R. and Perruci, G. (2015). *Understanding Leadership: An Arts and Humanities Perspective*. New York: Routledge.

Marques, J., Dhiman, S., and Biberman, J. (Eds.). (2012). *Teaching Leadership and Organizational Behavior through Humor: Laughter as the Best Teacher*. New York: Palgrave Macmillan.

Moore, K. (2012). *Effective Instructional Strategies: From Theory to Practice*, Third Edition. Los Angeles, CA: SAGE.

Poritz, J. and Rees, J. (2017). *Education Is Not an App: The Future of University Teaching in the Internet Age*. New York: Routledge.

Prensky, M. (2012). *From Digital Natives to Digital Wisdom: Hopeful Essays for 21st Century Learning*. Thousand Oaks, CA: Corwin.

Scarpaci, R. (2007). *A Case Study Approach to Classroom Management*. Boston, MA: Pearson/Allyn & Bacon.

Seeskin, K. (1987). *Dialogue and Discovery: A Study in Socratic Method*. Albany: State University of New York Press.

Shadel, M. (2013). *Finding Your Voice in Law School: Mastering Classroom Cold Calls, Job Interviews, and Other Verbal Challenges*. Durham, NC: Carolina Academic Press.

Shumer, R. (Ed.). (2017). *Where's the Wisdom in Service-Learning?* Charlotte, NC: Information Age Publishing.

Teays, W. (2015). *Business Ethics through Movies: Case Study Approach*. Malden, MA: Wiley Blackwell.

Tomei, L. (Ed.). (2008). *Adapting Information and Communication Technologies for Effective Education*. Hershey, PA: Information Science Reference.

Wagner, W. and Pigza, J. (Eds.). (2016). *Leadership Development through Service-Learning*. San Francisco, CA: Jossey-Bass.

Waldrop, J. and Bowdon, M. (Eds.). (2016). *Best Practices for Flipping the College Classroom*. New York: Routledge.

PART II

Building leadership capacity and competency

In the first part of this book, we explored the curricular side of our leadership programs. As is evidenced by the growing number of institutions embracing the curricular component of leadership studies, leadership education has become more visible on our campuses. Experiential learning is a key tool for bridging theory and practice in the field of leadership.

In Part II, we connect the study of leadership to its practice and offer a method for the development of leadership programming that draws upon the experiences of the Rockefeller Center at Dartmouth College and the McDonough Center at Marietta College. We begin by discussing the self-awareness, as well as the cultural and technical competencies, that educators must cultivate in themselves in order to model the values, attitudes, and behaviors the program seeks to develop in its learners. We suggest strategies for using this self-awareness to create an optimal learning environment. Once that foundational work is accomplished, the same clear-sighted planning must be applied to its implementation and assessment at the individual session level. Please adopt, adapt, and adjust concepts and ideas covered in this part of the book that will work for you and your organizational context.

5. The learning environment

Educators face an exciting challenge for creating program experiences that will foster the personal and professional growth of their learners, both now and into their future. The first step is to shape an optimal environment for teaching leadership. Above all, educators should aim to empower learners with a goal of nurturing, enhancing, and sharpening an evolving leadership mindset. Creating a learning environment necessitates an understanding of the interrelationship between the educator, learners, the physical set-up, and the emotional needs of participants.

The previous chapter focused on the techniques and methods to facilitate learning in classrooms and these can be applied to co-curricular programs as well. Before creating the content of these programs, educators must first assess their own leadership strengths and weaknesses. This may seem optional to some, but we believe it is foundational. The educator is the initial architect of the program, and it is inevitable that personal perspectives will be transmitted into whatever program is created. Educator self-reflection will inform program content creation and help educators hone their delivery. This chapter details the self-awareness, and the cultural and technical competencies educators must cultivate in themselves, so they may model the values, attitudes, and behaviors the program seeks to develop in its learners. Drawing on examples from the Rockefeller Center and experts in the field, the chapter presents strategies for using self-awareness to create an optimal learning environment.

Leadership educators in curricular and co-curricular programs need to continually assess their leadership presence, understand their audience, and strive to demonstrate congruence between values and behavior. They are self-aware, excellent communicators, use simple and direct language, and work hard on developing the skills to facilitate difficult conversations. They understand the difference between dialogue and debate. Dialogue between two people seeks to understand the other person's point of view. Debate, on the other hand, is when two people with opposing views try to win an argument or prove each other wrong. Educators work hard to create vibrant and shared experiences with their learners. They weave a tight-knit web that forms the support system for their values, attitudes, and behaviors, which results in an expression of their personal leadership presence.

The chapter begins with a discussion of what is meant by self-awareness, and then presents examples of how a number of educators have cultivated this awareness and effectively applied it in shaping their learning environments. The chapter concludes with reflection questions for educators to use in continually evaluating their effectiveness in creating an emotionally, socially, and intellectually supportive space for their learners.

EDUCATORS' SELF-AWARENESS

Self-awareness on the part of leadership educators is a critical factor in creating productive and supportive learning environments. Leadership is an inherently social process through which two or more humans interact; as humans, we have lives that are inherently social and not solitary. Therefore leadership cannot be exercised in isolation.

At the Rockefeller Center, self-awareness is defined as an understanding of:

1. who you are;
2. how you work with others; and
3. how you work within an organization to lead or follow in support of its mission.

Reflecting on Who You Are

> Leadership matters. It matters a great deal – to our organizations and institutions, to the people who work in them and to the people who are served by them. For our society to function effectively we need authentic leaders who can encourage people to perform at their best and step up and lead themselves. (George, 2008, p. xiii)

Authentic leadership requires exploring "who you are." Educators must reach deep inside and identify their own personal values and why these values are important to them. Exploring their values with a colleague can bring greater clarity and complement this kind of deep reflection; such a discussion might include sharing what motivated each to become an educator. The relative importance and influence of values such as integrity, a work ethic, steadiness, honesty, transparency, and authenticity should be discussed, as well as the challenges of upholding these values. Representative questions in the self-reflection could include the following:

- Do you believe that leadership can be exercised by everyone?
- Are there some people who have the capacity to be better leaders than others? To what end should we be seeking to build leadership?
- What is the value of leadership education? Of education?
- What are your top ten values and what matters to you and why?
- How are these values congruent or not congruent with your behaviors?
- How do people perceive you, your attitudes, and your behaviors, and is this perception in line with the way you want them to perceive you?

There are other illustrative reflection questions at the end of this chapter that can be used for self-reflection or in a group or even with learners. In this chapter, we have also provided examples of assessments frequently used with learners in the reflection process. We recommend that, as part of the self-awareness journey, you should first practice using these tools and learn from their insights before using them with participants in your programs. As a result, you will be better prepared to utilize them in your own leadership programs. Alternatively, you can find trained individuals who can administer these on your behalf.

Through these shared insights, leadership educators can come to recognize how both joyful and challenging experiences have shaped their values and contributed to their personal and professional identities. Educators should reflect on how their behaviors align with their values and whether the driving forces in their professional and personal lives affect this alignment (or lack thereof). This process can be lengthy, but it is worthwhile; leadership educators must build in time to intentionally reflect on these concepts.

In addition to identifying their core values, educators should understand their own technical strengths and weaknesses. While some literature suggests that educators should forget their weaknesses and simply play to their strengths, educators who are aware of their own weaknesses have the opportunity to address them and grow personally and professionally.[1] Recognizing both your strengths and your weaknesses are complementary components of the process of self-awareness. In fact, it can be said that even total mastery of one without the other is useless and will lead to incomplete reflection. It is often easier to understand our strengths because of our predisposition to accept and believe positive feedback. It may take a greater amount of work, but it is more holistic in the long run to also explore our weaknesses. Some educators understand their own weaknesses and seek out partnerships with individuals who have strengths that counterbalance them.

There are many exercises and assessments that can give educators clues about their own strengths and weaknesses. Instruments are helpful in analyzing our weaknesses because they help to illuminate our blind spots. "I have found 360 feedback processes, which are not linked to performance evaluations, to be particularly useful in illuminating my weaknesses and areas of growth. They are hard and a bit painful, but have been invaluable to my growth," says Renata Baptista, Acting Assistant Dean and Advisor to Latinx Students at Dartmouth College. Doing this sort of analysis requires grit and humility, which we believe to be fundamental competencies of strong leaders.

Kick-starting self-reflection with personality assessments

Many assessments can give educators clues about their own strengths and weaknesses. One well-known example is the Myers–Briggs Type Indicator (MBTI), which shows how individuals make meaning of the world around them and how they make decisions. Other instruments used in Rockefeller Center programs include the Intercultural Development Inventory® (IDI®), True Colors, StrengthsFinder, and the Native Compass.[2] Many times, these tools are seen as "reductionist" and participants question whether they are reliable, valid, independent, and comprehensive.[3]

Regardless, the process of taking an assessment can make participants think about themselves, their behavior, and their ideas; whether they agree or disagree with the results, this attention increases self-awareness. To identify whether such an assessment would be productive for a particular program, we suggest educators first take these assessments themselves and reflect on their own results before they administer one to program participants. Even if an educator ultimately decides not to use an assessment in his or her program, taking it encourages self-reflection and helps identify personal strengths and weaknesses for better teaching.

Based on our experience in administering these assessments, reactions from participants are mixed. Some learners are astounded with how accurately the results portray them, while others disagree with the outcomes. Both these reactions are instructive, creating an opportunity to explore and reflect on participants' personal strengths and weaknesses – either individually or in groups. The results of these assessments are only as good as the reflection and discussion that follow. The deeper the reflection, the better the self-awareness.

When done effectively, personality assessments can create a language around which lessons can be crafted. When used in the classroom setting, these assessments can help educators design programs that make the learning environment supportive for introverts and extroverts alike, and for a variety of learning styles.

Learning by listening and observing

In addition to formal assessments, educators must constantly accept and process feedback from their students. It is vital to understand how students perceive both our contributions to their personal and professional growth and what role our personal strengths play in this growth. This knowledge can be elusive, and it often comes from the most unexpected places.

For instance, during a conversation about this book, a colleague brought up the topic of student "thank-you notes" as an information-gathering opportunity. A quick look at a few of these notes revealed how they can help educators identify their inherent strengths and see what types of behavior are most conducive to student growth. A student research assistant analyzed 141 notes sent by students to 18 different educators in the fall of 2016. For the most part, the notes were written at the end of a program or class, or at the end of the student's time at Dartmouth. In these notes, students described how the educators had helped them to: shape their college experience; have a positive work experience; prepare for jobs or interviews; gain specific skills (communication, critical thinking, problem-solving); or develop an interest in a specific academic area.

Several common themes also emerged about what students valued in these educators. Educators had made time for the students regardless of their busy schedules. They had provided mentorship and support. They had expressed confidence in the students' abilities when they were grappling with a challenge or pushed the students beyond their comfort zone. They had demonstrated compassion, empathy, and kindness when they saw a student struggling with an issue.

Keeping an open mind to accept multiple sources of information, whether an assessment or a thank-you note, can provide rich, insightful, and useful information for educators' own self-awareness. Keeping an open mind also means being critically aware of the times you fail, as that is also a source of learning. Admitting failure, therefore, is an essential strategy in your toolkit as an educator that you can use to grow further as an individual and a professional. Admitting failure, developing the resilience to overcome it, and taking action to address it is a necessary skill for educators who seek self-awareness. Courageous educators are unafraid to own their failures and embrace them with humility. Modeling this behavior creates an environment for open dialogue in which participants know that it is all right to fail or make mistakes – so long as actions are taken to address these failures or mistakes.

Understanding How You "Work with Others"

Self-aware educators not only reflect about themselves, but also seek to understand their relationships with others with empathy and informed awareness of their needs, desires, and aims to reach a common goal. They observe how their words and actions influence others and what they can do to bring out the best in them. Self-awareness requires cultivating an appreciation of other individuals' contributions and talents, and sharing credit for success with them. Again, by engaging in this behavior themselves, educators model it for the young participants and their colleagues in their leadership programs.

On a university campus, young people are often confused about whether to present their work as an individual effort or as the product of a team. They may worry that sharing credit could adversely affect their status, and their image as a leader and as an individual. Recognizing this dilemma, the co-curricular team at the Rockefeller Center is intentional about modeling effective teamwork and mindful about sharing and acknowledging contributions of colleagues. For example, learners often see colleagues helping each other, complimenting, and celebrating the success of programs they are not responsible for with their own program participants, giving shout-outs to colleagues within their own programs, substituting for each other, and never criticizing each other in front of or to student participants. The co-curricular program staff annually revisit core values they have articulated as a team. For example, the current team etiquette is built on:

- respect;
- honesty;
- integrity/dependability/keeping your word;
- customer-service orientation;
- appreciation of other team members;
- graciously asking for and receiving help;
- being mindful of others and the situation;
- lifelong learning;
- staying positive – being the keepers of good morale in the workplace; and
- collaboration.

Team members also revisit business etiquette, including coordination of work schedules, how to share office space, efficiency of staff meetings, and other workplace expectations that enable them to address common goals. Student program assistants often comment that the atmosphere at the Rockefeller Center is collaborative, collegial, and cooperative. These are the very attitudes and workplace behaviors that our programs seek to instill in participants. In sum, working with others requires a thoughtful and systematic approach to empathetic relationship-building. This does not come without frequent and ongoing reflection and practice.

Understanding relationships requires additional reflection and assessment
The work of developing self-awareness in relation to working with others is difficult and ongoing. It demands a discipline of mind, asking educators to control their ego before it controls them. It requires educators to exercise self-compassion and self-forgiveness in the face of unexpected developments, and to provide the same compassion and forgiveness to their colleagues. It also requires educators to continually adapt to changing contexts and to become comfortable with ambiguity. Self-awareness and introspection practiced in this manner can help educators enhance their personal strengths, address their weaknesses, and ultimately emerge with an identity that is uniquely their own. Being clear about one's identity is critical to collaboration.

There are several assessments that can provide educators with insight into how they work with others and how they are perceived. The 360 review is one such tool that provides employees with feedback about their performance from several colleagues, many of whom would not traditionally review that person in other offices. For example, colleagues delivering feedback might include the person's boss, but also peers, direct reports, and anyone who works with the person regularly as an employee. Feedback is provided on qualities such as "leadership, teamwork, interpersonal communication and interaction, management, contribution, work habits, accountability, vision."[4] The Rockefeller Center co-curricular team recently completed the TriMetrix® HD assessment, which includes an exploration of behaviors (how you do things), driving forces (why you do what you do), acumen (your own personal strengths and weaknesses), and leadership competencies. This assessment helped team members understand one another's communication styles better through shared language, and developed opportunities to cooperate and collaborate on joint tasks.[5]

Most educators know that they need to have both hard and soft skills to exhibit strong leadership.[6] Educators should recognize power dynamics and their unique place in facilitating leadership education. They should also recognize how students perceive the interplay of power and influence in leadership programs and their role within it. The power dynamic of a person's identity reflects how the person interacts with others and needs to be a part of self-reflection, especially as educators increasingly work with diverse student populations. Brian Evje (2012) urges us to recognize that, "as a leader, you don't have the convenience of behaving only for yourself.

You must behave for others. Many leaders fail, or fail to develop, because they are stuck in an old mindset and continue to act for themselves." He goes on to call this the hard skills of leadership.

Considering How You Work within an Organization

Leadership programs thrive in a cultural environment that embraces excellence, innovation, and a desire for continuous quality improvement. This is an environment that strengthens the educator's ability to model collegiality and respect for others, and to demonstrate commitment to and passion for the work. In this type of culture, "joy in work" seeps into the programs offered within it. Transferred to the world of leadership, it is an educator's responsibility to create joy, hope, and optimism.

Striving for excellence, rather than perfection, is an effective guiding principle for most organizations (with some exceptions), but this can be a difficult mindset for high-achieving leadership educators, who naturally may strive for perfection at all times. Self-reflection is vital. An attitude that seeks perfection is aspirational, and individuals who focus on it are often unable to complete projects or even start them, particularly if they are driven by a fear of failure rather than joy. By contrast, a concentration on excellence promotes innovation, curiosity, and the desire to experiment with ideas. Educators who aspire to perfection while embracing continuous improvement and excellence in program development give themselves the space to grow and challenge their own assumptions, while minimizing the stress of trying to achieve an unattainable goal.

A team operating in a culture of excellence is likely to succeed in developing nimble leadership programs that are responsive to the learners and external environment. Team members demonstrate support for each other and feel pride, passion, and joy in their work. As Joanne Needham, Rockefeller Center Program Officer, said during an interview on June 20, 2017,

> Throughout my decades of working, I have established my work mantra as "Strive for excellence, not perfection." This results in a more productive and certainly less stressful work environment. I also believe that teamwork is essential to producing excellent outcomes. Each member of the team brings a different perspective and talent to any project, more brainpower, and trust in each other that each member is working for the greater good of the organization.

Driving a culture of supportive excellence through practice
At the Rockefeller Center, a standard agenda item for weekly meetings encourages educators to present a challenge faced in their daily work or a particular issue with a student. Team members bring up issues in order

to get input or support for a plan to move forward. Team members also deliver feedback to colleagues on their session designs (discussed in detail in Chapter 7). These conversations not only lead to the cohesiveness of program implementation, but also help achieve a team spirit, a commitment to doing things right, a cause for celebrating success, and educator self-assessment.

Creating and maintaining a culture of excellence demand time, energy, and effort. Educators pursuing this path can expect days in which they feel frustrated and confused, and in such instances their own level of self-awareness becomes a critical aid to understanding. They may reflect on how their personal attitude or behavior could have contributed to the frustration or confusion. Prepared with this knowledge, educators can approach the challenge at hand to resolve it.

Tying culture back to mission

When educators work in an environment where excellence is the goal and teams work together to continuously improve, they have the support to reflect on how their daily work supports the mission of the organization. Educators should self-reflect through the exercises described above, but also gather their superiors' and colleagues' perspectives on how they are using their time, their talents, and their resources to contribute to the organization's mission. Periodic reflection and discussion will help to align personal behaviors and tasks to maintain or enhance a culture of excellence. When personal and team values align to an organizational mission, it builds synergy and excitement around commonly developed goals and programs.

CREATING AND MANAGING A LEARNING ENVIRONMENT

Learning about leadership is best done in an environment that is non-judgmental, yet questioning. It challenges participants, but does not make them so uncomfortable that they find themselves stressed and unable to grow. Tom Senninger describes this concept in his learning zone model.

The learning zone model in Figure 5.1 is depicted in concentric circles, with the innermost circle as the "comfort zone." Next is the "learning zone," and the outermost circle is the "panic zone." Senninger suggests that, when participants are in their comfort zone, they are dealing with issues familiar to them and do not need to take risks. When they transition to the learning zone, they are presented with possibilities outside of their known experience and outside their comfort zone. When educators create

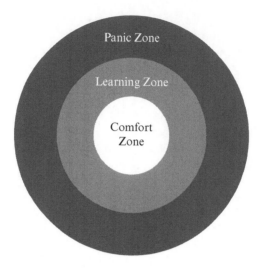

Sources: Senninger (2000); ThemPra Social Pedagogy (2009). The Learning Zone
Model (available online at: http://www.thempra.org.uk/social-pedagogy/key-concepts-in-
socialpedagogy/the-learning-zone-model). Accessed May 15, 2017.

Figure 5.1   The learning zone model

an intellectually and emotionally supportive environment by encouraging
them to grow, participants expand their learning beyond their comfort
zone. Beyond this lies the panic zone, where learning stops as participants
find themselves crippled by a fear of the unknown. In such situations,
the energy that should be invested in learning is diverted into managing
anxiety and distress. Such situations often result in inaction or resistance,
which is commonly referred to as "flight, fight, or freeze."

An educator's task is to maintain a delicate balance among these zones.
The educator must promote the learners' curiosity and sense of adventure,
lead them from their comfort zones, and at times stretch the boundaries of
their learning zones while being continually aware of the danger of pushing
them too far toward panic. As learners grow, what was once a learning zone
will eventually become a comfort zone, and what was once a panic zone
will become a learning zone. In this way, learning can be scaffolded to help
students reach concepts that might seem immediately out of their reach.

Navigating Difficult Subjects with Students

The balance between the comfort zone, learning zone, and panic zone often
becomes relevant in discussions about the role of leadership in matters

related to race, religion, politics, and campus violence. Difficult conversations are increasingly becoming a part of campus life and our global society at large. They are one of the high-impact practices used to develop leadership capacity in learners, as demonstrated by the Multi-Institutional Study of Leadership (Dugan et al., 2013).

Leadership educators should devote time to honing their facilitation skills and fostering them in their learners as well. Developing these skills begins with an understanding of the circumstances in which a difficult or "crucial" conversation takes place, and progresses to a deliberate action to deal with it. Having a plan to reach a positive conclusion to the conversation will guide the discussion, even if it gets messy.

In their book *Crucial Conversations*, Patterson et al. (2002) describe the conditions in which crucial conversations take place. They propose a series of actions that can be taken to come to an understanding at the conclusion of difficult conversations. Their perspective is especially applicable in situations where opinions differ, when there are strong emotions about it, and when the perceived stakes are high. In these situations, the authors suggest the need to:

- guide the conversation with facts and not emotions;
- listen actively; and
- work together to focus on creating constructive dialogue and not debating just to win a point about an issue. In this context, dialogue is about having a conversation with the intent to understand the other person's point of view. Debating is conversation with the intent to prove you're right.

Stone et al. (2010) suggest another way to understand the internal workings of a difficult conversation. In effect, they say that *three* conversations are taking place at once. The first conversation is the apparent dialogue about the subject of discussion, which involves analyses of different points of view: that of a given person, that of the person with whom they disagree, and the third point of view which really gets to the truth that lies somewhere in between. The second conversation, or "feelings conversation," involves the emotions of the participants and how they handle them. The third conversation is the "identity conversation." It is the most challenging because it looks inward and makes a person think about who she is, what the conversation says about her, and how open she is to the "truth."[7] The idea then suggested by Stone et al. is to shift to a "learning conversation," by sharing one's point of view, sharing and understanding the feelings of the two people involved in the conversation, and finding a way to move forward. This requires participants and educator facilitators to have self-awareness, empathy for others, and curiosity to learn about new points of view.

In a leadership program, the concepts related to difficult conversations imply that, in order for such conversations with learners to have a successful outcome, educators need to approach the conversation from a position of integrity, authenticity, and authentic listening. They need to understand their own habits and triggers, know how to recognize and respond to different forms of conflict, and understand their own personal style of working with others. Educators should consider how their ethnic and cultural background influences how they interact and converse with students and peers. The more educators know themselves in several contexts, the better prepared they are to deal with the complexity of conversations with their participants.

For example, educators may themselves feel uncomfortable during a difficult conversation with a student that might evoke memories of a personal experience similar to the learner's. We suggest that educators have strategies in place in advance for addressing how they will manage their personal discomfort. We believe that visualizing such conversations beforehand can help them use the right words and help to minimize emotional responses such as sweaty palms, feeling flushed, or even feeling breathless. At the Rockefeller Center, Rev. Dr. Nancy Vogele skillfully facilitated a discussion after the 2016 U.S. presidential election by creating space for participants who were very upset with the results.[8] She led them to reflect on actions they could take to ground their emotions and reactions using self-care and mindfulness. Gradually, participants opened up to share their embarrassment, concerns, fears, and uncertainties about having to navigate situations in which their personal political ideology was at odds with that of their friends or family members. In this situation, Vogele artfully invited participation into the discussion and, when the emotions were high, she used short meditations, silence, and quotations from different faiths and religions.

Vogele demonstrated an understanding of how far she could stretch the discussion, guiding the participants from the panic zone to the learning zone, and from the learning zone to the comfort zone. She also demonstrated the art of facilitating difficult conversations from a position of integrity, authenticity, and authentic listening. After the session, many participants openly expressed their gratitude for how the session had helped them to manage their anxiety, to make meaning of their emotions, and to gain self-control and self-awareness as a result. Vogele has this advice for educators:

> In developing a session like this, it is crucial to process your own thoughts and feelings about the subject ahead of time so that you don't, even unintentionally,

insert them into the program and thereby prejudice students' own engagement with the subject. Pre-processing enables educators to be fully present in order to develop and maintain an open space. This will allow for a most fruitful discussion with discoveries on the part of students and presenter alike. (Vogele, email to author, June 20, 2017)

Inspiring Educators Who Build Effective Learning Environments

Higher education institutions have the privilege of extensive networks of alumni and community leaders beyond just faculty or staff members. Engaging individuals through dialogue or experiential learning outside the classroom can enhance the learning environment for students to experience transformative leadership from multiple perspectives. The Rockefeller Center has been fortunate and honored to work with a number of inspirational educators across its programs. In this subsection, we highlight three effective educators from the military, religious, and business arenas. We invite you to look at the characteristics of these three presenters, because not only do they have compelling stories to tell, but also these stories are a result of deep personal reflection and the ability to engage with their participants. Everyone has a transformational story to tell. We invite you to look for such presenters in your community, or become one yourself!

LEADERSHIP CASE STUDY 1: LEADERSHIP IN THE MILITARY

Nate Fick is a Dartmouth alumnus and current member of the College's Board of Trustees. He is also a former Marine captain. Despite his busy schedule, for the past decade Fick has committed to leading an annual session for the Rockefeller Leadership Fellows Program titled "In the arena: translating thought into action as a young leader."[9]

In a typical session, he walks into the room greeting the people he knows, and then he joins the circle of Fellows and immediately establishes a relaxed environment before his session begins. In the first 15 minutes, Fick shares lessons he has learned as a Marine officer, as well as his executive experience in a nonprofit organization and a tech company. He discusses leadership concepts such as moral authority, legal authority, diversity, and the importance of being technically competent. He emphasizes how critical it is to explain to followers the rationale for taking an action and the need to be transparent, by over-communicating if necessary. He insists that leaders must take care of their followers. At the end of his presentation, he calls on Fellows to ask questions. They eagerly jump into the discussion with him for the next 20 minutes. By this time, they are fully engaged with the content. Fick then uses two short case scenarios of situations he experienced as a Marine officer, as shown below:

- *Complex decision-making in military leadership 1: Nate Fick session*. The Saddam Hussein regime collapsed a week ago. Your platoon is tasked with investigating a deserted amusement park on an island in the Tigris River near Baghdad. Intelligence is reporting that *fedayeen* militiamen are using the park to plan and launch attacks throughout the city. Orders require you to be back at your base by dark, and it is currently 2:00 PM, leaving you only about four hours to search the multi-acre amusement park. Just as you are about to cross the bridge leading to the island, a red sedan screeches to a halt next to you. A man and woman are in the front seat, and a young girl is sprawled in the back. She has a cast on her leg and looks to be in great pain. As you approach to look more closely, you can smell the infection. She is nearing septic shock and will die without immediate care. Do you continue with the mission or stop to help the girl?

- *Complex decision-making in military leadership 2: Nate Fick session*. You are a Marine platoon commander. For the past week, you've battled your way through central Iraq, witnessing your enemy wearing civilian clothes, fighting from mosques and ambulances, and using children as human shields. You are responsible for accomplishing the missions you are assigned, and also for ensuring the safety of the 22 Marines in your charge. An hour before sunrise, you are hurriedly ordered to seize an Iraqi military airfield. There are reports of tanks and anti-aircraft guns on the field. You have only unarmored Humvees and light weapons. As you crash through the airfield fence, you receive a radio call from your commander. The rules of engagement, which previously required that you be attacked before firing, have been changed. All personnel on the airfield, you are told, are "declared hostile." That is, they can be fired at without provocation. You are potentially vastly outnumbered by Iraqi forces, and the nearest American help is miles away. The first sign of trouble at the field may be your lead vehicle disappearing in a ball of fire. The platoon has not yet heard this change to the rules of engagement. It came over a radio monitored only by you. Do you pass it on to them?

Both scenarios required Fick to make difficult decisions. He asks Fellows to place themselves in his position and poses this question: "What would you do?" After many ideas are shared and discussed, Fick openly talks about the choices and concerns he had in both situations. In the first case, he decided to help the young girl, and in the second case he passed on the message to his platoon. He opens the floor up for further questions from participants, and then he ends the session by thanking the participants for their engagement and for attending the session.

Some educators might find these two scenarios too jarring or realistic to be used as case studies in a classroom for students. While we recognize those concerns, these two scenarios have tremendous educational value for the following reasons. First, students can build empathy with people, military or civilian, who suffer in regions of conflict. Presented in an intellectually challenging environment, scenarios such as the ones presented here invite students to reflect on the complexities of decision-making in a hierarchical structure. It also opens up the space for reflective discussions on the relationship of war and unrest with global issues such as humanitarian crises, food security, or extreme poverty.

Second, both scenarios selected by Fick challenge students to weigh the ethical and the practical impact of difficult choices. We acknowledge that there are risks in taking students outside their comfort zones, and we also believe students learn best when they wrestle with ideas that they are uncomfortable with. Leaders who face these issues often find it difficult to reconcile their values with how they are being asked to act. Many find that these situations are humbling, as Fick often reflects.

Third, lessons from military leadership often provide insights into managerial and organizational challenges in the civilian world. For example, to address the constant choice between career and family faced by working parents, Dowling suggests in her 2017 *Harvard Business Review* article that many lessons can be gleaned from the U.S. military, which has extensive experience in taking care of working-parent difficulties (Dowling, 2017).

Fick's session continues to be one of the most popular, not only because of the content, but because of who Fick is as a person. While one might presume being a military officer isn't the same thing as being head of the debate team, the takeaways about leadership that students glean from this session suggest otherwise.

At the end of the session, students reflect on the intimate relationship between leaders and those who follow or work with them. This becomes especially important when there is no manual to follow or when leadership is messy at best; in these types of situations, solitude and mindfulness can be vital in bringing clarity to complex issues that need further exploration and reflection. This space can also provide leaders with the capacity to develop self-confidence in trusting their own decisions, a confidence that ideally is passed on to others around them. As one student said:

> [The session] made me think more about how being a leader is not only about being an enabler/facilitator so that people can do their jobs, but one so that people can lead themselves.

From Fick's involvement with learners, we also gain a few insights on how to foster a learning environment. Learning about leadership starts from the very moment inspirational educators step into a relationship with their learners. This relationship involves humility and, at the same time, creates trust and confidence in the content being delivered. In this example, when Fick entered the room, he greeted the participants as equals and joined their circle. Through skilled facilitation, he drew out good perspectives and useful comments. He also engaged them and validated them as learners. Such actions bring down barriers and create open dialogue. Additionally, for successful educators, this relationship is one that transforms learners and educators alike and creates a path to lifelong learning. There is no question that this session is transformative and impactful, as evidenced by how participants frequently cite this session in the program's evaluation and discuss the impact it had on them.

Fick is also effective in capturing participant attention because he demonstrates his self-awareness, his authenticity, and "his leadership presence." He communicates his strengths without arrogance and, during the session, demonstrates his humility by admitting mistakes he has made in his career and what he learned from them. He is a master storyteller, uses humor in the right places, and draws upon dramatic case situations that capture all the leadership concepts he is trying to communicate. In a short 90-minute session, he is able to build a connection with Fellows who remember him even ten years after they attended his session, as evidenced by a survey of alumni conducted recently.

Fick is an excellent example of one who has "leadership presence," explored further by Halpern and Lubar (2004) in their book *Leadership Presence*. The authors' experiences as stage artists led them to define leadership presence in their PRES model as "the ability to connect authentically with the thoughts and feelings of others" (Halpern and Lubar, 2004, p. 8).[10] One of the behaviors they propose further includes being present, which requires the ability to be in the moment and demonstrate the ability to listen authentically. When Halpern and Lubar talk about reaching out to others, they are also referring to an educator's ability to build relationships with empathy. The authors believe that leadership presence combines power with humility, and Nate Fick shows this is true.

LEADERSHIP CASE STUDY 2: LEADERSHIP, CULTURE, AND RELIGION

As the United States becomes more culturally diverse, educators need to develop a higher level of cultural competence and the ability to empathize, understand, and successfully teach students who come from cultures different from their own.[11] Thoughtful educators recognize how their own culture, as well as those of their learners, plays a critical role in shaping a worldview and a particular understanding of a problem or issue being considered. Educators need a keen understanding of how to facilitate conversations amongst participants from different backgrounds. This recognition helps them develop relevant experiences both in and out of the classroom, as well as on and off campus, and it enriches learning as a result.

Near the end of the Rockefeller Center's eight-session Global Leadership Program, its 25 participants travel to New York City for an experiential learning weekend. The overall goal of the program is to help participants move from theoretical discussions about intercultural competence to "practice and experience" by engaging with a culture that feels unfamiliar, uncomfortable, and outside most learners' frame of reference. In the experiential learning weekend, the specific focus is to learn about American Muslims living in NYC. The program features activities where a risk of failure is part of the experiences for the learners. Included is a panel session called "Falafels and fatwas: Why are Americans so afraid of Muslims?" led by Haroon Moghul, a scholar in the Muslim American experience, and Hanadi Doleh, Program Manager for Park 51, a mosque in NYC.[12] Together, these educators illustrate how to encourage learners to think about cultural differences and how they affect people. The session takes place at a mosque, and many students in the program have never entered a mosque or any other place of worship different from their own. They walk in quietly and are greeted warmly by Moghul and Doleh. After a brief welcome, participants learn they will witness a call to prayer, tour the mosque, and be free to ask Moghul and Doleh questions.

Moghul and Doleh speak about their work and the importance of fostering open and honest dialogue about Muslims and their culture. Using their personal stories, they trace the current hostility, misunderstanding, and misinformation toward

Muslims back to 9/11 and describe how every American can remember exactly where they were when the terrorist attacks took place. The participants are transfixed and, while their discomfort with the discussion and the newness of their surroundings can be sensed, they begin to engage in conversation with Moghul and Doleh.

When it is time for the call to prayer, Doleh helps the women to cover their hair with scarves and leads men and women into the mosque. Both groups are invited to participate in the prayer. There are others who stay behind to continue their conversation with Moghul. When students return from the prayer, they look quieter and more reflective. When asked how they felt about this experience, two quotes provide a sample of how the participants responded:

> It really helped me to understand the America[n] Muslim experience . . . and gain insight into how to better advocate for American Muslims as a whole, especially given today's political and social climate.

> This program was great in giving people a framework in which to engage other cultures without making judgments. Especially in an age where cultural differences are highlighted and [are being] used to divide people, being able to communicate across cultures without causing offense or adding to discomfort is important in creating meaningful dialogue.

What were the ingredients that created an environment that was conducive to learning and engagement? As with Fick, Moghul's authenticity, honesty, and willingness to share his experiences made others feel open and comfortable in asking the hard questions that are too often neglected in today's world. They were the sort of questions that it is safe to ask in an intellectually supportive environment and would be considered in the "learning zone." Both Moghul and Doleh were extremely observant about the participants' body language and helped students reflect and make meaning of the uncomfortable conversation that was taking place. Moghul also is gifted with using his unique sense of humor, which brings levity to an otherwise difficult conservation. At the same time, the gravity of the conversation is not lost. For her part, Doleh created an environment where no one felt uncomfortable or intimidated about learning things unfamiliar to them. This was demonstrated by the way she welcomed them, helped women to wear the hijab, and answered questions candidly and respectfully.

Both these examples underscore the importance of educator selection. Educators should be skilled facilitators, have a leadership presence, be inviting, and be hospitable. They should be transparent and skillful at dealing with questions that are raised during conversations and welcome all perspectives. At the same time, they should be curious and open to learning about the perspectives of others who are different from them. These characteristics are critical to helping participants understand the importance of dealing with ambiguity in unfamiliar situations, and challenging them without pushing them from the learning zone into the panic zone.

LEADERSHIP CASE STUDY 3: LEADERSHIP AND BUSINESS

David Ager is a Senior Fellow in Harvard Business School's Executive Education Program and has participated as an educator in the Rockefeller Leadership Program for the past decade. In his session, Ager uses a Harvard Business case study to demonstrate challenges leaders face in managing people, as well as the consequences that can result from failing to do this well. The Harvard Business case study highlights events that unfold when a high-performing individual was hired by an organization and promised a promotion if he were to produce a financial turnaround in a branch of that organization. The employee achieves this goal but, at the same time, his co-workers describe his style as abrasive, volatile, and at odds with the vision of the organization's CEO, who emphasizes the importance of teamwork and respect in the workplace.

The case challenges students to decide whether or not to promote the high-performing employee. Through discussion and analysis, students learn about the potential for damage to the CEO's reputation as a fair and trustworthy person. They consider the possibility that the high-performing employee could leave the firm – possibly resulting in decreased financial productivity of the branch. And they wonder whether the high-performing employee, if promoted, would start to conform to the "rules" of the organization.

On the assumption that the employee was promoted and did not conform to the "rules," students reflect on the implications of a message that the firm's internal rules do not apply to those who produce financial success and its resulting effect on the organization's morale. They also consider the possibility that, through leading by example, the high-performing employee would end up developing a "toxic cell" within the firm or that the other employees of the branch would be emboldened to follow their leader's behavior.

Students learn that the culture of an organization is critical to its productivity, and the people within the organization play a paramount role in defining this culture. Productivity is impacted by several things, one of which is keeping your word. In the session evaluation one student reflected:

> Leaders can be trained; however, it is as important for leaders to develop growth as it is for them to meet business targets.

Ager also introduces the importance of the ability to give and receive honest feedback through a role-play scenario. In this role-play, a Fellow playing the role of the superior is required to give feedback to the other playing the role of the high-performing employee as described in the case study. Again, through this exercise, Fellows learn how crucial it is for leaders to give constructive and specific feedback, how hard it is to do, and how one needs to practice continuously to be skilled at it.

In his session, Ager's high energy and enthusiasm are infectious and charge the learning environment with an air of anticipation. His method of calling on students at random, combined with his playfulness, engages all participants to get involved in the discussion, including the introverts, who are willing to participate because of Ager's facilitation method. His style of moving about the room and engaging with each participant in a quick conversation makes everyone accountable for the decisions they make about the case study. This pushes participants beyond their comfort zones, but the supportive environment avoids sending students into the "panic zone" discussed earlier.

Ager's careful attention to mixing methods (brief lecture, case method, one-to-one discussion, a discussion in triads, role-play) within a 90-minute session addresses different learning styles of the students and supports critical thinking, decision-making, and reflection on personal leadership action. In his closing remarks, Ager links the session to broader leadership concepts, synthesizes the learning from the session, and makes it applicable to the for-profit, not-for-profit, and government sectors. Students leave this session thinking all lessons learned were applicable to them in their life after graduation.

Finding Themes across Case Studies

All educators highlighted in this chapter had a few things in common. All of them:

- demonstrated technical competence in the issues they were presenting and discussing;
- dissolved the traditional power gap between educators and learners and became equal partners in powerful exercises;
- invited an exploration of ideas, respect for diverse perspectives and individuals, critical thinking, and reflection;
- exhibited introspection and humility that was evident in the way they conducted themselves and supported the learners in mutual discovery; and
- showed a very high level of emotional intelligence.[13]

In a learning environment, this reflective and supportive behavior pays rich dividends because these educators model and demonstrate that it is acceptable not to have all the answers – it is all right to make mistakes, and it is all right to seek help.[14] By doing these things, the educators quickly gained credibility and the trust of learners, helping them to open up and share their thoughts and opinions without fear of feeling embarrassed.

The educators described above each clearly had spent time reflecting on their own experiences, cultures, and values, which came through in how they connected with students. They each were also effective in considering that individuals learn differently. Students have different styles and absorb information in various ways. For this reason, it is important to use a mix of methods for delivering content. As Wagner says, "facilitating learning is not about finding the 'one great method' that works universally but about understanding the ways in which students differ and shaping the environment to stimulate more complex thinking when students are developmentally ready" (Wagner, 2011, p. 85). This might involve calling on all students to encourage broad participation, uncomfortable silences that force people to consider new ideas, experiential learning, visual and physical displays of information, and others used by the leaders described in these case studies.

As a result of understanding the background of the learners and understanding their needs, educators and learners can together create learning communities in which respect for opinions, elegance in the manner in which they are stated, and critical examination of issues become the driving forces for learning and transformation through this learning.

Strategies to Build a Learning Environment

The learning environment takes on a different atmosphere when educators make an effort to gain an understanding of themselves and their participants. Creating opportunities for understanding the culture and context in which participants were raised generates dialogue in which educators and learners develop shared experiences during the leadership course and program. Taking the time to have this conversation with learners before the course or program helps educators and learners alike to establish a relationship at the early stages. It also helps them to clearly articulate hopes, concerns, and expectations. For example, in the Rockefeller Leadership Fellows Program, a newly selected Fellow meets individually with the program's educators for 20 minutes each to begin establishing these relationships. In larger programs, it is possible to develop strategies such as using alumni, student leaders, or student assistants to reach the same goal. Also, we invite you to consider other ways to build relationships that work for your particular cultural context.

Methods of learning that can fully capture a learner's attention to analyze a problem, internalize information, and discover solutions should be used to build a learning environment. Educators should limit the use of what Paulo Freire (2015), a Brazilian educator, described as the "banking" method in his celebrated *Pedagogy of the Oppressed*. In this traditional educational method, the learner is the passive recipient of knowledge, and the teacher/educator is the keeper and provider of all information. This "dehumanizes" the students and changes them into objects because they do not have the opportunity to think critically about any issue. Freire encourages educators to use the problem-posing and consciousness-raising method to enable educators to fully engage learners.

Freire's ideas have shaped the modern concept of education today, including the curricula of the Rockefeller and McDonough Centers' programming. Use of various techniques such as role-playing, simulations, immersion, or case studies enables learners to analyze problems and transform their thoughts about an issue. Improvisation ("improv"), a teaching technique quite on the opposite end of the spectrum to the "banking" method, is used by the Rockefeller Center in both its Management and Leadership Development Program and the Rockefeller Leadership Fellows Program.[15] It enables participants to get to know each other in a fun, yet meaningful, way and explore key leadership ideas at the same time. This segment is run by student facilitators in an improv group on campus. A student facilitator from the Class of 2018, Connor Lehan, describes his experience as both a learner and a leader in these exercises:

> When I first began leading improv workshops, I had a lot of trouble getting students to participate. I empathized completely with those who stared at their shoes, or hid in the corner, or fled to the bathroom when I asked for volunteers. These workshops were usually for large groups of people who did not know each other very well. Doing improv for the first time is stressful enough without being watched by 30 people you just met. The challenge I faced was transforming an environment that encouraged conformity into one that encouraged taking risks.
>
> I learned to begin my workshops with activities designed to get the students comfortable with looking foolish. For example, I have students walk around the room while I give them increasingly ridiculous scenarios ("Walk as if you are on the moon . . . as if you are a crab . . . as if half your body is a fashion model and the other half is a baby . . ."). I have found that starting with these simple exercises makes the rest of the workshop much more successful. Before students can most effectively work together, they must first overcome their fear of embarrassing themselves in front of the group.

Lehan continues his session by using improv techniques to help participants reflect on thoughts for making an environment open and inclusive of different perspectives, and the implications for leadership and for working as a team. Improv has shown to be an effective tool to increase participation and engagement within the group, which helps build a learning community. For example, since the introduction of improv in the Rockefeller Leadership Fellows Program, the sense of community and camaraderie is much stronger in the program, and to this day many alumni within a cohort or even across cohorts have kept in touch with each other. This camaraderie has led many Fellows to continue to serve as informal mentors and coaches for each other for many years. In *Improv Wisdom*, Patricia R. Madson (2005) shares many techniques educators can incorporate in their classrooms or co-curricular programs.

Challenges to Creating an Effective Learning Community

Building a learning community is not without its challenges. Educators must be vigilant and take action if the environment becomes divisive. For instance, when the development of cliques was becoming evident in a leadership program offered by the Center, the educator created new small groups that dispersed the existing team members. The educator also created a seating plan in which members of cliques could not sit together. During a teamwork session, the educator introduced a discussion on the sociology and psychology of in-groups and out-groups and their impact on a work environment. Implementing these strategies led to positive change, and the cohort began to work well together.

Educators often discuss amongst themselves how difficult it is to create accountability and commitment in co-curricular leadership programming. Many learners begin a leadership program with enthusiasm, but quickly drop out. There are several reasons why this occurs. Some learners are struggling with the academic workload. Others are simply involved in multiple activities. Still others feel the program does not meet their expectations. It is important for educators to understand reasons why students drop out so they can check in with them and take appropriate actions to improve the program if needed. Dropping out of a large program has a relatively small impact on the learning environment, but educators should still be concerned and seek to understand why and whether adjustments can be made. Dropouts from smaller programs have a larger impact. In a cohort of 20–25 participants where the program relies on peer-to-peer learning, dropouts will have an effect on the learning community and group dynamics. When students are not prepared or are inconsistent in their attendance, it creates a sense of resentment in those who have invested their time and effort and made the commitment to participate. If not addressed, dropouts can affect a program's reputation and its enrollment in future cycles.

Fostering Accountability Requires Feedback and Self-Reflection

There are strategies for making learners more accountable to themselves and their commitment to the program. The first is to understand the student's situation. If students are stressed with their academic load and performance, connect them to resources that can best address their needs. If they are involved in multiple activities, help them in developing time management and prioritizing skills. If the program is not meeting their expectations, educators should listen without being defensive or stubborn that the program is "perfect as is."

Listening to students' feedback can make them feel heard and, in the long run, become supporters of the program. Accountability goes both ways: students are expected to show up and participate; and, at the same time, leadership educators are responsible for creating a positive learning environment that is continuously improving and providing value to the students.

Fostering accountability and commitment begins with providing clear expectations about fulfilling requirements for the program. In large programs with open enrollment, we recommend establishing expectations of the program with each student before he or she begins. The Rockefeller Center often uses student program assistants for this purpose. Past participants, if available, in a program can assist with this as well. This strategy is helpful because students feel less pressured to give a "correct answer" to their peers. Requirements should be made clear in the opening session, and learners should be invited to discuss any conflicts or constraints they might face. In smaller programs, the educator should meet individually to establish a relationship with participants and share expectations of the program before it begins.

In the Rockefeller Leadership Fellows Program, for instance, educators make it clear in meetings with newly selected Fellows that they have an opportunity to refuse participation in the program after being presented with the expectations regarding their commitment. Acceptable reasons for student absences should be made clear. In the Rockefeller Leadership Fellows Program, for instance, varsity athletic commitments, job interviews (as only seniors are eligible to participate in this program), conflicts with class meetings or scheduled exams, and illness are acceptable absences. If a session is missed for any of these reasons, Fellows are required to submit a 350-word summary of the session they missed after completing the required assignments and meeting with peers who attended that session. Each Fellow signs an agreement about his or her commitment to participate in the program. In sum, participants must recognize that they are valued as active contributors, and what they stand to gain as a result of their participation. The individual meeting approach is time-intensive at first, but it pays off in the long run. Word spreads quickly about the need to be accountable and committed, which increases the value of the program for personal and professional growth.

Again, accountability goes both ways. If session facilitators are unable to attend a meeting for any reason, they should be transparent with the students about the reasons why they were unable to meet their obligations as leader educators. Acknowledging personal faults or limitations, if they result in missing a scheduled session, and sharing them with the students are opportunities to model self-reflection and humility to program participants.

Don't Forget to Address the Physical Environment of Your Learning Space

Effective learning environments often organize students into small groups
of five to seven participants. Organizing learners in this manner offers
several opportunities to create a positive learning environment. It quickly
sets the tone for establishing a group identity and a foundation for
developing a sense of belonging in a community of learning. Small group
work in which participants are seated in a circle and can make eye contact
promotes dialogue and discussion. If the program extends over a term or
over a year, this seating arrangement and group size facilitate the building
of trust, honesty, and openness.

   We would add a final note about the importance of paying attention
to the physical setting. Every effort should be made to make the learning
environment inviting, accessible, comfortable, and conducive to conversations. We have observed, for instance, after the Management and Leadership
Development Program moved from a classroom setting to a smaller intimate
setting, that the quality of conversations and retention of learners participating in the program improved significantly as a result of the change. Educators
may face constraints in the type of facility available to them, so creativity in
session location and design may be required. If the physical setting consists
of a classroom with theater-style seating in which desks are bolted down,
there are several facilitation techniques which can encourage dialogue even
within these limitations. These techniques are provided in Appendix 5.1, and
educators are invited to adopt or adapt them for their own specific needs.

REFLECTION QUESTIONS

1. How do you define your leadership style? Consider your areas of
    strength and how your leadership presence plays into them.
2. In what ways are you leveraging the perspectives and experiences of
    educators around you to guide students to the learning zone? What are
    some factors you might consider to push them out of the comfort zone
    but not to the level of the panic zone?
3. Consider what pedagogical methods can create an optimal learning
    environment. What kind of learning techniques, methods of learning,
    and physical space might you use to foster curiosity, innovation, trust,
    and learning?
4. What strategies do you have in place to set clear expectations, create
    group cohesion, set up accountability, nurture commitment, and build
    a relationship with participants that set the stage for transformative
    learning?

5. How do you seek feedback from superiors, colleagues, and students to improve your effectiveness as an educator? How do you incorporate this feedback into your leadership style and relationships?

NOTES

1. "Studies show that trying to improve a weakness is far less effective than spending time building up your strengths. Working on weaknesses can become frustrating and may even lead to withdrawal. Research and performance consulting firm Gallup Inc., for instance, found that employees who are given the opportunity to focus on their strengths every day are six times more likely to be engaged in their jobs as those who aren't" (quoted in Murray, 2017). See also https://hbr.org/2005/01/how-to-play-to-your-strengths. Accessed May 17, 2017.
2. These inventories may be found in campus student life offices or counseling services, and some require trained facilitators. For different types of inventories, see: Intercultural Development Inventory (IDI), https://idiinventory.com/; Myers–Briggs Test, http://www.myersbriggs.org/; True Colors, https://truecolorsintl.com/; StrengthsFinder, https://www.gallupstrengthscenter.com/?gclid=CjwKEAjwja_JBRD8idHpxaz0t3wSJAB4rX-W5Vd3RrmnsvHCJTlqfT2k12NdbajY5_tFd3nbX5e6F4RoC4S7w_wcB; and Native Compass, the Personality Compass. Content has been adapted from Turner and Greco (1998). Accessed May 29, 2017.
3. See Grant (2013).
4. See Heathfield (n.d.).
5. Website (https://www.ttisuccessinsights.com/research/). This assessment looks at four dimensions of behavior and provides recommendations for best ways to communicate with an individual. It also provides a comparative assessment of self-perception and others' perception of the individual, and discusses natural and adapted styles of dealing with problems, people, pace, and response to rules and procedures.
6. Hard skills are teachable skills that are measurable or quantifiable. Examples include reading, writing, arithmetic, and machine operations. Soft skills are related to personal characteristics and traits and include such things as a person's ability to communicate, work with others, and fit into an organization's culture, and the person's leadership abilities.
7. Stone et al. (2010) describe the three conversations as the "what happened" conversation, the "feelings" conversation, and the "identity" conversation.
8. Nancy A.G. Vogele is the former Director of Religious and Spiritual Life at Dartmouth College and an Episcopal priest with 20 years of experience in parish ministry. Throughout her career and in her personal spiritual journey, Dr. Vogele has sought to make connections between her religious profession and social justice. Provided by Nancy Vogele via email on June 20, 2017.
9. For Nate Fick's biography, see http://www.dartmouth.edu/~trustees/biographies/fick.html. Accessed May 24, 2017.
10. Belle Halpern and Kathy Lubar describe the PRES model as "P – *Being Present*, the ability to be completely in the moment, and flexible enough to handle the unexpected. R – *Reaching Out*, the ability to build relationships with others through empathy, listening, and authentic connection. E – *Expressiveness*, the ability to express feelings and emotions appropriately by using all available means – words, voice, body, face – to deliver one congruent message. S – *Self-knowing*, the ability to accept yourself, to be authentic, and to reflect your values in your decisions and actions" (Halpern and Lubar, 2004, p. 9).
11. Van Roekel (2008). See https://www.psychologytoday.com/blog/sideways-view/201511/self-awareness. Accessed May 24, 2017.
12. For Haroon Moghul's biography, see https://www.google.com/search?q=haroon+moghul&ie=utf-8&oe=utf-8. Accessed May 24, 2017. Hanadi Doleh is a long-time veteran

of Park51, having been a part of the organization since its opening in September 2011. Since then Doleh has taken a leading role in managing the organization's weekly prayer services and oversees all of its programming and internal administrative functions. Doleh also serves as Park51's main liaison with various interfaith organizations across NYC, specializing in informational sessions that are catered to visiting groups wanting to understand aspects of the American Muslim perspective. Doleh has also forged relationships with several universities in the tristate area and across the nation for similar purposes. She holds a Master's degree in International Relations from CUNY Brooklyn College. Her graduate thesis was titled "The interplay between religion and politics in Palestinian–Israeli history."

13. Goleman (2006) describes emotional intelligence as self-awareness, empathy, self-regulation, motivation, and social skills in his book *Emotional Intelligence*. For related sources, see Goleman (2014) and Malcolm Higgs and Victor Dulewicz (2016).

14. Website (https://www.inc.com/resources/leadership/articles/20071001/musselwhite.html). Accessed June 25, 2017.

15. Improvisation, or improv, is a form of live theatre in which the plot, characters, and dialogue of a game, scene, or story are made up in the moment. Often improvisers will take a suggestion from the audience, or draw on some other source of inspiration, to get started. Website (http://www.hideouttheatre.com/about/what-is-improv). Accessed May 27, 2017.

REFERENCES

Dowling, Daisy W. (2017). What the U.S. Military Can Teach Companies about Supporting Employees' Families. *Harvard Business Review*. May 11. Website (https://hbr.org/2017/05/what-the-u-s-military-can-teach-companies-about-supporting-employees-families). Accessed May 11, 2017.

Dugan, J.P., Kodama, C., Correia, B., and Associates. (2013). *Multi-Institutional Study of Leadership Insight Report: Leadership Program Delivery*. College Park, MD: National Clearinghouse for Leadership Programs.

Evje, B. (2012). The Skills Most Leaders Don't Have. *Inc.* November 7. Website (https://www.inc.com/brian-evje/the-skills-most-leaders-dont-have.html). Accessed June 23, 2017.

Freire, P. (2015). *Pedagogy of the Oppressed*. Transl. by M.B. Ramos. New York: Bloomsbury.

George, B. (2008). Why a Personal Guide to True North? In B. George, A. McLean, and N. Craig, *Finding Your True North: A Personal Guide*, First Edition (pp. xiii–xviii). San Francisco, CA: Jossey-Bass.

Goleman, D. (2006). *Emotional Intelligence: Why It Can Matter More than IQ*. New York: Bantam Books.

Goleman, D. (2014). *What Makes a Leader: Why Emotional Intelligence Matters*. Florence, MA: More Than Sound.

Grant, A. (2013). Goodbye to MBTI, the Fad That Won't Die. *HuffPost*. September 18. Website (http://www.huffingtonpost.com/adam-grant/goodbye-to-mbti-the-fad-t_b_3947014.html). Accessed May 23, 2017.

Halpern, B.L. and Lubar, K. (2004). *Leadership Presence*. New York: Avery.

Heathfield, S.M. (n.d.). What Is a 360 Review? Website (https://www.thebalance.com/what-is-a-360-review-1917541). Accessed June 23, 2017.

Higgs, M. and Dulewicz, V. (2016). *Leading with Emotional Intelligence: Effective Change Implementation in Today's Complex Context*. Cham, Switzerland: Palgrave Macmillan.

Madson, P.R. (2005). *Improv Wisdom: Don't Prepare, Just Show Up*. New York: Bell Tower.

Murray, B. (2017). Forget Your Weaknesses ... Focus on Your Strengths! *Mind Tools* Blog. March 9. Website (https://www.mindtools.com/blog/forget-weak nesses-focus-strengths/). Accessed May 29, 2017.

Myers & Briggs Foundation. (n.d.). Website (http://www.myersbriggs.org/home. htm?bhcp=1). Accessed June 23, 2017.

Patterson, K., Grenny, J., McMillan, R., and Switzler, A. (2002). *Crucial Conversations: Tools for Talking When Stakes Are High*. New York: McGraw-Hill.

Senninger, T. (2000). *Abenteuer leiten – in Abenteuern lernen: Methodenset zur Planung und Leitung kooperativer Lerngemeinschaften für Training und Teamentwicklung in Schule, Jugendarbeit und Betrieb*. Münster: Ökotopia-Verlag.

Stone, D., Patton, B., and Heen, S. (2010). *Difficult Conversations: How to Discuss What Matters Most*. London: Penguin.

Turner, D. and Greco, T. (1998). *The Personality Compass: A New Way to Understand People*. Boston, MA: Element.

Van Roekel, N.P.D. (2008). *Promoting Educators' Cultural Competence to Better Serve Culturally Diverse Students*. Washington, DC: National Education Agency.

Wagner, W. (2011). Considerations of Student Development in Leadership. In S. Komives, J. Dugan, J. Owen, C. Slack, W. Wagner, and Associates (Eds.), *The Handbook for Student Development* (pp. 85–107). San Francisco, CA: Wiley.

The Nelson A. Rockefeller Center at Dartmouth College
The Center for Public Policy and the Social Sciences

APPENDIX 5.1 FACILITATION TECHNIQUES

As a facilitator of programs or discussions, when you work with people, you can make the experience enjoyable. Your goal is and should be to bring out the best in people, help them to think about things they are concerned about, and create an intellectually supportive and non-judgmental environment in which they can freely express their thoughts. Provided below are some techniques that you can use to keep the conversation flowing. You can use one technique or combine techniques. Feel free to experiment. Finally, remember to always keep the purpose of the discussion in mind and what you and your participants hope to achieve. Have fun doing this.

1. Icebreaker

When to use it: You can use an icebreaker when: 1) you want to energize participants; 2) you want to help them get to know one another; 3) you want to do some type of team-building; 4) you want to have participants practice a particular skill.
Instructions: There are many options for icebreakers. Look for books on icebreakers.

2. Popcorn (also Known as Group Brainstorming)

When to use it: When you're interested in quickly generating new ideas in a large group.
Instructions: Ask participants to simply throw out any ideas that they have on a topic. Encourage them to not worry about organizing their idea beforehand. Tell them that there are no correct or incorrect answers. Write down each idea on a flipchart or dry erase board.

3. Parking Lot

When to use it: Use this when participants come up with ideas that are not the focus of the topic of discussion. Can also be used when you run out of time and would like to remember to come back to a topic in the future.
Instructions: Write down on a flipchart or piece of paper any ideas that you

would like to come back and talk more about. Make sure that you do come back to address the parking lot.

4. Small Group Discussion

When to use it: Use it anytime you think it would be helpful to have more active participation in the group. Participants are often more comfortable sharing in small groups than in a large group. The advantage of small groups (groups of three or triads, four, five, six) is that you can still hear from a broad range of ideas in a relatively short period of time. Small group discussions are often accompanied with sharing highlights with the larger group.

Instructions: Break the larger group into small groups and ask them to discuss their thoughts or ideas with one another. You may want to give them a time-limit for their discussion and encourage them to make sure that everyone has time to share. It's often helpful to also give the group a minute or two heads-up to wrap up their conversations.

5. Pairs or Dyads

When to use it: Use this any time you think it would be helpful to have more active participation in the group. As with small groups, participants are often more comfortable sharing in pairs than in large groups. This format is most helpful when you're asking participants to share something more sensitive or personal. Pair discussions are often accompanied with sharing highlights with the larger group.

Instructions: Just ask participants to get into groups of two (you can invite them to pair with the person next to them or to just find a partner).

6. Think, Pair, Share

When to use it: Use this when it would be helpful to have more active participation in the group. As with small groups, participants are often more comfortable sharing in pairs than in large groups. This format is also very helpful when you're asking participants to share something more sensitive or personal.

Instructions: Give all participants a time to think about the question you are posing and write down their thoughts. Then participants get into groups of two (you can invite them to pair with the person next to them or to just find a partner) to discuss the thoughts they wrote down. Finally invite participants to share thoughts from their discussion with others in the larger group.

7. World Café

When to use it: Use this anytime you would like to quickly get participants to brainstorm ideas or share opinions in a creative and efficient manner. This format is most useful when the group's energy is low and you want to get participants moving a little bit and focus on one or two issues.

Instructions: Break the large group into small groups of four or more. Maximum number for a small group should not exceed five. Pose the question you want all the groups to consider. Give them five to ten minutes for discussion and ask one person to note key points on the flipchart provided to them. When the time is up, ask the recorder to stay at the table and ask other members to switch and join other groups. The newly formed groups can continue discussion on the same question, and the recorder can add new points. After two to three rounds, discuss common themes and new ideas participants heard during various discussions. There are many variations for using this technique, and we encourage you to experiment with it!

8. Gallery Walk

When to use it: This is a great technique to use when you're interested in having participants nonverbally reflect on the ideas, thoughts, and opinions shared.

Instructions: There are two ways that you could do this. 1) Invite participants to write their thoughts related to an issue individually on post-it notes or on flipchart papers. Ask participants to stick the post-it notes or flipchart paper up on the walls and ask the group to review the information in silence. Encourage participants to notice themes and things that stood out or surprised them. Then ask the larger group to verbally discuss their reflections. 2) You could put topics on different flipcharts and ask participants to go around the room and put comments on them. Then invite participants to read through them. As a larger group, you could discuss themes or what stood out for them.

9. Index Cards

When to use it: Index cards are a great tool to use when discussing sensitive, taboo, or personal topics. 1) They can be used effectively to help participants list questions or share ideas anonymously. 2) They can also be used to help participants to write down their personal reflections after they have participated in an activity.

Instructions: There are several ways that you can use index cards. 1) When participants first come in, hand them a blank index card and ask them to write down any questions they have about the topic (no names). You could then collect and redistribute the cards so others could help read the range of questions or you could collect and read them yourself. It's helpful to ask the group to help you identify the themes of the questions. 2) Another option is to ask the group to write down their hopes and fears on the index card. 3) Give participants blank index cards and invite them to write down their thoughts and feelings related to the topic. Often this is for them only, but you could collect and redistribute the cards without names as well. 4) You can also make name tents for participants attending a meeting with index cards. It instantly makes group members feel as though they know each other's names and creates a nice welcoming environment for all. Please provide permanent markers (not pens or pencils) to participants and ask them to write their names.

10.   Journaling

When to use it: This is a great technique to use when you would like participants to privately reflect or process what they have learned. This is particularly useful when you're talking about personal or sensitive topics.
Instructions: Ask participants to write down in a journal, on an index card, or on a piece of paper their thoughts, feelings, questions, etc.

11.   Drawing or Visual Aids

When to use it: Many participants are visual learners and appreciate the opportunity to reflect or share information through images. This can be a great way to allow individuals to reflect, but it can also be a way to do an individual or creative group activity.
Instructions: Pose a problem or solution you want participants to consider. Ask them to draw the problem or solution showing its causes and effects with arrows or symbols. They can use words as well or you can instruct them to not use words. The key is to provide different colors and an opportunity for participants to visually map their thoughts. After they have finished their drawing or visual aid, either do a gallery walk or ask participants to describe what they have produced to a smaller group or to the rest of the group. Important: if you instruct them to not use words, make sure you tell them that it is not a competition to see who draws the best. Rather, it is another way to think about issues.

## 12.	Report Back

When to use it: This technique is often used after you break the group into pairs or small groups. It's a great way to allow the larger group to hear summaries of what participants discussed. This can help the group identify themes rather than specifics.

Instructions: After you have broken the group into small groups or pairs or had participants reflect individually, ask participants to verbally share themes or highlights of what they discussed. If you use small groups, you could consider giving them flipchart paper on which to write down what they discussed. There are several ways that you could structure the sharing. 1) Ask each group to share what they discussed to the larger group. 2) Ask one group to share what they came up with and then ask others to add to the list. 3) Ask for a few volunteers to share some highlights with the larger group.

## 13.	Chalk Talk

When to use it: Use this when you would like to generate a lot of thoughts or ideas quickly. It's also a great way to get all participants to share their personal views efficiently.

Instructions: Write down a word or topic on the chalk or dry erase board. Invite everyone to come up and share ideas, reflections, or thoughts related to the word or topic. Invite the group to read them and reflect on themes.

## 14.	Take a Break and Move Around

When to use it: This is a great technique to use when you expect that your discussion will be over an hour long. It's also helpful to use when you feel that the group is losing energy or seems disengaged. Finally, it might be something to try if the discussion has been very heated or off topic. This can give everyone time to reflect, reenergize (wake up), touch base with a co-facilitator, and refocus.

Instructions: When there is a break in the discussion suggest that the group take a moment to take a break (ten-minute food or bathroom break) or sometimes you will want to imbed this into the schedule if the discussion is expected to last longer than an hour. There may be times when you stop the group and encourage participants to get up and jump around. Finally, you could also schedule quick wake-up icebreakers periodically in order to reenergize and focus the group.

15. Silence

When to use it: This is very useful when discussion has been very heated on a topic or too many thoughts have been expressed and everyone in the room (you as well as participants) has not had the time to catch up with them.

Instructions: Tell the group that the topic has raised so many emotions that the group needs a moment of silence to reflect. In the case where too many thoughts have been expressed, inform the group that you are providing a minute of silence to reflect on all the thoughts that have been expressed. This will help you to bring the discussion back on track.

Note: Sometimes, when you pose a question as a facilitator, no one responds. In such cases, learn to feel comfortable with silence and know someone or another will say something.

16. Call-Outs or "Cold Calling"

When to use it: When you are trying to hear from more members of the group – particularly those who may be less likely to be the first to speak.

Instructions: Call on individual members of the group to share their thoughts. Most effective when some degree of comfort has been established but folks are still hesitant to speak up. It is helpful to call on a few participants in succession so individuals don't feel specifically targeted.

17. Around the Horn

When to use it: When you are trying to hear from all members of the group – particularly when you would like everyone's thoughts out on the table.

Instructions: Going in a circle, ask each member of the group to share their thoughts in a few words or one sentence. Most effective when some degree of comfort has been established but folks are still hesitant to speak up.

Revised from original version created by Nora Yasumura and Sadhana Hall. This handout is used for a training in the Rockefeller Center's program, Dartmouth Leadership Attitudes and Behaviors (D-LAB).

6. Program conceptualization and development

In this chapter, we describe how to conceptualize and develop co-curricular leadership programming. First, steps should be taken to identify and understand the target population for the program. Then educators should assess the available resources and assemble a team of similarly motivated individuals to assist in the development process. From there, research should be conducted to help further conceptualize the program. Finally, educators should establish initial program goals and student learning outcomes for their program to ensure that the needs of both the students and the educators will be fulfilled by the proposed design.

The opportunities for implementing leadership initiatives at the undergraduate and graduate levels have increased significantly in recent years. Leadership programming is at the core of leadership education, training, and development. Leadership programs should be conceptualized in several ways. They can range from well-defined curricula that focus on individual, team, or organizational growth all the way to mentoring programs that help to develop networks and support systems. While they can be either curricular or co-curricular in nature, leadership programs should all be developed with the same level of intensity and expertise.

In developing leadership initiatives, academic institutions need to address issues related to the size of the program, the resources required to sustain it – compared to what is actually available – and the location of the programming within the institution's organizational structure. Regardless of size, location, and resources, all effective leadership programs must be conceptualized and developed using a consistent, systematic approach that is guided by a clear understanding of the program's place in the institution's overall mission and vision.[1]

This chapter presents a method for the development of leadership programs that draws on the experiences of the Rockefeller Center at Dartmouth College and the McDonough Center at Marietta College. It provides a discussion of the activities that set the stage for effective program design:

- identifying and understanding the need of the target population;
- assessing resources;
- assembling the planning and development team;
- research and benchmarking; and
- developing goals and learning outcomes.

With this foundation, the chapter then provides a systematic path forward based on seven core pillars of program design that the Rockefeller Center has identified over the course of more than a decade of running leadership programs. Using these seven pillars facilitates conceptualization and development of a strong program design:

1. intentionality of programs;
2. theoretical grounding;
3. rigor;
4. structure;
5. reflection;
6. community; and
7. assessment and evaluation.

Below are several lessons learned from implementing leadership programs at the Rockefeller Center, as well as a case study illustrating how the Management and Leadership Development Program from the Center uses these principles in practice. The chapter concludes with reflection questions that can be used during the development phase for a new or existing program.

ELEMENTS OF PROGRAM DESIGN

In Chapter 2, we explored the historical processes that give rise to unique leadership programs from distinct institutional contexts. While each institution's circumstance shapes its programmatic preferences, in this section we propose developmental factors that should be common to all programs.

Identifying and Understanding the Target Population

The characteristics of an intended audience influence each phase of the program, from initial enrollment, to engaging with the content, and finally to the transformation of attitude, thought, or behavior. Jane Vella (2002) explains that adults learn when the content has immediate use and is relevant to their lives. Educators should develop an understanding of the varied characteristics, motivations, and perspectives of different generations, as identified by scholarly research. This understanding can be a valuable tool in designing leadership content that is relevant to the target audience, as well as improving intergenerational communication.[2]

Seemiller and Grace (2016), in their work on intergenerational characteristics, provide insight on every generation's perceptions about the world, motivations, attitudes, beliefs, and working styles.[3] Reviewing generational trends aids in the establishment of a general context for the program and enables the planning team to create an audience profile. Other things to consider include the gender/sexual identity, cultural background, and ethnic traditions of the audience. These social identities and experiences work together to create a worldview and perspective that make an individual unique. Furthermore, to create an environment for constructive discussion, educators should consider how their own worldview and perspectives are similar or dissimilar to those of their learners.

Although the information is an aid to understanding learners and how to engage their interest, Seemiller and Grace (2016) caution that the insights on generational trends should not be used to stereotype or box learners into categories. They also remind educators to review and revise systems, processes, and structures based on evolving trends. Learners have varying levels of knowledge, maturity, and experience, and may excel with different learning styles. There is some controversy over learning styles, as discussed by Pashler et al. (2008) in "Learning Styles: Concepts and Evidence." Based on their research, they conclude that:

> At present, there is no adequate evidence base to justify incorporating learning-styles assessments into general educational practice. Thus, limited education resources would better be devoted to adopting other educational practices that have a strong evidence base, of which there are an increasing number. However, given the lack of methodologically sound studies of learning styles, it would be an error to conclude that all possible versions of learning styles have been tested and found wanting; many have simply not been tested at all. (Pashler et al., 2008, p. 105)

Educators can gather additional information specific to their potential participants in a variety of ways. In small or large schools or institutions offering leadership programs, we encourage educators to identify sources that can yield the information discussed previously. For example:

- Admissions offices and departments of institutional research may be able to share valuable information about enrolled students, although privacy concerns may inhibit the type of information that can be shared.

- Colleagues who have invested in developing the leadership capacity of students in other programs can provide educators with insights into their needs and strengths.
- Information can be gathered through the application process and through focus groups with potential participants to learn more about their background and their perceived needs.
- Human resources departments may gather information that might be useful in learning the background and demographics of participants.

In this phase of identifying the audience, educators must consider how they will develop inclusivity in the classroom. University leadership programs increasingly need to feature dialogue surrounding issues that may be difficult and polarizing. These discussions can only be enriching if there is a strategy in place to create a diverse pool of program participants, which is an endeavor aided by deliberate, inclusive design.[4] Inclusive design is the development of activities and programs that acknowledge the ways in which individual social identity shapes the way that students learn. Through inclusive design, we actively seek different perspectives that move leadership learning forward. Educators can then develop the aspirational vision of what they hope to accomplish for their learners.

Assessing Resources

Educators should be very clear about the human, financial, and material resources needed for a potential leadership program in order to match the size and the scope of the program to the resources available. A preliminary budget and establishment of budget and expenditure by funding source and program(s) are essential to prioritize the flow of resources and focus the program team on overall mission and values. While the budget often highlights direct costs related to the program, don't forget about the additional cost of compensating educators and staff involved in the design, implementation, and management of the program. Funders and potential funders for the program should be part of the assessment, and systems should be built early on to ensure their participation in the process.

To be frank, assessing and managing resources may be the most unexciting part of conceptualizing a leadership program. Educators may see themselves solely as being responsible for the curriculum and content of programs and may not embrace the logistical and administrative aspects of program implementation. This may be the reason why stewardship of resources is often low in the priority of implementation tasks that need to be done. Yet it is essential, because dealing with these tasks at the conceptualization stage enables educators to think creatively and build a program to scale with a view to expanding it in the future.

The setting of your program – quite literally where you will deliver the lessons – is another key resource. Where leadership programs are physically housed depends on context, financial resources, and the culture of the institution, as we discussed in Chapter 2. Leadership programs are housed within centers (e.g., Rockefeller and McDonough), within departments, or within individual organizations, which are connected within or beyond the campus and share a common purpose (Komives et al., 2011, p. 232).

Assembling a Planning and Development Team

To carry out an effective program-planning process, it is important to solicit the views of individuals representing faculty, staff, and students. The diversity of thought from such a group will ensure the development of a program that incorporates several points of view in the continuum from theory to practice. Educators can create a formal team or an informal network that informs program conceptualization decisions. Over time, this planning process can foster a collaborative spirit that extends into program implementation.

The first step in this process is for the educator, with the help of the formal team or the informal network, to develop a common understanding of the need for the program and its alignment with institutional mission and values. A statement of need (a document describing the need) can later be used for public communications, discussions with other campus partners, fundraising, measurement, and evaluation.

For example, Dartmouth College has assembled a development team of faculty, staff, and students to explore how to offer a continuum of programs across the undergraduate students' time on campus. Team members have been chosen for their experience with leadership programs and represent a diversity of roles on campus.

Research and Benchmarking

Researching existing programs, guidelines, and standards creates the foundation for strong programs. Relevant research should include studies or surveys involving students, faculty, employers, and alumni that draw out information and expectations which will help conceptualize the program. For example, a quick web search of colleges that offer leadership programs with similar-size or program goals can be a source for identifying a host of programmatic topics.

Surveying students can help educators identify their specific management and leadership concerns. Employers who have hired students from the college for entry-level positions or internships can also provide information about the leadership skills they want to see in the workplace. Employers may be able to offer insights into the management and leadership gaps they see in their young employees. Information can also be drawn from alumni surveys or focus groups. Educators should reach out to colleagues to learn about their personal best practices for developing programs. A SWOC (strengths, weaknesses, opportunities, constraints) analysis with a formal or informal team of educators can further give shape to the program.

Information from all these sources should be analyzed and used to form the basis for developing a list of topics and creative methods for implementing the program. The research, combined with the understanding that has been developed about the target audience, forms the basis for the next subsection on developing program goals and student learning outcomes.

Developing Goals and SMART Student Learning Outcomes

Program goals are general statements that articulate an expectation of what students will learn, understand, or appreciate as a result of their participation. For example, the program goal of the Management and Leadership Development Program offered by the Rockefeller Center is to "develop practical competencies and capacities that students can apply in real time within their leadership and management roles on campus, during leave-term internships, and in their careers beyond Dartmouth."

Tied closely to such program goals are SMART student learning outcomes. SMART student learning outcomes are:

- *Specific*: This includes information about who will be involved and for what intended outcome.
- *Measurable*: The outcome can be quantifiably evaluated.
- *Attainable or Appropriate*: The learning outcome is logically constructed and aligned with goals.
- *Realistic*: Desired outcomes are informed by audience maturity level and time allotted to meet the learning outcome.
- *Time-bound*: The outcome is attainable within a defined period.

With SMART learning outcomes, educators and learners can fully commit to program goals with confidence. SMART learning outcomes create a sense of urgency because they are time-limited; this only works when learning outcomes are well communicated publicly, however. They also create accountability for both educators and learners. Provided below are some examples of SMART learning outcomes:

1. Students will describe key terms ("global awareness," "global attentiveness," "global consciousness," and "global citizenship") associated
   with globalization.
2. Students will examine some of their cultural assumptions using
   role-play.
3. Students will draw conclusions about different leadership strategies
   when developing a global consciousness.

There are other versions of the SMART acronym, but the key is to use
well-defined learning outcomes to frame lesson plans that will need to be
in place to achieve a program goal. Chapter 7 provides additional examples
of SMART learning outcomes.

THE SEVEN PILLARS OF PROGRAM DESIGN

With the initial planning work accomplished, it is time to design the
program's content and structure. The following seven core pillars create
a strong foundation for a leadership program. Even though content and
structure can vary across institutions and programs, paying close attention
to these concepts helps educators build strong programs. In our experience,
these have proven to be the seven most important pillars as we develop
programs at the Rockefeller Center and the McDonough Center, but in the
process of implementing them you may discover others that are important
to you.

We suggest these concepts are interrelated and sometimes overlap.
However, we have described the seven pillars so that educators may pay
close attention to them when they are conceptualizing their programs.
The International Leadership Association (ILA) has developed "Guiding
Questions: Guidelines for Leadership Education Programs," which also
help in the thoughtful design of programs.[5] Wherever appropriate, these
have informed the development of the seven pillars.

Throughout this section, we have provided an example of a program
focusing on public speaking, a competency the student leaders believe is
important for a leader. This example is used to highlight each one of the
pillars of program design. It was chosen because of the importance of
public speaking in both formal and informal leadership situations. The
goal of the program would be to strengthen a leader's capacity to mobilize
and inspire followers through effective communication. The intention of
this example is not to be exhaustive, but rather to provide further clarity
on the application of each pillar.

Pillar 1: Intentionality of Programs

Intentionality is important when creating leadership programs. Strong leadership programs are intentional when they take into consideration audience characteristics, comprehensively target the leadership educational needs of the participants, and hold these participants accountable for their own learning. Leadership programs are also intentional when their selection and outreach processes succeed in gathering learners from different backgrounds with diverse perspectives, resulting in greater peer learning.

Intentional leadership programs are based on perceived needs within a modern college campus and are tied to the needs of the workplace. They are based on articulated values, have SMART learning outcomes, address key concepts, have a clear methodology, and offer activities that continually reinforce previous learning.

It is important to consider the research you gathered regarding participants' maturity levels and other characteristics to meet the students at their particular stage of leadership development. In the example of the public-speaking program, first and foremost, the formation of such a program would address the need for students to become proficient at public speaking. Once formed, the facilitator would be intentional with:

- articulated values: the group's focus would be on clear and honest communication, respect for multiple perspectives, constructive feedback, and the ethical presentation of information;
- establishment of SMART learning outcomes: students will be able to describe the rationale for considering audience characteristics; describe the relationship between tone, body language, and message; develop a message for a three-minute speech; deliver a speech and receive feedback on its message, tone, and body language;
- inclusion of key concepts: information about verbal and nonverbal communication, audience participation, delivery, reflection, and constructive feedback;
- a clear methodology: weekly sessions would be offered at a set time on a set day; sessions would be participatory and experiential in nature; and
- reinforcement of previous learning: through recap of earlier sessions, examples, stories, and simulations.

Pillar 2: Theoretical Grounding

Leadership programs with theoretical grounding allow learners to translate theory into practice and create a space for transformative learning.[6] They help learners connect general concepts to their own personal or distinctive experiences. Thus learners are provided with a systematic framework for analyzing and reflecting on experiences in order to reach higher levels of achievement and deeply internalize the learning. As an example of such a framework, the co-curricular programs at the Rockefeller and McDonough Centers use Kolb's cycle of learning (see Figure 6.1). We also encourage educators to consider how to incorporate foundational concepts such as Bandura's self-efficacy (1977) and leader identity development (Komives et al., 2006) in their theoretical grounding.

The model emphasizes the importance of experience and the applications of that experience in life to advance one's own learning. This cycle

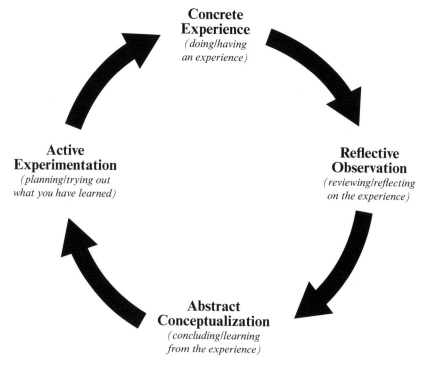

Concrete Experience
(doing/having an experience)

Reflective Observation
(reviewing/reflecting on the experience)

Abstract Conceptualization
(concluding/learning from the experience)

Active Experimentation
(planning/trying out what you have learned)

Source: McLeod (2013).

Figure 6.1   Kolb's cycle of learning

reinforces that learners are active and unique. At the same time it encourages them to take the time to reflect and act on their learning – both in and out of the classroom, and on and off campus. To explain how this model could be used in a session of our public-speaking program, imagine that you have a large group of 20 participants divided into smaller groups of five, with four members in each group. They first practice public speaking and give each other feedback on clarity of message (concrete experience). They discuss and reflect on their observations from the practice session (reflective observation). In their small groups, they form conclusions based on what they learned from this experience (abstract conceptualization). Finally, they use new insights gained (active experimentation) to develop a work plan to further improve their skills (concrete experience), thus completing the cycle of learning.

To take our public-speaking program further, we developed several learning outcomes. Public speaking for leadership has its own body of relevant theory and knowledge that can be applied to the development of this competency. The program would also use Kolb's cycle of learning as the methodology for the delivery of the outcomes listed above. Using both the content knowledge (e.g., communication theory) and the process of delivering it, we can imagine a systematic way in which learning outcomes are met for the public-speaking program.

SMART learning outcomes have been documented according to the broadly applied Bloom's taxonomy (Bloom, 1956). According to this taxonomy, there are three domains of learning: cognitive, affective, and behavioral.

The well-known Bloom's taxonomy emphasizes different levels of critical thinking within the cognitive domain. Bloom identifies six levels of behavior – knowledge, comprehension, application, analysis, synthesis, and evaluation. The complexity of learner skills increases as one moves up the levels, and each level adds on to the foundational skills of the prior one (Komives et al., 2011). This allows for more focused and effective learning outcomes. Anderson et al. (2001) have revised Bloom's work, providing robust examples and descriptions in the affective and behavioral domain, respectively. This pillar addresses the guiding question: What is the conceptual framework of the leadership education program?

Pillar 3: Rigor

Program development is rigorous when it follows a systematic framework, with content based on research about participant needs, and establishing best practices from other institutions using information from professional organizations such as the ILA, the National Association of

Campus Activities (NACA), or the National Clearinghouse for Leadership Programs (NCLP). The content should challenge participants to go beyond their comfort zones, as described in Chapter 5. This could entail incorporating concepts that are complex, ambiguous, or contentious. These activities should not paralyze learners, but drive them to explore and acquire skills that they can apply in personal or professional contexts.[7] Ultimately, such programs create a space for learners to wrestle intellectually with problems and identify creative solutions to them. The exercises chosen for administering rigorous programming should be deliberate, focused, and chosen to enhance the understanding of leadership in different fields of endeavor.

Rigorous programs should have systems in place to make them dynamic and allow for periodic review and revision to meet changing workplace needs. They should tie together the learners' programming options and, in this process, ensure that curricular and co-curricular offerings inform each other. This pillar addresses this guiding question: What is the content of the leadership education program and how was it derived?

In the public-speaking program example, we would be demonstrating rigor if we had ensured that we had gathered relevant information about the participants through a pre-assessment and had conducted research on possible topics to be covered in the sessions for the program. In this case, we would be covering information about audience, verbal communication (tone), nonverbal communication (body language), and message (content). Further, the public-speaking program would have assessment methodologies in place to gauge participant learning. For instance, an evaluation sheet would be used for providing written feedback to participants after they deliver their speeches. Participants would also receive verbal feedback. This feedback would be used to adjust future sessions to reflect students' real-time learning.

Pillar 4: Structure

The structure of leadership programs is critical because it determines how they are implemented. Being able to answer questions like why, what, when, where, and how is vital to creating structure at the program conceptualization stage.[8] Educators must identify ideal numbers of participants to optimize the program's impact, and consider options for the timing and layout of each session. Having a consistent day and time that is convenient for participants makes the program more accessible and enhances the learning environment. Constant awareness of the next step in the established planning sequence is also a keystone of structured programming.

Structuring programs also includes sequencing sessions or activities within a program into manageable lessons that build from simple to complex concepts. The learning path should be well established and follow a natural progression, taking into account the learners' stages of education, maturity, and experience. Sequencing enables educators to determine where to specialize and offer more in-depth programming. It also facilitates continued engagement in the overall program because learners understand what their next option is for further learning. As part of a continuum of programs within an organization, individual offerings within a program relate clearly to one another, to a shared framework and set of values, and to expectations amongst program implementers.

In the example of the public-speaking program, budget and staffing considerations would define the number of sessions. Let's say we have resources available for six one-hour sessions. We would limit the sessions to 20 participants so that they can practice lessons learned in each session. The first session would focus on an overview of public speaking and an assessment of participants' skill levels. Session two could cover audience characteristics and why it is important to consider them. Participants would continue the session by applying this knowledge through an actual review of their intended audiences' characteristics. Session three would highlight their intended message and how delivery is adjusted for identified audiences. Session four would include delivery of the speech and methods for crafting word structures. Session five would aim at working on body language, and the final session would include presentations in which participants demonstrated an alignment with all three chosen areas (body language, message, and tone).

All sessions would use Kolb's cycle of learning as the methodology, with intensive practice and feedback built into each session. In this example, we would sequence and build student experiences to end with the most complex presentation. We took our participants through content starting from an introductory level; however, if our participants were at an intermediate or even advanced level, we would scaffold the curriculum to meet their needs. We would also determine how the content of this program fits within a continuum of programs offered by the organization.

Pillar 5: Reflection

Leadership programs should help their participants to develop the practice of reflecting on their actions. It is critical to incorporate reflective components in leadership programs that create the space for learners to slow down and evaluate what they have learned. This will help learners take future purposeful actions that address personal and professional growth. When personal reflection is incorporated into the learning outcome of a session, learners become aware of their personal strengths and weaknesses.

They may also become aware of those of their team, organization, or community, depending on the focus of the session, which further helps them understand how they can better fit into a team and collaborate. Reflection allows learners to examine current experiences and new insights in the context of their previous knowledge, facilitating the transformation of thoughts, attitudes, and actions necessary for the development of problem-solving skills (Kinefuchi, 2010).[9]

Reflection would be built into the public-speaking program example. Every time students attended a session, they would be given opportunities to explore how the content is relevant and applicable to them. For reflection purposes, these questions can be used: How do I make my audience feel? How clear and concise is my message? Given the content, how was the delivery of the message received? These reflection exercises are critical to ensuring that learners synthesize the competencies and knowledge to which they are exposed.

Pillar 6: Community

Leadership depends on a community of leaders and followers, and leadership education should also embrace this. The role of community on leadership can be seen in the effect of campus involvement on student leadership. Dugan and Komives (2007) find that "students that reported any level of involvement in campus clubs and organizations demonstrated higher scores across all of the Social Change Model values" (p. 15). The social change model values most improved were collaboration, common purpose, and citizenship (Dugan and Komives, 2007). For programs, building community involves nurturing familiar relationships and mutual support between learners and educators within and beyond the leadership program and between learners themselves. Learners and educators serve as current and future resources and mentors to each other. These relationships depend upon a level of trust being established early on in a program, so that learners feel comfortable asking questions that lead to greater growth for themselves and their peers. It is therefore important during the planning phase to build in strategies that promote the creation of networks of community.

In the public-speaking program example, we would work hard to establish a sense of community. Giving and receiving constructive feedback would be one mechanism through which students would work together and help each other to build their own skills as well as the skills of others. As educators, we would create experiences which would help them develop a cohesive understanding of the topics which are going to be covered and create processes for participants to support each other throughout the learning process. The goal in this instance would be to create an intellectually supportive environment that group members use to help each other grow in their public-speaking competencies. One example would be coming together to co-create guidelines for how they would like to give and receive feedback. Another example could include the development of the assessment tool by the group.

Pillar 7: Assessment and Evaluation

Programs must have clear assessment and evaluation procedures that focus on the individual learner, program, alumni, and institutional levels. Learners can be expected to learn and grow personally, academically, and intellectually as a result of participating in such programs. This model is intended to augment traditional course-evaluation mechanisms based on specific and actionable feedback on learning objectives. Very often, systems to assess and evaluate a program are put in place only after it is well underway and are added only as an afterthought. Strong leadership programs, in contrast, begin with a clear articulation of what participants can expect to learn.

Program planners must articulate how participants can expect to grow personally and professionally. They should also have systems in place to capture this information before, during, and after the program. This allows managers to clearly measure program effectiveness and articulate a link to the institution's mission. This pillar addresses a guiding question: What are the intended outcomes of the leadership education program, how are they assessed, and how will they be used to ensure continuous quality improvement?

Finally, effective assessment is linked to learning objectives. As Combs et al. (2008) suggest, "The [successful] model employs an assessment tool that measures student perceptions of importance and their current competence in course-specific learning objectives both pre- and post-course" (p. 87). Information gained from this assessment also allows for modification in delivery and/or content of the current course.

In the public-speaking program example, written and verbal evaluations created by the group would be provided to each participant for every speech delivered. A post-assessment in the last session would determine the improvement in skill levels of the participants. Throughout the program we would assess how well sessions are working, and how the logistics have been implemented. Finally, we would see whether the program addresses the organization's mission of educating, training, and inspiring leaders.

In sum, the roadmap to effective program design begins with conception, followed by design and assessment. The roadmap that outlines program conceptualization and development is illustrated in Figure 6.2.

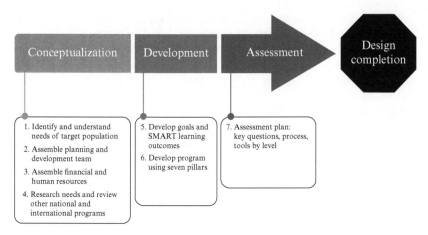

*Figure 6.2   Roadmap for effective program conceptualization and
            development*

CASE STUDY: ROCKEFELLER'S MANAGEMENT AND LEADERSHIP DEVELOPMENT PROGRAM

The following case study brings together all the concepts surrounding program conceptualization and design as discussed in this chapter.

Creating the Management and Leadership Development Program

As described at the beginning of the chapter, the Management and Leadership Development Program (MLDP) at the Rockefeller Center was developed in the fall of 2008 after assessing the available resources. The program was conceived of as a response to the unmet need for preparing sophomores, juniors, and seniors with management and leadership principles for successful performance in internships and for personal and professional growth as leaders. Having identified the target need with thoughtful consideration of excluding first-year students given their particular need to focus on acclimating to higher education, a planning and development team was assembled which consisted of students, faculty, and staff working in the Rockefeller Center.

After identifying the target population, assessing the human and financial resources, and confirming that the Center had the capacity to offer such a program, the team's next task was to gather information through research and benchmarking that would help shape the new program. The group surveyed other higher education institutions. They also received feedback from other members of the Dartmouth community. In addition, the National Association of College Employers (NACE) survey provided insight into what skills and competencies employers look for in their employees. If you are looking for a comprehensive collection of competencies from a wide variety of accreditation agencies, we recommend considering Seemiller's

(2013) *The Student Leadership Competencies Guidebook: Designing Intentional Leadership Learning and Development*. This provides an index of 60 leadership competencies organized within eight broad themes. These may prove useful in your own program design.

Mapping key topics offered by other higher education institutions and using this information with feedback given by educators, students, and alumni enabled the planning team to narrow a large potential program content down to a smaller initial set of topics. Next, they considered the SMART learning outcomes for the program and then used the seven pillars of program design to develop a set of nine mandatory, 90-minute sessions:

- What makes a good leader?
- Analytical/critical thinking.
- Writing in the workplace.
- Diversity in the workplace.
- The art of public narrative.
- Facilitation.
- Problem-solving, decision-making, and negotiation.
- Strategic planning and systems thinking.
- Business etiquette.

The planning team also designed a menu of "special sessions," with a requirement for students to select at least two, according to their interests:

- Time and stress management.
- Word hero.
- Interview skills.
- Grant writing.
- Excel.
- Finding your passion.
- PowerPoint.
- Global leadership.
- Event planning.
- Fundraising.
- Writing resumes.
- Ethics in leadership.
- Recruiting prep super-day.
- Social media tools.

The special sessions were open both to participants of the Management and Leadership Development Program and to non-participating students. The content of all these sessions highlighted how each topic directly connected to leadership development.

With the sessions identified, the group selected speakers with demonstrated expertise in the topics and gathered them together to discuss how the sessions would flow and be sequenced. Kolb's cycle of learning served as each speaker's framework for content delivery. SMART learning outcomes were refined at this time, and the assessment framework was developed using Bloom's revised taxonomy. Chapter 7 illustrates how Kolb's cycle of learning is used in developing the session design, and at the Rockefeller Center all programs use this framework to deliver the specific content for each session.

The pilot offering of the program was conducted during the fall term of 2009 with 21 participants. At the end of the pilot, the speakers met again to make revisions based on feedback from participants and their own observations. In the winter term of 2010, the Rockefeller Center opened the program to all interested participants, and this program has been continually offered every term since. Today, about 50 students complete the program in each of the three terms in a given academic year. Similar to other programs at the Rockefeller Center, the Management and Leadership Development Program has a rigorous assessment process and has gone through several revisions.

The program is designed using the seven pillars as its foundation. It is intentional because it takes into consideration the maturity of the learners and pegs the curriculum at an intermediate to advanced level based on that maturity level. It invites students to go beyond their comfort zone, provides them with a challenging yet supportive environment to learn new material, and applies it to their leadership experiences and internships within their chosen fields.

Creating a space for students to reflect is an important feature, and program officers pay close attention to it. In the words of Eric A. Janisch, Program Officer, MLDP, May 2017;

> The personal leadership challenge is the most beneficial reflection tool for MLDP students. During their reflection with me students are asked what kind of leader they think they should be, and what steps they need to take to be that leader. I then ask them to reflect on the reasons they might have not taken those steps. These questions more often tease out a student's values, force them to reckon with their evolving identity in college, and place the onus and power for change in their hands.

The program maintains its quality and rigor by ensuring that each speaker who has agreed to facilitate the content of a session during a particular term commits to offering the same session in the remaining terms of the academic year. Speakers ascertain that the content related to each session is current and updated. Also, based on student and educator feedback, the program is changed if necessary after each offering to ensure that the SMART learning outcomes are met. Logistically, it is structured to take place over dinner at a specific day and time each week (every Tuesday) to enable students to plan their schedules. Every session incorporates a reflection component, which helps learners to apply information gained during the session to their personal and professional situations.

Originally, building community was not considered to be a core requirement of the program, but it quickly became evident that this pillar was necessary for group learning, growth, and building commitment to the program. As a result, strategies to create a more intimate learning environment now include increasing small group discussions and dividing the large number of participants into two sections. The two sections are offered back to back to use speakers' time effectively and to manage the logistics related to the program sessions efficiently.

The pilot session provided administrators with insights about which changes to the seven pillars they would need to implement before the Center offered the program campus-wide. Sometimes mistakes made in early program implementation reveal important information that should be heeded to continually improve. For the MLDP, feedback from a first-year student who had been inadvertently signed up for the pilot program revealed that the program was more appropriate for sophomores, juniors, and seniors because of the maturity level and experience required for the program content. Active reflection of students, staff, and speakers helped to guide other program innovations. The team incorporated small group projects, clarified expectations for completion, and developed approaches that would mobilize and inspire students to attend sessions utilizing the same experiential learning model that MLDP built upon. They explored using technology to deliver content to expand the reach and potential for MLDP, trying to "flip the classroom." This incorporated video segments for asynchronous learning and used the time together in the sessions for clarification and practical application of the themes. They identified new ways to reach out to different groups of students who were not currently represented fully in student participant groups. They discovered the need to make a clear distinction between core mandatory MLDP sessions offered on Tuesday nights each term from one-off, stand-alone special sessions. They also continued to use the special sessions as an outreach avenue for MLDP participants, MLDP alumni, and other students on campus.

Key details related to program conceptualization and development are provided in Table 6.1, with notes identifying unchanged or changed features about the program. This program has undergone many changes every year to make it more responsive to participants and to data from alumni surveys and employers of recent graduates. To demonstrate how evaluation of the program has informed implementation in practice, this table compares features of the program in 2010 and 2017.

A very important feature of this program is an ongoing effort to build a diverse community by reaching out to African American, Asian American, Latinx, and Native American students, and others, to engage all communities on campus. Intellectually diverse fields of study are also considered. Strategies have included: inviting enrolled students in the program to "nominate" others from their communities who would benefit from the program; advertising the program through faculty, staff, and students; and conducting short presentations in large classes. The result is a campus-wide representation of students with different perspectives and backgrounds. To further deepen this outreach effort, at the time of this writing, the Center is looking at active ways to partner with programs for first-generation students and students from low socioeconomic backgrounds.

Table 6.1   Management and Leadership Development Program features

Features	Winter term of 2010	MLDP 2017	Notes
Goal	Create an understanding of management and leadership.	Create an understanding of management and leadership.	No change.
Audience	Sophomores, juniors, or seniors.	Sophomores, juniors, or seniors.	During the pilot in the fall term, we had inadvertently signed up a first-year student.
Mandatory sessions	1. What makes a good leader? 2. Writing in the workplace. 3. The art of public narrative. 4. Problem-solving, decision-making, and negotiation. 5. Analytical/critical thinking. 6. Diversity in the workplace. 7. Facilitation. 8. Strategic planning and systems thinking. 9. Business etiquette.	1. What's your "why" of management and leadership? 2. Using your strengths for effective personal communication. 3. Understanding your strengths in the context of management and leadership. 4. Presenting yourself professionally. 5. Being an effective team player. 6. Authentic exchanges: the science and art of building relationships. 7. Negotiating for success. 8. Writing and workplace etiquette.	Using the annual NACE survey and looking at feedback from employers and students, Rockefeller Center staff made relevant changes to the session.

Table 6.1 (continued)

Features	Winter term of 2010	MLDP 2017	Notes
Mandatory sessions		9. What happened? So what? Now what?	
Optional sessions	Time and stress management, interview skills, Excel, PowerPoint, event planning, writing resumes, recruiting prep super-day, word hero, grant writing, finding your passion, global leadership, fundraising, ethics in leadership, and social media tools.	None.	These sessions are no longer tied to MLDP, as we learned that participants could not devote additional time for them. As a result, such sessions are now offered as special workshops and are open for campus-wide participation. MLDP participants are encouraged to attend.
Structure	All participants met together and attended 90-minute weekly sessions that met on Tuesdays for mandatory sessions. In addition, participants were required to attend two special sessions. All sessions model Kolb's cycle of learning.	Program divided into two sections. One section meets from 4:30 to 6:00 PM and the other section meets from 6:30 to 8:00 PM on Tuesdays. The same speaker facilitates both sessions. Speakers present the same topic three times a year. All sessions model Kolb's cycle of learning. Students identify a personal leadership challenge that they plan and work	Structure changed to build relationships, a sense of community, and camaraderie. Location also changed to help with facilitating this process. Personal leadership challenge strengthened as a reflection tool.

Table 6.1 (continued)

Features	Winter term of 2010	MLDP 2017	Notes
		to address during the ten weeks of the program.	
Student/learner selection	Short application with multiple-choice questions and a short statement.	Short essay applications and a ten-minute interview with student assistants.	Builds commitment and camaraderie.
Registration goal	31 students.	65 students.	Changed from 95 to 65 because many more programs.
Completion	12 students; 39% of students participating.	48 students; 74% of students participating.	Likely owing to improved monitoring and communication between educators and participants.
Student program assistants	Two per term.	Four per term. Four "student ambassadors" are also selected per term who serve as program assistants and facilitators for activities and discussion.	The student assistants were increased to three for spring and fall terms of 2015, and increased again to four in winter term 2016.
Assessment and evaluation plan	Session surveys on content, process, and logistics; meetings with speakers; end-of-program evaluation.	Session surveys on content, speaker, application of previous session material, program logistics, status of personal leadership challenge. Peer nominations for excellence.	

Table 6.1   (continued)

Features	Winter term of 2010	MLDP 2017	Notes
		Bi-weekly feedback sessions with student ambassadors. Personal leadership challenge reflections.	

LESSONS LEARNED

Several lessons can be gleaned from the experience of conceptualizing and developing leadership programs at the Rockefeller Center:

1. Get input and commitment from relevant players at the early stages of program development. This includes potential funders whose commitment could play a critical role in ensuring the sustainability of the program. Involve faculty, students, and staff in conceptualizing and developing a vision for the new program. Stakeholders who make human and financial resource allocations must also be involved in developing the vision for a new program. Current students and alumni provide valuable perspectives in shaping the program. Paying close attention to what employers are looking for in entry-level candidates provides useful perspectives.
2. Annually assess program content to see how well it addresses the skills employers want in entry-level positions using the NACE survey and feedback from internship supervisors and alumni. This action always helps to keep the program vibrant and relevant to the needs of the participants.
3. Learn as much as possible about the target audience when conceptualizing and designing a program and look for a variety of methods for gaining insights. This is an ongoing process and, as the program matures, so will the sophistication of understanding the needs of learners and educators.

> "I learn about what sessions and content are most applicable to students from their Personal Leadership Challenges (identification paper, one-on-one meetings, and reflection paper) and from regularly asking each student

participant, 'How have you used what you learned in the program so far during this past week?' Through these avenues, I hear about what they do on campus, what they are passionate about, and what they are currently struggling with in their leadership development" (Robin Frye, Program Officer, personal communication, June 20, 2017).

4. Once a need is recognized, secure institutional will and funding. At the same time, consider how to place the program in the larger institutional context. Program conceptualization and development depend on a strong institutional commitment and vision. Support from senior leadership provides educators with the inspiration and the physical, human, and financial resources to develop and conceptualize these leadership programs. If there is no institutional will and support, there is no program.
5. Strong leadership programs do not necessarily need vast amounts of financial resources. What is needed is a clear approach to program conceptualization and development.
6. Start small with a few students and then expand to program capacity. This will help to establish what works, discard what does not work, and test new ideas before the program is formally implemented.
7. Defining program goals is an iterative process that begins with a needs assessment, but needs can change over time. Incorporate ongoing assessment with input from key stakeholders, including funders of the program.
8. Program conceptualization and development are hard work. Educators working to develop programs should be supported in taking calculated risks and encouraged to rework program conceptualization and development until they meet the needs of the learners.

REFLECTION QUESTIONS

Although these reflection questions are created particularly for conceptualizing and developing new programs, educators can also use them as a quick assessment of programs both new and mature, and anywhere in between.

1. What group of individuals are working together to develop a rationale, vision, and goals? How did our team share the leadership function? Which parts need more attention? How has our team handled Tuckman's stages of group development discussed in Chapter 1 (i.e., forming, storming, norming, performing, adjourning)?
2. Is there institutional will and funding for the program? In what ways have you sought stakeholder input and buy-in to ensure human and

financial support? In what ways does the program conceptualization fit into the broader vision of the program?

3. Given the specific needs of your target audience, how does the learning framework meet them? What have other organizations done well with similar groups and in similar contexts?

4. How will the program learning outcomes help to shape content and how will they be assessed? What does success look like to you?

5. How might the "seven pillars" help to develop your program? Are there other considerations that you might focus on for your particular cultural and institutional context?

NOTES

1. The value of the vision lies in increasing program effectiveness. In Komives et al. (2011)'s *The Handbook for Student Leadership Development*, Chapter 6: Establishing and Advancing a Leadership Program, the authors advise that creators would be well served by developing a clear vision statement to establish concrete direction for program planners and participants.

2. This is important because strong leaders emerge from reflection and self-awareness. This is discussed in Brown's "Leadership for Social Justice and Equity: Weaving a Transformative Framework and Pedagogy" (2004). The article cites pragmatic approaches to shaping successful and transformative leaders. Brown focuses on a process-oriented model applied to educational leaders in particular. The critical theory she uses is rooted in the daily lives of people and cultures. The model she proposes promotes "awareness through critical reflection, acknowledgement through rational discourse, and action through policy praxis" (Brown, 2004, p. 78). Brown emphasizes the need to constantly reflect and consider change. The strongest leaders, she says, are stretched outside of their comfort zones in thought and experience. In the context of social-justice leaders, this leads to true change in oppressive structures. So, to effectively structure a program, it is critical to gain an understanding of the issues facing the program participants.

3. In their book *Generation Z Goes to College*, Seemiller and Grace (2016) address questions about social issues students care about, what motivates them, how they prefer to learn, and their use of technology.

4. The importance of identity is discussed in Pendakur and Furr (2016). Critical pedagogy utilizes themes and principles in designing curricula, tying in various ideologies and cultural frameworks into the learning process. Leadership education, the authors suggest, is inextricably linked to personal culture and identity. The authors aim to apply this type of pedagogy to curricula designed for students of color, integrating elements of critical race theory in determining leadership identity. In practice, the engagement of power, identity, and culture allows for empowered leaders, centering social issues at the core of their foundation. This allows for leaders making challenging decisions, considering the power relationships among themselves and others, and bringing in voices of all members of the community.

5. You can find this document on the ILA website (http://www.ila-net.org/Communities/ LC/GuidingQuestionsFinal.pdf). Accessed June 25, 2017.

6. As discussed in Brookfield (2005). Brookfield cautions against the idea that theory and theorization are processes restricted only to certain intellectuals. Theory should be both accessible and pragmatic, as all actions and decisions are based on understandings or assumptions held about how the world works. Brookfield states that adult educational

theory, in particular, is practical in that we can critically evaluate and reevaluate our values, understandings, and judgments.

7. This is achieved through learning activities. Hmelo-Silver and Barrows expand on this in "Goals and Strategies of a Problem-Based Learning Facilitator." They write: "[In facilitation of a student-centered problem-based learning group], specific strategies were used to support the goals of helping students construct causal explanations, reason effectively, and become self-directed learners while maintaining a student-centered learning process" (Hmelo-Silver and Barrows, 2006, p. 4).

8. These elements of structure are supported by program frameworks as described in Dennis Roberts's *Student Leadership Programs in Higher Education* (1981). The author analyzes various empirical student leadership programming models and establishes three broad areas through which to reach students: purpose, strategies, and populations. Roberts uses a few theories for the framework of his conceptualization, including Perry's cognitive developmental scheme. Each chapter outlines individual parts of the process of program building, with Chapter Four focusing most on implementation of the programs. Chapter Four begins by assessing the needs, expectations, and goals of the students at the beginning of the program, and in the final stages it suggests methods for effective follow-up evaluation.

9. Kinefuchi applies a learning scholarship that stresses the need for applied learning in critical consciousness and change. Kinefuchi discusses this in the context of phenomenology, which primarily deals with subjective meanings of life by examining "descriptions of and reflections on experiences." A critical consciousness requires challenging conventionally accepted discourse. Kinefuchi's article not only recognizes the subjective experiences of individuals, but stresses the importance of gathering multiple experiences to understand the range of subjective meaning. In Kinefuchi's practice, creation of a space for written student reflections revealed productive meanings for service-learning experiences. Some of these reflections dealt with dominant racial representations, and some dealt with other institutional practices that marginalize immigrants.

REFERENCES

Anderson, L.W., Krathwohl, D.R., Airasian, P., Cruikshank, K., Mayer, R., Pintrich, P., Raths, J., and Wittrock, M. (2001). *A Taxonomy for Learning, Teaching and Assessing: A Revision of Bloom's Taxonomy*. New York: Longman Publishing.

Bandura, A. (1977). Self-Efficacy: Toward a Unifying Theory of Behavioral Change. *Psychological Review*, 84 (2), 191–215.

Bloom, B.S. (1956). *Taxonomy of Educational Objectives*, Handbook I: *The Cognitive Domain*. New York: David McKay Co.

Brookfield, S.D. (2005). *The Power of Critical Theory*. San Francisco, CA: Jossey-Bass.

Brown, K.M. (2004). Leadership for Social Justice and Equity: Weaving a Transformative Framework and Pedagogy. *Educational Administration Quarterly*, 40 (1), 77–108.

Combs, K.L., Gibson, S.K., Hays, J.M., Saly, J., and Wendt, J.T. (2008). Enhancing Curriculum and Delivery: Linking Assessment to Learning Objectives. *Assessment and Evaluation in Higher Education*, 33 (1), 87–102.

Dugan, J. and Komives, S. (2007). *Developing Leadership Capacity in College Students*. College Park, MD: National Clearinghouse for Leadership Programs.

Hmelo-Silver, C. and Barrows, H. (2006). Goals and Strategies of a Problem-Based Learning Facilitator. *Interdisciplinary Journal of Problem-Based Learning*, 1 (1), Article 4.

Kinefuchi, E. (2010). Critical Consciousness and Critical Service-Learning at the Intersection of the Personal and the Structural. *Journal of Applied Learning in Higher Education*, 2, 77–93.

Komives, S.R., Longerbeam, S.D., Owen, J.E., Mainella, F.C., and Osteen, L. (2006). A Leadership Identity Development Model: Applications from a Grounded Theory. *Journal of College Student Development*, 47 (4), 401–18.

Komives, S.R., Dugan, J., Owen, J., Slack, C., and Wagner, W. (2011). *The Handbook for Student Leadership Development*, Second Edition. San Francisco, CA: Wiley.

McLeod, S.A. (2013). Kolb – Learning Styles. *Simply Psychology*. Website (www.simplypsychology.org/learning-kolb.html). Accessed June 1, 2017.

Pashler, H., McDaniel, M., Rohrer, D., and Bjork, R. (2008). Learning Styles: Concepts and Evidence. *Psychological Science in the Public Interest*, 9 (3), 105–19.

Pendakur, V. and Furr, S.C. (2016). Critical Leadership Pedagogy: Engaging Power, Identity, and Culture in Leadership Education for College Students of Color. *New Directions for Higher Education*, 174, 45–55.

Roberts, D.C. (1981). *Student Leadership Programs in Higher Education*. Washington, DC: American College Personnel Association.

Seemiller, C. (2013). *The Student Leadership Competencies Guidebook: Designing Intentional Leadership Learning and Development*. San Francisco, CA: Jossey-Bass.

Seemiller, C. and Grace, M. (2016). *Generation Z Goes to College*. San Francisco, CA: Jossey-Bass.

Vella, J. (2002). *Learning to Listen, Learning to Teach: The Power of Dialogue in Educating Adults*, Second Edition. San Francisco, CA: Jossey-Bass.

7. Planning effective sessions: strategies, tools, and logistics

As described in the previous chapter, the design of robust curricula that meet defined goals and learning outcomes is essential to the development of an effective leadership program. Once that foundational work is accomplished, the same clear-sighted planning must be applied to its implementation at the individual session level – the main focus of this chapter.

Excellent leadership programs are developed through rigorous attention to detail. The sessions within a syllabus are the building blocks for sound programs. If sessions are not carefully designed and executed with proper attention to composition and logistics, participants will not only have a weaker understanding of the content being covered, but also receive the implicit message that the educators are not committed to the learning that should be taking place. As a Dartmouth student from the Class of 2019 says, "Participants can tell when a session has been developed hastily – without a clear roadmap or goal. Interest wanes as they become disengaged from the material, which may ultimately result in disenrollment from the course."

Well-designed sessions convey the educator's dedication to the material and respect for the learners' time and effort. Put simply, by intentionally crafting and organizing each session, we communicate a devotion to doing things right, which puts us well on our way to establishing trust, credibility, and respect as stepping-stones to leadership.

It is therefore vital for educators to give adequate thought to the individual sessions within a curriculum, and in this chapter we will offer one strategy we use at the Rockefeller Center for ensuring maximum impact. We will begin with a general overview of the components of effective session design: assessing audience maturity level and readiness; establishing SMART learning outcomes; identifying key concepts; incorporating leadership categories and competencies; outlining content and roles; and creating time for reflection within a session. With a session design in place, we then discuss logistical considerations for its implementation, including some tools used by the Rockefeller Center for organizing each session within a program. We end the chapter with a few reflection questions.

COMPONENTS OF EFFECTIVE SESSION DESIGN

Developing effective sessions requires an understanding of those sessions from various angles. Through our experience, we have learned how important it is to take into consideration audience maturity and a clear understanding of the session content. This is an ongoing process. We encourage educators to reflect deeply about changes they want to make to the session after delivering it and how to incorporate those changes in the next round. Taking these steps often improves a session's quality.

Assessing Audience Maturity Level

Assessing your learners' maturity level will help ensure the concepts delivered are at a level of complexity (introductory, intermediate, or advanced) that will best fit their needs. Patton et al. (2016, p. 61) describe the importance of student development theory by saying that "listening to students' stories over time and in multiple contexts will foster deeper understanding of their development and the resources they need to promote more developmental growth." There have been many models for the application of student development theory in leadership programs, but the following are the two we find most relevant to our personal experiences as educators.

The first is the leadership identity development model, which frames programs in terms of the six stages learners pass through during participation (Komives et al., 2006). These stages are awareness, exploration/ engagement, leader identified, leadership differentiated, generativity, and integration/synthesis. By identifying where students fall in these six stages, educators can offer the most appropriate programs for their maturity level. The second model is Evers, Rush, and Berdow's bases of competence, which is typically used to develop leadership programs. However, the bases can also be a useful framework for thinking about student development and the maturity level of your incoming cohort. These bases of competence center around four key competencies: managing self, communicating, managing people and tasks, and mobilizing innovation and change (Komives et al., 2006). Educators can ask students to identify situations where they have employed one or more of these competencies, and from there work toward placing students in beginner, intermediate, or advanced leadership programs. Table 7.1 illustrates how educators at the Rockefeller Center have addressed these student development theories in three areas of proficiency – data analysis, professionalism, and negotiation.

Taking the first area of data analysis as an example, we encourage first-year students and those students who have not been exposed to using Microsoft Excel to develop some basic proficiency with the software in the

Table 7.1   Examples of maturity-level assessment and audience identification

Level	Data analysis	Professionalism	Negotiation
Introductory	Ability to conduct basic spreadsheet functions.	Ability to manage their tasks and complete them in a timely fashion.	Ability to articulate importance of negotiation strategies.
Intermediate	Ability to understand and manipulate pivot tables.	Ability to follow directives and manage a pre-existing team.	Ability to negotiate between two individuals.
Advanced	Ability to develop models based on data.	Ability to create innovative programs and bring together people on their own initiative.	Ability to negotiate between multiple parties, and know stakeholder roles and leadership implications.

introductory phase. We have included this in our programming because a majority of employers we have surveyed state that understanding, organizing, and presenting data is an important skill for young managers and leaders.

Alumni have also reported that proficiency with this skill leads to higher levels of responsibility. At the intermediate level, students who will be participating in internships are encouraged to be proficient with pivot tables and, at the advanced level, students should demonstrate their deep understanding of Excel as a database for developing or interpreting models. The second and third examples of areas of proficiency (i.e., professionalism and negotiation) follow the same logic of progressing from simple to complex information, from less to more experience, and from lower to higher levels of maturity. This kind of audience experience and maturity-level assessment is highly contextual and will vary from institution to institution and from session to session, but in all instances educators should set the bar at a level that challenges but does not paralyze learners.

Whether educators plan to facilitate the session or invite speakers to facilitate it, this type of initial assessment is crucial. As educators delve deeper into session design, having a clear understanding of audience and maturity level provides a strong platform for tailoring the information to the specific needs of the participants.

Establishing SMART Learning Outcomes

As with articulating program goals at the macro-level, it is important to outline SMART learning outcomes for each session that align with a specific program goal. A detailed explanation of SMART learning outcomes was provided in the previous chapter. Here, we set the model into practice as illustrated in Table 7.2.

When developing session content for the Rockefeller Center, we have determined through experience that three SMART learning outcomes are typically sufficient for a 90-minute session that allocates 80 percent of its time to active audience participation.

Developing SMART learning outcomes using Bloom's revised taxonomy helps develop learning objectives because it explains the process of learning. It is initially labor-intensive, but less time is required with practice. Provided in Table 7.2, we include some SMART learning outcomes from three sessions within a leadership program offered by McDonough and Rockefeller Center educators. We selected them because they exemplify learning outcomes that target the knowledge, attitude, and application we seek from our participants through the sessions, which employ different levels of Bloom's taxonomy.

We have observed that, when session content is designed with appropriate SMART learning outcomes and an awareness of the needs of the audience according to their stage of maturity and learning, subsequent dramatic adjustments are not necessary. However, successful sessions also depend on the educator's awareness of the environment and an ability to respond to participants' needs, which we previously discussed in Chapter 5.

Experienced educators will recognize when to build in a discussion that takes longer than initially planned and thus effect small changes within the session itself, but in some cases radical changes need to be made in session delivery even though the session's SMART learning outcomes remain the same. For example, a session and its speaker may meet the stated learning outcomes, but participant feedback on the delivery of the content may necessitate its revision before that session is presented again.

Identifying Key Concepts

Once SMART learning outcomes are established, it is useful to identify the key concepts related to them. Articulating three to five key concepts helps concentrate the learning on essential information so that learners can formulate key takeaways from each session. The following are some examples of key concepts identified by speakers in selected sessions offered by the Rockefeller Center:

Table 7.2   Examples of SMART learning outcomes

Example one: Learning outcomes for the Management and Leadership Development Program session, *Understanding your strengths in the context of management and leadership* led by Gama Perruci

Category	Level	SMART learning outcomes
Knowledge	Recalling	Each student will identify their top five strengths related to management and/or leadership, and potential areas of improvement.
	Comprehending	Students will examine how identified strengths may be categorized into the areas of management, leadership, or a combination of both management and leadership. Students will explore similarities and differences between management and leadership.

Example two: Learning outcomes for Rockefeller Leadership Fellows Program session, *Negotiate this: getting to "yes" is no accident* led by John Garvey

Category	Level	SMART learning outcomes
Knowledge	Recalling	Students will identify their personal negotiation style and how it plays out in communication with other people through the management of differences exercise.
Problem-solving	Evaluating	Students will examine best negotiation practices (BATNA; research; self-awareness; firm, fair, and friendly).
Application	Applying	Students will practice applying this information through the Sally Soprano negotiation exercise.

Example three: Learning outcomes for the Management and Leadership Development Program session, *Using your strengths for effective communication* led by Jennifer Sargent

Category	Level	SMART learning outcomes
Knowledge	Recalling	Students will identify at least two personal areas of growth related to their MBTI type and professional communication style.
Problem-solving	Analyzing	Students will analyze at least two personal strengths related to their MBTI type and professional communication style.
Application	Applying	Students will integrate one or more strengths and one or more areas of growth into their personal leadership challenge.

Session on effective teamwork:

- Hallmarks of a great/close team: trust, working together to accomplish a mission, executing tasks thoroughly and quickly, meeting demanding challenges, learning from experience, and developing pride in accomplishments.
- Four stages of leadership development in teams: lead yourself, be a good teammate, be a great teammate, be a team leader.
- Leadership: leaders provide vision, direction, and motivation to a group of people toward a chosen goal.
- "Growth mindset" is the opposite of "fixed mindset." This is the concept that every challenge is an opportunity to learn and develop leadership skills. Individuals with a growth mindset internalize this concept and seize these opportunities when presented.
- Mental toughness: persevering in the face of adversity, and performing at the same level, regardless of external stressors.

Session on management versus leadership:

- Strengths: a preferred way of thinking, feeling, and behaving (Sessa, 2017).
- Manager: a person responsible for planning and directing the work of a group of individuals, monitoring their work, and taking corrective action when necessary (Reh, 2016).
- Leader: a person who has a vision, a drive, and a commitment to achieve that vision, and the skills to make it happen (Reh, 2017).

Emergent leadership for life:

Distributed leadership: a social process by which many people, across group boundaries and levels within a social system, interdependently create the conditions to accomplish shared purposes, in which:

- leadership is a set of social functions, not a position;
- leadership is shared among many people in different places in the system; and
- leadership is exercised interdependently by sharing resources, expertise, and authority with each other.

In addition to maintaining the focus on student learning, identifying key concepts directs the educator's attention to content areas that need to be covered within a session. It also helps to keep the session on track with learning outcomes.

Incorporating Leadership Categories and Competencies

Within the context of a leadership program, the *Student Leadership Competencies Guidebook* defines competencies as the "knowledge, values, abilities and behaviors that help individuals to contribute or successfully engage in a role or task" (Seemiller, 2013, p. xv). When designing program content, it is important for educators to have a clear idea of the specific leadership competencies each session will focus on advancing in its participants. Further, competencies identified across all sessions within a program should indicate how that overall program will help prepare its participants for future careers.

Seemiller (2013) provides an analysis of how competencies are used in leadership programs across the country and identifies 60 competency areas within eight categories. We have found this list very useful, and we encourage others to consider these competencies according to their own needs and resources. In its co-curricular programming, the Rockefeller Center uses seven categories and 43 competencies (see Table 7.3).

These competencies represent a menu of options when we build programs. Some programs sample across different categories, while others focus heavily on competencies within one category. They represent a culmination of two processes, one at the institutional level and the other at the departmental level. This list of competencies is based on a review of Council for the Advancement of Standards (CAS), Learning Reconsidered, and Liberal Education and America's Promise (LEAP) standards. Different universities will highlight different areas of competencies, all of which should align with the broader institutional priorities. These competencies also translate well to rubrics for assessment of self and others. Regardless, clarifying these at the outset is important to developing and guiding content design.

Outlining Content and Roles

Once learning outcomes, concepts, and competencies are established, you will develop qualitative and quantitative measures that reflect these learning outcomes. This process will be discussed fully in Chapter 8. With the key components of measurement and evaluation established (learning outcomes, concepts, competencies), the focus can turn to the development of the content.

At the Rockefeller Center, leadership program content is based on Kolb's cycle of learning, as described in Chapter 6. Typically, speakers devote 20 percent of the session to providing an overview of key concepts that incorporates a multimedia format, and then devote the remaining 80 percent of the time to structured activities and reflection related to the particular content area. Provided in Table 7.4 is an example of a lesson plan that demonstrates this allocation of time for activities, reflection, and action.

Table 7.3   Leadership categories and competencies used by the Rockefeller Center

---

Collaboration
- Builds and maintains partnerships based on shared purpose.
- Acknowledges and listens to different voices when making decisions and taking action.
- Facilitates collective action toward common goals.
- Encourages, supports, and recognizes the contributions of others.
- Fosters a welcoming and inclusive environment.

Effective communication
- Writes and speaks after reflection.
- Clearly articulates ideas in a written and spoken form.
- Exhibits effective listening skills.
- Influences others through writing, speaking, or artistic expression.
- Acknowledges and appropriately communicates in situations with divergent opinions and values.

Effective reasoning
- Employs critical thinking in problem-solving.
- Employs creative thinking in problem-solving.
- Develops personal reflective practices.
- Engages in inquiry, analysis, and follow-through.
- Integrates multiple types of information to effectively solve problems or address issues.

Management
- Develops and implements a plan for goal attainment.
- Develops appropriate strategies for capitalizing on human talent.
- Stewards and maximizes all resources.
- Manages multiple priorities.
- Prepares for leadership transition.
- Develops appropriate strategies for effective teamwork.
- Evaluates efficacy of current course(s) of action.
- Identifies structure and culture of organization.
- Demonstrates effective and appropriate use of technology.
- Demonstrates financial, task, and resource-management skills.

Self-knowledge
- Continually explores and examines values and views.
- Understands social identities of self and others.
- Demonstrates realistic understanding of one's abilities.
- Seeks opportunities for continued growth.
- Takes appropriate action toward potential benefits despite possible failure.
- Shows self-respect and respect for others.
- Moves beyond self-imposed limitations.
- Practices self-compassion, friendliness, ease with self, and vulnerability.

Table 7.3 (continued)

Principled action
● Identifies and commits to appropriate ethical framework.
● Demonstrates congruence between actions and values.
● Demonstrates personal responsibility.
● Appropriately challenges the unethical behavior of individuals or groups.
● Bases actions on thoughtful consideration of their impacts and consequences.
● Seeks appropriate and mutually beneficial solutions when conflict or controversy arises.

Intercultural mindset
● Contextualizes social identities and experiences.
● Understands, communicates with, and respectfully interacts with people across identities.
● Actively engages in opportunities to expand worldview.
● Applies intercultural knowledge and skills in local, national, and/or global contexts.

Session title: Public speaking for leadership
SMART objectives: The presenter has laid out the following SMART learning outcomes:

1. Describe three concepts needed for effective presentations.
2. Practice a model for giving and receiving feedback.
3. Practice the concepts by presenting in small groups, giving and receiving feedback.

Key concepts: The speaker hopes to cover these key concepts: alignment of mind, heart, and body and their connection to public speaking; the relationship between verbal and nonverbal communication; framing a message; and giving or receiving feedback effectively.
Competencies: The presenter addresses these four competencies: clearly articulates ideas in a written and spoken form; influences others through writing, speaking, or artistic expression; demonstrates a realistic understanding of one's abilities; and shows self-respect and respect for others.

Required readings and additional resources
In the outline, educators should also include recommendations about additional readings and resources related to the topic covered, as shown in Table 7.5. These should be organized to have information available for learners at different stages of engagement. These recommendations can be mentioned at the end of the session, emailed to participants after the

Table 7.4 Session outline or lesson plan

Please provide an outline of how you will use the time to present your material. What types of activities will you utilize, and in what order will you use them? Total programming should not exceed the session duration listed on page 1 of the session proposal form.

Time required (minutes)	Description
20 minutes	Welcome participants. Start lecture. Key points: Most people get anxious about public speaking. It is also a natural feeling that comes when you are about to deliver a speech that is very important to you. Public speaking aligns three things: mind, heart, and body. Explain how the three are connected. **Mind:** The mind is about crisp thinking and good writing. The content will make people want to listen to you. This makes the content look good. You need to make people care by having great content and great delivery. Get comfortable. Appearing nervous can ruin how the audience perceives your content. **Heart:** Connect content to emotion; this entails the willingness to refine your written content by editing ruthlessly and to frame your message to the needs of the audience. This also requires you to be thoughtful about modulating and varying the tone of your voice to accentuate key points and messages. It is vastly preferable to speak with your own authentic voice rather than attempt to emulate someone else. **Body:** Posture and hand gestures will also determine whether the audience will be distracted or not. **General advice:** Always be well prepared for the physical setting. Know the room setting before you give your speech. Practice makes perfect. More experience will help you improve on your weakness in public speaking. Obtaining feedback from peers can be a valuable tool. Incorporating video review into your arsenal is the single most powerful way to get an objective view of your performance.
20 minutes	Instruct learners to frame their message and ask them to develop an answer to the common interview question "Tell me about yourself." Use a handout that asks students to answer the following questions: What frame are you going to use? What implicit question are you going to answer? What topic are you most passionate about? What values are most important to you? Why are you passionate about it? What stories or examples exemplify you? Now break the students up into groups of three or four.
35 minutes	Students present. Record presentations for personal reflection later. Students give each other feedback based on three elements: body language, tone, and content.
10 minutes	Wrap up by summarizing key learnings and tying the importance of good communication to leadership. Ask students to think about three things they will do to improve their public speaking.
5 minutes	Students complete a session survey with key takeaways and evaluation related to speaker content and session process.

Note: This is an example of a session plan for *Presenting yourself professionally* developed by David Uejio.

Table 7.5   Required readings and additional resources

Required readings (optional): Please limit required reading to a total of 20 pages.	*Video for reading ahead or after the session*: *Think Fast, Talk Smart: Communication Techniques*, https://www.youtube.com/watch?v=HAnw168huqA
Additional resources: What resources would you recommend on this topic? Please feel free to include books, articles, websites, multimedia, TED Talks, etc.	*Public Speaking: An Audience-Centered Approach*, https://www.amazon.com/Public-Speaking-Audience-Centered-Approach-Standalone/dp/0205914632

Note: This is an example of required readings or additional resources for *Presenting yourself professionally* developed by David Uejio.

session, or be made available for easy reference through online platforms (e.g., Blackboard, Canvas) used by the institution.

Session title and description
Assigning a title and description to the session are often the final tasks in the content development phase. Their importance is often overlooked, but in fact this is the key information that will drive the learner's decision to participate. The session title frames the expectation for what the learner will take away from the session. Titles should be short, concise, and informative, and use plain language. Readers should get a clear understanding of what they can expect from the session content. Provocative or thought-provoking titles are most effective, leading participants to look forward to the session and consider it worth their time. These example titles are taken from program sessions facilitated by McDonough and Rockefeller Center educators:

- Networking: the art of give and take.
- Manager or leader? Understanding your strengths.
- Dream teams versus scream teams: the science and art of building effective leadership.
- Leadership: establishing credibility and building power.
- Don't go it alone: effective delegation and empowerment for leaders.
- Making your ideas stick.
- The art of telling people what they don't want to hear.
- Facilitative leadership: blending individual styles to achieve common goals.
- Leadership in civil society.

For the session description, the identified SMART learning outcomes and key concepts can be helpful in crafting the language. Again, the description should be short, descriptive, comprehensive, and free of jargon. Educators can use this session description in multiple ways to market the program to potential participants and to ensure content is not being duplicated within other sessions or in other programs. They can even be used for fundraising purposes. The following are examples of titles and descriptions taken from Dartmouth and McDonough Center sessions, and they demonstrate the different styles in which information can be conveyed:

Session title: Leadership, personal development, and the feedback cycle
Session description: This session will briefly review leadership theory to establish a framework for assessing leadership that involves striving for excellence in four areas: personal excellence, situational control, managing relationships, and achieving results. The session demonstrates giving and receiving feedback, which is essential in all four areas. Students will learn about best practices and then practice providing feedback using role-playing and scenarios provided by the instructor.
This example outlines the activities participants can expect to participate in during the session.

Session title: The naked leader
Session description: What inner work is necessary to be a leader? Is it all about the accumulation of knowledge, skills, and contacts, or is there also a simultaneous, somewhat paradoxical, stripping away that is crucial to being a leader? Is there a spirituality to leadership?
This description poses a set of questions for participants to consider, and participants recognize that it will be a reflective exercise.

Session title: Leadership and the curse of natural resources
Session description: There are many circumstances in which communities are blessed by the presence of natural resources. However, many of the worst examples of leadership are found in exactly those communities. This presentation will discuss examples of the "natural resource curse" from economics and other fields and ways that leaders can avoid falling victim to it.
This description helps participants to understand that they will be analyzing information using examples.[1]

Session title: Framing global leadership and developing a global consciousness
Session description: This session introduces the concept of "global consciousness" to students participating in the Rockefeller Global Leadership

Program. Participants are introduced to the historical evolution of four key terms: global awareness; global attentiveness (also referred to as a global mindset); global consciousness; and global citizenship. Students first think about how they use cultural assumptions to interpret human interaction. Next, they are invited to explore ways in which they can expand their global awareness, global attentiveness, and global consciousness. Finally, they consider factors affecting and impacting global citizenship.

The final description frames key concepts related to global leadership and helps participants to analyze what these concepts mean to them.

One approach is not preferred over another. Being deliberate in tone, style, and word choice can entice participants with opportunities to learn different content with different modes of content delivery.

Role of alumni and students in session engagement and facilitation

In addition to including experienced educators in programming, consider inviting alumni who have previously participated in the programs and are now serving as faculty or staff in higher education or are working in fields of interest to the participants. Alumni can be invaluable resources to a leadership program, they are typically invested in the success of the institution, or they may have participated in the program and have first-hand knowledge of it.[2] They also have instant credibility with and "relatability" to the learners. Finally, involving alumni creates an opportunity to build lasting networks between different cohorts participating in your program.[3] In Chapter 11, we expand on how we encourage alumni to become engaged with our centers as a way to promote lifelong learning.

Similar to alumni, students can play a powerful role as facilitators, because program participants find it easier to relate to them. These facilitators rise to the challenge of making each session experience relevant and meaningful, and they play an important role in building community. At McDonough, student leaders have played a crucial role in shaping its EXCEL program for incoming first-year students. In another example, the Dartmouth Leadership Attitudes and Behaviors (D-LAB) Program at the Rockefeller Center is facilitated by students in their sophomore, junior, and senior years. In the most complex example of student engagement, current Fellows in the Rockefeller Leadership Fellows Program practice and demonstrate their leadership skills by selecting their successors. Relationships established as a result of participating in these programs last long after their completion.

Session Reflection

True learning happens when participants have a chance to reflect on the session content and apply it to new situations, resulting in personal and professional growth (Kolb and Kolb, 2005).[4] When selecting questions for reflection, consider which might lend themselves to private insight and which are better suited for group discussion. Our examples have been taken from different sessions and have inspired thoughtful discussion, either by helping participants to become more self-aware or by helping them develop a deeper understanding of team or organizational dynamics. They are categorized around major themes covered in these offerings: self-awareness, group dynamics, and organizational behavior.

Reflection relating to self-awareness

Example 1   Focus is on negotiation as it relates to leadership.

- What have I learned about myself which will help me to become a successful negotiator?
- What negotiation techniques can I use to address the goals of my personal leadership challenge?
- What personal barriers did I find that may get in the way of a successful negotiation?

Example 2   Focus is on values and behaviors that form the backbone of a leadership philosophy.

- What leads to incongruence between values and behaviors?
- What are my core values?
- What does integrity mean to me? To us?

Example 3   Focus is on project management and its significance to leadership.

- What are my skills as a project manager? What do I need to focus on?
- How well do I use my critical-thinking skills in outlining assumptions and becoming proactive about anticipating problems?

Reflection relating to teamwork or organizational dynamics

Example 1   Focus is on teamwork and dynamics.

- How did it feel to discover your leadership style? Were you surprised with what you learned about yourself?

- What are some of the strengths and weaknesses of your style?
- What are some strategies for collaborating with people who have different styles?
- What do people need to understand about you and your work style?

Example 2   Focus is on teamwork and dynamics.

- Thinking about the roles teammates play, where would you place yourself on this continuum?
- Thinking about the hallmarks of a great team, how did your team measure up?
- How can you apply what you learned about teammate roles and the hallmarks of a great team to address your personal leadership challenge?

There are many factors that contribute to boosting engagement in the reflection questions. Within the session itself, it's important to allot sufficient time for this activity. Reflection can happen in different formats: participants could write down their thoughts during the session, or in response to administered surveys, or the questions can be discussed in small groups or one-on-one conversations. Whatever method is chosen, educators should ensure that the questions are clear and participants know why they are being asked to reflect on a particular topic. If the rationale for the exercise is not clear, it will often be confusing to participants and will lower the level of engagement. Finally, reflection exercises should always end with an action plan outlining one or two steps participants can take individually once the session has concluded.

LOGISTICAL CONSIDERATIONS AND RECOMMENDATIONS

For the successful delivery of a session, the importance of logistics cannot be overstated. The details matter, and good leaders pay close attention to them. All the attention to careful design will have been wasted if the sound system doesn't work, if the speaker biography in the handout is incorrect, if the materials aren't printed in time, or if the speaker gets lost en route to the venue.

The essential logistical considerations in preparing for the delivery of a session can be captured in the following main categories:

- Faculty/speaker coordination: the right people in the right place at the right time, with a shared understanding of expectations and individual roles. Also, speaker accommodation and travel.
- Preparation and distribution of publicity and session materials: complete and correct information, prepared to professional standards, available on time and in sufficient quantity, and distributed effectively.
- Preparation of venue: a comfortable environment for both participants and faculty/speakers, a set-up conducive to session type and size (classroom, lecture, discussion, etc.), equipment that functions properly, and professional and competent coordination of any catering provided.

Such details may seem trivial but, in fact, they are as important as every other aspect of session development. Without effective coordination of logistics, the quality of the content cannot shine, and the overall success of the session is at risk.

Tips and Tools: Session Proposal Form

This chapter has focused on all the details an educator or a manager needs to keep in mind when designing an individual session, but within the typical leadership program there are multiple sessions to be designed and implemented every term. Tracking all their details can be challenging, and poor organization causes unnecessary frustration. To remedy this, the Rockefeller Center uses a set of tools to aid in the effective collection and use of information for programmatic development.

The first is the session proposal form, which has proved useful at every stage of teaching leadership – from session conceptualization, to delivery, to marketing, to assessment. Its strengths lie in its ability to create intentionality in programming, as well as an organizational framework for logistics. The form has also been used to shape detailed sessions, place them neatly into a broader program context, and facilitate discussions about session delivery with educators. Most recently, it has been adapted by other departments on the Dartmouth campus and has been used in collaborative programming. The session proposal form is just one example of a tool that can be used for planning and implementation of programs, and we encourage educators to use it or adapt it to meet their needs. If this way of organizing information does not meet one's working style, we encourage educators to develop or create a tool that better suits their needs. Such tools often save significant time and energy, allowing these resources to be devoted to developing learner knowledge and growth.

From a management perspective, the form has many strengths. Developing one for each session within a program ensures consistency by collecting the same categories of information for each. This leads to a shared understanding among educators within a program, allowing them to sequence sessions that work in concert toward achieving the goals and learning outcomes of the program. For instance, Dartmouth's Management and Leadership Development Program (MLDP) consists of nine different sessions which all align with the overall goal of the program.

The session proposal form also serves as an aid to program evaluation and coordination. Reviewing the proposal forms as a team gives educators a greater knowledge of each other's sessions and programs. It thereby improves their ability to give feedback to strengthen content, identify gaps or duplicative efforts, and develop a common understanding of language and key concepts. This helps a programmatic team ensure quality and continuity, and it allows the team to assess how competencies are addressed. At the Rockefeller Center, this has elevated our desire to build a team culture of learning, accountability, and continuous improvement. Since instituting this process, we have observed that team members exhibit increased confidence in leading and driving the further development of the programs for which they are responsible. From a delivery standpoint, educators have used this form to initiate conversations with outside speakers to spur creativity in session development. A completed session proposal form and the case scenario can be found in Appendices 7.1 and 7.2 respectively.

Educators who use the session proposal form are able to keep information related to a particular session in one place and retrieve it in a timely manner. It becomes an electronic record for institutional history that is updated regularly to record adjustments made based on speaker and staff observations and feedback from session participants. This contributes to a continuous, overarching assessment and analysis within and between programs to ensure activities align well with learning objectives and outcomes.

While providing educators with a valuable tool, the session proposal form presents some challenges as well. We recognize that people have different work styles, and therefore the tool is not always conducive to the planning methods of individual educators. Ensuring consistency in filename conventions and the number of versions created across a team of educators can also be difficult. Keeping the forms updated requires commitment and discipline, and the level of detail can vary. Before implementing any widespread use of the form, program managers may find it helpful to pilot the tool with a few educators and engage in an inclusive process to tailor it to the program's particular needs.

Tips and Tools: Gantt Charts

Once the design phase is completed and a session is moving toward implementation planning, the need for organization and coordination among team members becomes critical. One helpful method to stay organized in this phase is to develop a simple system that outlines activities, deadlines, and the leaders responsible for each task. The system used by some of the educators at the Rockefeller Center is a simple Gantt chart (see an example in Figure 7.1).

Although an implementation plan can be as detailed as desired, we prefer this simple tool to organize and visually depict high-level tasks. It demonstrates the interdependency of certain tasks – and thus of team members – by illustrating those that cannot begin until the previous one is completed. A Gantt chart also helps its users to set timelines and judge whether they are realistic, to understand when key decisions are needed, and to balance the task load against the session's completion date. We would add a word of caution when using a tool such as a Gantt chart: the bars in the chart do not indicate the complexity of tasks, meaning that additional information is often necessary to determine the difficulty of accomplishing a given task in the allotted time. Many other organizational tools exist (PERT charts, Asana, Trello, Microsoft OneNote, Azendoo, Producteev, etc.). It is important to select the one that best meets the particular characteristics and habits of the team members who will be using it.

REFLECTION QUESTIONS

1. In what ways have you matched your program's content to the maturity level and cognitive complexity of your learners?
2. What tools are you utilizing to ensure logistical synergy and efficiency to ensure that your program aligns with learning outcomes and competencies?
3. How might you leverage the expertise of alumni and other students? In what ways does this relationship benefit all parties?
4. How have you integrated reflection questions to encourage participant engagement, learning, and growth? How might you also creatively use these reflection questions for assessment?
5. How have your programs helped participants to develop an action plan?

TASKS				April				May				June				
DESCRIPTION	Person(s) Responsible Primary/Alternate	Start Date	Deadline	Week 2–8	Week 9–15	Week 16–22	Week 23–29	Week 30–6	Week 7–13	Week 14–20	Week 21–27	Week 28–3	Week 4–10	Week 11–17	Week 18–24	Week 25–1
Develop Detailed Budget	Leshawna/Devin	1 Apr	15 Apr	███												
Confirm Speaker	Joshua/Heorold	15 Apr	22 Apr		███											
Complete Speaker Proposal Form or Forms If There Are Multiple Sessions Within a Program	Michael/Timothy	15 Apr	28 Apr			███										
Develop Monitoring and Evaluation Plan	Jane/Phillip	10 Apr	15 Apr	██												
Book Space	Phillip/John	15 Apr	19 Apr		██											
Confirm AV	Timothy/Michael	17 Apr	25 Apr			███										
Book Travel and Accommodation	Devin/Leshawna	17 Apr	25 Apr			███										
Develop and Implement Outreach Plan	Phillip/Jane	27 Apr	15 Jun				████████████████									
Send Reminder to Speaker a Week Before Session	Jane/Joshua	15 May	22 May							██						
Choose Specific Dates to Monitor Progress	John/Heorold	15 May	22 May							██						
Before Session Begins, Ensure AV and Supporting Materials, and Water for Speaker are Available and in Place	Timothy/Michael	14 Jun	15 Jun												▌	
Evaluation Plan is in Place	Jane/Phillip	14 Jun	15 Jun												▌	
Session Evaluation is Completed	Devin/John	15 Jun	19 Jun												██	
Thank Speaker and Ensure a Summary of the Evaluation From Learners. Follow Up With Speaker Regarding Adjustments to the Session	Devin/John	15 Jun	22 Jun												███	

Figure 7.1   Example of session planning and implementation Gantt chart

NOTES

1. Felder and Silverman (1988) say: "Much research supports the notion that the inductive teaching approach promotes effective learning. The benefits claimed for this approach include increased academic achievement and enhanced abstract reasoning skills; longer retention of information; improved ability to apply principles; confidence in problem-solving abilities; and increased capability for inventive thought" (p. 678).
2. The value of alumni in education processes is also referred to in Mizikaci (2006). She describes that the transformation process of a program includes "evaluation of the program, the courses, and the professors (through student surveys, alumni, parents, employers)" (p. 48).
3. Seeking out alumni increases their engagement with the institution as a whole, as Heckman and Guskey describe here: "The significance of active participation of customers [in this case, alumni] in an institution or organization is emphasized by the results of the study. The importance of shared values, effective communication, and participation in social activities was consistent in all equations" (Heckman and Guskey, 1998, p. 110).
4. Kolb's work describes learning thus: "The process is portrayed as an idealized learning cycle or spiral where the learner 'touches all the bases' – experiencing, reflecting, thinking, and acting – in a recursive process that is responsive to the learning situation and what is being learned" (Kolb and Kolb, 2005, p. 194).

REFERENCES

Felder, R. and Silverman, L. (1988). Learning and Teaching Styles in Engineering Education. *Engineering Education*, 78 (7), 674–81.

Heckman, R. and Guskey, A. (1998). The Relationship between Alumni and University: Toward a Theory of Discretionary Collaborative Behavior. *Journal of Marketing Theory and Practice*, 6 (2), 97–112.

Kolb, A. and Kolb, D. (2005). Learning Styles and Learning Spaces: Enhancing Experiential Learning in Higher Education. *Academy of Management Learning and Education*, 4 (2), 193–212.

Komives, S.R., Longerbeam, S.D., Owen, J.E., Mainella, F.C., and Osteen, L. (2006). A Leadership Identity Development Model: Applications from a Grounded Theory. *Journal of College Student Development*, 47 (4), 401–18.

Mizikaci, F. (2006). A Systems Approach to Program Evaluation Model for Quality in Higher Education. *Quality Assurance in Education*, 14 (1), 37–53.

Patton, L.D., Renn, K.A., Guido, F.M., and Quaye, S.J. (2016). *Student Development in College: Theory, Research, and Practice*. San Francisco, CA: John Wiley & Sons.

Reh, F.J. (2016). The Role and Responsibilities of a Manager. *The Balance*. Website (https://www.thebalance.com/what-is-a-manager-2276096). Accessed May 13, 2017.

Reh, F.J. (2017). Understanding the Role and Responsibilities of Leadership. *The Balance*. Website (https://www.thebalance.com/what-is-a-leader-2275811). Accessed June 6, 2017.

Seemiller, C. (2013). *The Student Leadership Competencies Guidebook: Designing Intentional Leadership Learning and Development*. San Francisco, CA: Jossey-Bass.

Sessa, V. (2017). *College Student Leadership Development*. New York: Routledge.

The Nelson A. Rockefeller Center at Dartmouth College
The Center for Public Policy and the Social Sciences

APPENDIX 7.1 RLF SESSION PROPOSAL FORM

Thank you for contributing to the success of our program. Please complete the following proposal form, which ensures consistency throughout our program and facilitates the overall assessment of our program's learning objectives and competencies.

Program-specific criteria:

- Session duration is one hour.
- Target level of complexity of session content is advanced.
- Please note that audience is generally composed of 20–24 seniors.
- Primary point of contact for RLF is Tatyana Bills, Program Officer.
- For more information about RLF, please visit: http://rockefeller. dartmouth.edu/studentopps/rlf.html

Co-curricular programs at the Rockefeller Center follow the Kolb cycle of learning: theory-based knowledge, experiential learning, reflection, and concrete application.

Part 1. *Speaker Information and Session Administration & Logistics*

Your Name:	Philip J. Hanlon
Your Title:	President
Your Institution or Affiliation:	Dartmouth College

Brief Bio: *Please provide a brief bio of 200 words or less.*	Philip J. Hanlon became the 18th president of Dartmouth College in June 2013. He is the 10th Dartmouth alumnus to serve as its president and the first since the 1981 to 1987 tenure of David T. McLaughlin. President Hanlon, formerly the Donald J. Lewis Professor of Mathematics at the University of Michigan, earned his Bachelor of Arts degree from Dartmouth, from which he graduated Phi Beta Kappa. An accomplished academic and administrative leader, Hanlon served in a

	succession of administrative leadership roles at Michigan for more than a decade, most recently as provost and executive vice president for academic affairs. He had been a member of the faculty there since 1986, and continues to teach as a Professor in the Mathematics department at Dartmouth in addition to his role as President. Hanlon has earned numerous honors and awards for his mathematical research, including a Sloan Fellowship, a Guggenheim Fellowship, a Henry Russel Award, and the National Science Foundation Presidential Young Investigator Award. He is a fellow of the American Academy of Arts and Sciences and held an Arthur F. Thurnau Professorship, the University of Michigan's highest recognition of faculty whose commitment to undergraduate teaching has had a demonstrable impact on the intellectual development and lives of their students.
Photo: *Please provide a photo to be used in our program information. The picture should be high resolution, 300 dpi or more. Please insert the photo here and resize to a height of 2.5 inches, if needed.*	
A/V or Other Needs: *Please list your A/V or classroom needs. Additionally, please specify if your slide presentation includes multimedia such as video clips to ensure audio will be set up for this purpose.*	None

Part 2. *Session Proposal*

Session Title: *Maximum 10 words*	*Managing Stakeholders: Leadership Lessons in Navigating Competing Interests*

Session Description: *Please provide a brief description of the session, maximum 150 words.*	In this session, Fellows will be exposed to a realistic scenario that will require them to consider competing stakeholder interests in making a key decision as leaders of an academic institution. Faced with constraints, risks, and mounting pressure from various stakeholder groups, students will discuss how much weight to give each group's concerns and anticipate possible outcomes, while identifying key elements of effective decision-making.
Learning Objectives: *Objectives should be **SMART**:* **S**pecific, **M**easurable, **A**ppropriate, **R**ealistic, and **T**ime-bound. *Please limit to 3 objectives.*	• Analyze stakeholder interests and identify and evaluate effective strategies for navigating through intense moments of competing stakeholder interests. • Examine the benefits of asking the right questions and having all the necessary information to inform decision-making. • Reflect on personal leadership experiences in higher education.
Key Concepts and Definitions: *Please list up to 3 key concepts that your session will focus on and how you define those concepts.* *Examples of key concepts may include authenticity, integrity, empowerment, creativity, risk taking, results, autonomy/ independence, accuracy, growth, excellence/mastery.*	Balancing stakeholder interests, analyzing risk, effective communication
Reflection Questions: *What questions should our students be asking themselves when the session is over? Please limit to 3 questions.*	• Should you direct the General Counsel of the university to challenge the unionization effort or should you let it go forward? Why? • Is there more you can or should learn to help you make this decision? If so, what information might help you make a better decision? • How much weight do you give to each of your stakeholders (GSRAs, Faculty & Deans, Regents) in making a decision? • To what extent should your own personal

| | feelings toward unionization of GSRAs influence your decision?
● If you were the key decision-maker, what would you do? |

Session Outline or Lesson Plan: *Please provide an outline of how you will use the time to present your material. What types of activities will you utilize, and in what order will you use them? Total programming should not exceed the session duration listed on page 1.*

Time Required (*mins*)	Description
5 minutes	● President Hanlon (PH) will introduce himself and address the continual need for leaders to manage multiple stakeholders. ● PH will describe his personal path through administrative leadership positions in higher education.
15 minutes	● PH will provide Fellows with a handout containing a scenario about multiple stakeholders with competing interests; he will ask them to read it and discuss in groups of three; and he will ask them to answer key questions to clarify the case even more.
20 minutes	● PH will invite groups to share their answers/decisions as part of a broader discussion.
10 minutes	● PH will then introduce a decision, and a consequence of that decision, asking follow-up questions of the group about how they would respond given the new information.

10 minutes	● PH will highlight the importance of understanding stakeholder viewpoints, communication, and anticipating (and planning for) possible outcomes.
	  ● PH will reflect on his own personal experiences with the scenario at hand and how it played out, sharing the important lessons learned.
	  ● PH will invite questions from the group.

Time Required (*mins*)	Description
Required Readings (*optional*): *Please limit required reading to a total of 20 pages.*	None
Additional Resources: *What resources would you recommend on this topic? Please feel free to include books, articles, websites, multimedia, TED Talks, etc.*	None

Leadership Competencies Addressed:

Please indicate which of the following leadership competencies your session focuses on and seeks to develop within students.

Collaboration	*Effective Communication*
● Builds and maintains partnerships based on shared purpose ☑ **Acknowledges and listens to different voices when making decisions and taking action** ● Facilitates collective action toward common goals ● Encourages, supports, and recognizes the contributions of others ● Fosters a welcoming and inclusive environment	● Writes and speaks after reflection ● Clearly articulates ideas in a written and spoken form ● Exhibits effective listening skills ● Influences others through writing, speaking, or artistic expression ☑ **Acknowledges and appropriately communicates in situations with divergent opinions and values**
Effective Reasoning	*Management*
● Employs critical thinking in problem-solving ● Employs creative thinking in problem-solving ● Develops personal reflective practice ● Engages in inquiry, analysis, and follow-through ● Integrates multiple types of information to effectively solve problems or address issues	● Develops and implements a plan for goal attainment ● Develops appropriate strategies for capitalizing on human talent ● Stewards and maximizes all resources ● Manages multiple priorities ● Prepares for leadership transition ● Develops appropriate strategies for effective teamwork ● Evaluates efficacy of current course(s) of action

	Management ● Identifies structure and culture of organization ● Demonstrates effective and appropriate use of technology ● Demonstrates financial, task, and resource-management skills
Self-knowledge ● Continually explores and examines values and views ● Understands social identities of self and others ● Demonstrates realistic understanding of one's abilities ● Seeks opportunities for continued growth ● Takes appropriate action toward potential benefits despite possible failure ● Shows self-respect and respect for others ● Moves beyond self-imposed limitations ● Practices self-compassion, friendliness, ease with self, and vulnerability	**Principled Action** ● Identifies and commits to appropriate ethical framework ● Demonstrates congruence between actions and values ● Demonstrates personal responsibility ● Appropriately challenges the unethical behavior of individuals or groups ☑ **Bases actions on thoughtful consideration of their impact and consequences** ● Seeks appropriate and mutually beneficial solutions when conflict or controversy arises
Intercultural Mindset ● Contextualizes social identities and experiences ● Understands, communicates with, and respectfully interacts with people across identities ● Actively engages in opportunities to expand worldview ● Applies intercultural knowledge and skills in local, national, and/or global contexts	

Thank you!

APPENDIX 7.2   CASE SCENARIO FOR RLF SESSION PROPOSAL FORM – MANAGING STAKEHOLDERS: LEADERSHIP LESSONS IN NAVIGATING COMPETING INTERESTS

Led by Phil Hanlon, President, Dartmouth College
Please organize yourselves into groups of three. You have 15 minutes to read the following scenario and arrive at answers to the questions below.

Scenario

You are the President, Provost, and Executive Vice-President (EVP), respectively, of a well-known state university. Both the EVP and Provost report to the President, who reports to a Board of Regents.

The Regents are elected to their posts in statewide elections. A majority of the Regents are Democrats, having been nominated to stand for election by the Democratic Party. These Regents have a history of being strongly supportive of unions.

The teacher's union is mounting an effort to unionize the Graduate Student Research Assistants (GSRAs) on your campus. The faculty and deans are strongly opposed to unionization of GSRAs.

The State Labor Relations Board blocked an attempt to unionize GSRAs several decades earlier on the grounds that their work is more educational, and thus beneficial to them personally, than it is work that benefits the institution (i.e., they are more students than employees). Because of the prior ruling, you have grounds to challenge the current effort to unionize the GSRAs. However, the Board of Regents passes a motion that forbids the Administration from challenging the current unionization effort with the Labor Relations Board or in court.

A number of deans vow to step down and a number of key faculty vow to seek employment elsewhere, unless you defy the Regents' directive and try to block this unionization effort.

Questions

- Should you direct the General Counsel of the university to challenge the unionization effort or should you let it go forward? Why?
- Is there more you can or should learn to help you make this decision? If so, what information might help you make a better decision?

- How much weight do you give to each of your stakeholders (GSRAs, faculty and deans, Regents) in making a decision?
- To what extent should your own personal feelings toward unionization of GSRAs influence your decision?
- Discussion on implications for leadership.

8. Program assessment and evaluation

Leadership educators should create a robust program assessment and evaluation culture at the launch of a leadership program. Ideally, such a culture promotes an ethos of continuous quality improvement and evidence-based decision-making. The data and information it yields form the basis for understanding the program's achievement of goals and its impact. It helps educators or a planning team to determine how well the content is advancing student learning and how program results satisfy the interests of key stakeholders. An evidence-based plan that measures learning, satisfaction, and program efficiency can play a critical role in promoting the program and providing funding justification to donors. Thus, a well-designed assessment and evaluation system plays a critical role in measuring outcomes for the participant, for the department, and for the institution.

In committing to efforts that continually improve the quality of our programs, educators also develop entrepreneurial attitudes and behaviors that enable them to keep a critical eye on data gathering. If they prioritize data gathering and evidence-based evaluation, educators can flexibly and effectively modify programs. We become fearless in creating nimble and responsive systems to address opportunities or gaps. We also become brave when it is time to discontinue programs that no longer fit our participants' needs and organizational priorities, because our decisions are evidence-based. By embracing a systematic framework that makes the phrase "We always do it this way" obsolete, we become deliberate and reflective in the way we revise our programs to improve outcomes and achieve lasting impact.

Too often, a planned assessment and evaluation is a late addition, implemented when the programs are already well underway. As described in Chapter 6, assessment and evaluation should be built into the program conceptualization and design phase. In that phase, broad, high-level goals are taking shape, and this is the ideal time to begin creating linkages to concrete, granular outcomes, and to identify tools and processes needed to effectively measure the established goals. Ideally, assessment should be considered from the very beginning, but it is never too late to begin the process.

The ability to articulate successes and failures in meeting goals is vital to implementing changes to improve outcomes. This begins with a clear definition of assessment and evaluation terminology, clarity about how each stage in an assessment framework feeds into the next, and an understanding of how the method influences the ability to improve programs and their outcomes.

This chapter will present a systematic assessment framework that thrives on a culture of continuous quality improvement and can be implemented within a single program or across multiple programs. It begins with a brief definition of terms, to ensure a common understanding of how they are used in the context of the framework. Next, an outline of the framework is presented, along with useful tools and processes for its implementation at the participant level, the center level, and the institutional level. The chapter then shares lessons learned from the use of this framework at the Rockefeller Center and ends with reflection questions. Beginners might use the contents of this chapter and the reflection questions to build a strategy from the ground up. Educators charged with developing a leadership program might make the assessment plan more rigorous by adding or revising qualitative and quantitative tools to measure learning, program and system improvements, and outcomes. Educators with established leadership programs might revisit and refine their strategy to determine which tools are relevant and which information is no longer needed on a regular basis. Ultimately, the goal is to create a culture that is responsive to the question "If this is not working as well as it can be, where are the gaps, and how might we change our approach to further improve our programs to meet the needs of our students?"

DEFINITION OF KEY TERMS

We reiterate the importance of creating a culture of continuous quality improvement because, without a "growth mindset," any kind of assessment plan becomes a chore or one more task to accomplish.

For the purpose of this chapter, we will focus on the Rockefeller Center's program assessment and evaluation experience. This approach can be adopted, adapted, or adjusted by any organization and depends on organizational context and available resources. The Rockefeller Center assessment framework operates at three different levels: the participant level, which focuses on capturing student learning, competencies, and satisfaction; the center level, which seeks to measure the efficiency and effectiveness of programs offered through the Rockefeller Center; and the institutional level, which enables the Center to review how well it is addressing the mission and institutional priorities set by the College's senior leadership. The Rockefeller Center assessment framework uses the following terms, definitions for which are provided below: "impact," "assessment," "evaluation," "efficiency," "effectiveness," and "learning outcomes." Multiple definitions exist for the terms listed. Therefore, it is useful to establish a common understanding of how they will be used in the discussion of the Rockefeller Center's particular assessment framework.

Impact

This term encompasses our understanding of what success looks like upon completion of a program, and it is defined as a measurable change (ideally positive) in an outcome of interest. For example, at the participant level, an outcome of interest might be an improvement in the measure of the learner's self-awareness over the course of a program. At the center level, it might be an increase in participants compared to the previous year or an increase in the number of times competencies are reached within each of the seven categories addressed over the course of the program. At the institutional level, it may be measured as a change in the levels of financial support or recognition as a result of the program. While we always work toward positive outcomes, we acknowledge that impact can also capture unintended consequences or negative outcomes.

Assessment

Schuh and Upcraft (2001, p. 17) define assessment as "any effort to gather, analyze, and interpret evidence which describes institutional, departmental, divisional, or agency effectiveness." This definition aligns closely with how assessment is defined in this chapter.

Assessment should be distinguished from research, which is defined as "any effort to gather evidence which guides theory by testing hypotheses" (Upcraft and Schuh, 1996, p. 21).

We define assessment as a systematic process of data collection and analysis that allows us to:

- determine and measure student learning;
- monitor the effectiveness and efficiency of programs;
- articulate the achievement of program outcomes;
- state how programs meet organizational and institutional missions; and
- determine long-term program impact among participants (current students and alumni).

Evaluation

"Assessment" and "evaluation" are often used interchangeably, but, while assessment involves the effort to gather, analyze, and interpret evidence, evaluation is the effort to use this assessment evidence to improve the effectiveness of programs. This definition is consistent with the work of other researchers who have explored this topic (Komives et al., 2011). In the context of the framework presented, evaluation is an annual decision-making process derived from qualitative and quantitative assessment that promotes program improvement, inclusion, and modification.

Efficiency and Effectiveness

Efficiency and effectiveness are equally important when assessing and evaluating programs (Chavan, 2009). Efficiency measures how well a program uses its human, material, and financial resources, while effectiveness refers to how well the organization and its programs align to meet the organizational mission along with program goals and learning outcomes (Komives et al., 2011). By ensuring that programs are both efficient and effective, we can help to maximize their impact on our learners.

Learning Outcomes

According to a framework established by the National Institute for Learning Outcomes Assessment (2016), student learning-outcomes statements

> clearly state the expected knowledge, skills, attitudes, competencies, and habits of mind that students are expected to acquire at an institution of higher education. Transparent student-learning-outcomes statements are:
>
> - Specific to institutional level and/or program level;
> - Clearly expressed and understandable by multiple audiences;
> - Prominently posted at or linked to multiple places across the website;
> - Updated regularly to reflect current outcomes; and
> - Receptive to feedback or comments on the quality and utility of the information provided.

Additionally, as described in Chapter 6, SMART learning outcomes are defined as specific, measurable, appropriate, realistic, and time-bound.

CASE STUDY: THE ROCKEFELLER CENTER ASSESSMENT FRAMEWORK

The Rockefeller Center has developed a culture of evidence-based assessment by requiring that all decision-making be grounded in a systematic use of qualitative and quantitative data collected in its leadership programs. An important factor in creating that culture was an acknowledgment that data should only be collected when it is needed, and only when a measurement is designed to inform decisions (Twersky et al., 2010). Added to valuing educators' time (because it takes some time to collect data), we also involve educators to take ownership of the assessment of programs to which they are assigned. This practical approach allows educators to stay focused on relevant program measures and analyze data efficiently so that new knowledge can be quickly incorporated.

In the assessment framework used for co-curricular leadership programs at the Rockefeller Center, key questions are developed for each of the relevant levels (participant, center, institution) to assess student learning, impact, efficiency, and effectiveness. This is in line with Anderson and Krathwohl's revised Bloom's taxonomy, which incorporates both the kind of knowledge to be learned (knowledge dimension) and the process used to learn (cognitive process). It allows the educator to efficiently align objectives to assessment techniques (Cruz, 2003). With the questions established, quantitative tools, qualitative tools, and methods are then identified to capture the information required. Figure 8.1 illustrates the Rockefeller Center's assessment framework.

The Center's Dartmouth Leadership Attitudes and Behaviors (D-LAB) Program is used as an example to demonstrate how each stage can be developed and implemented.[1] Offered to first-year students with small group facilitation by upperclass students, the D-LAB Program encourages participants to explore their individual beliefs, values, and identities through discussion and interactive exercises, and examine how to act in line with these ideals within the greater community. Six sessions cover the content.

Stage One: Determine Assessment Questions

The assessment framework begins with understanding what questions need to be asked at the participant, center, and institution levels. For example, at the participant level, we are interested in understanding what students are learning and what competencies are being gained by the students.

As described in Chapter 7, the Rockefeller Center programs use 43 competencies, which are organized into seven categories. The D-LAB Program addresses 18 of the 43 competencies within broad categories of collaboration, effective communication, effective reasoning, management, self-knowledge, principled action, and intercultural mindset. These are illustrated in Table 8.1.

Expectations for achieving competency in these areas are established by the educators, who identify and develop SMART learning outcomes. For example, the first session, "Leadership from within," focuses on the following SMART learning outcomes:

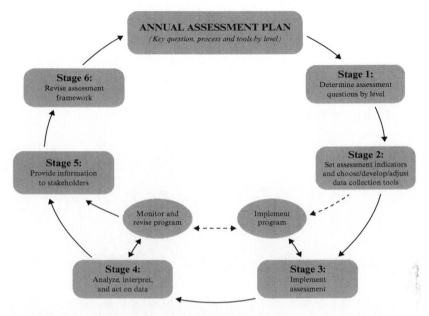

Figure 8.1   Rockefeller Center assessment framework

By the end of this session, participants will:

1. Identify three or more factors that influence their values and personality (consider experiences, identities, character traits, context, etc.).
2. Identify at least three attributes of their core identity and three attributes of their social identity.
3. Discuss and identify and rank at least ten important personal values.

The Rockefeller Center's co-curricular team analyzes competencies within each program annually, and across programs periodically, to answer this question: Is the Center providing the opportunity for its students to develop a defined set of competencies? It is not the intent of every program to cover all of our identified leadership competencies. Tracking them, however, helps us to get an overview of how the competencies are being covered across the continuum of programs being offered. The team maps competencies across sessions within a program to get an understanding of which are emphasized, which are under-represented, and where there are future programming opportunities. Figure 8.2 illustrates the mapping of competencies across programs.

To measure efficiency, we are concerned with answering questions related to the adequacy of staffing, material, and financial resources dedicated to achieving learning outcomes for a program or for co-curricular programs in general. We also want to measure program coverage, the cost of the program, and participant satisfaction with the programs offered by the Center. This information is very helpful for discussions with other colleagues from the College, and also with colleagues

Table 8.1 D-LAB competencies

Dartmouth Leadership Attitudes and Behaviors	Session 1	Session 2	Session 3	Session 4	Session 5	Session 6
Competency	Leadership from within Part I	Leadership from within Part II	Leadership with others	Leadership for others Part I	Leadership for others Part II	Leadership in practice
Collaboration						
Builds and maintains partnerships based on shared purpose						1
Acknowledges and listens to different voices when making decisions and taking action					1	
Encourages, supports, and recognizes the contributions of others	1					
Effective communication						
Exhibits effective listening skills	1	1				
Influences others through writing, speaking, or artistic expression						
Acknowledges and appropriately communicates in situations with divergent opinions and values			1		1	
Effective reasoning						
Develops personal reflective practice	1	1	1			

	1	2	3	4	5	6
Engages in inquiry, analysis, and follow-through	1					
Integrates multiple types of information to effectively solve problems or address issues		1				
Management						
Develops and implements a plan for goal attainment	1					
Self-knowledge						
Continually explores and examines values and views				1	1	
Seeks opportunities for continued growth	1					
Principled action						
Identifies and commits to appropriate ethical framework			1			
Demonstrates congruence between actions and values				1	1	
Demonstrates personal responsibility	1		1		1	
Appropriately challenges the unethical behavior of individuals or groups			1			
Bases actions on thoughtful consideration of their impact and consequences		1		1		
Intercultural mindset						
Understands, communicates with, and respectfully interacts with people across cultures		1				1

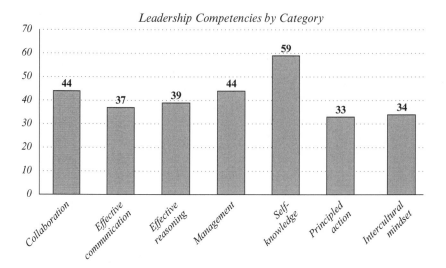

Leadership Competencies by Category

Note: The Rockefeller Center staff conduct an annual assessment of how often a leadership competency within seven broad categories is touched upon during programming. A count is taken of each time a program session or event provides an opportunity for students to practice a specific leadership competency in each category. Figure 8.2 depicts the 2016 annual assessment, which included 61 sessions across the leadership programs offered by the Center. The category "self-knowledge" had the highest representation, which reflects the Center's opinion that leadership development begins with self-knowledge and awareness.

Figure 8.2   Leadership competencies by category reflected across co-curricular leadership programs 2016

from other institutions, potential donors, and parents of prospective students. It also helps us decide which program strategies are cost-effective and replicable. As a result, we can drop those which are not cost-effective. At this stage, we acknowledge that all programs are built to address specific student learning outcomes, and we caution educators not to measure the effectiveness of one program against another based only on cost considerations. Put simply, one program can cost more than another but be very effective in meeting stated student learning outcomes because of the strategies used to achieve them. For example, the Rockefeller Center offers leadership programs that are taught over a term and over a year. Learning activities within programs include retreats, immersion, and site visits, and costs for such activities vary. Each program offered has been found to be very useful in meeting desired outcomes.

Cost-effectiveness should be considered in different ways, and educators should consider the trade-offs when they measure the cost-effectiveness of activities between programs. For example, the Management and Leadership Development Program is offered on campus and costs less compared to the Rockefeller Global Leadership Program, which includes an international immersion. The on-campus offering meets the program goal of creating an understanding about management and leadership effectively. On the other hand, the Global Leadership Program meets its goals effectively by tying classroom discussions with an international immersion component that serves to crystallize the importance of understanding intercultural differences and how to operate in a culture that is different from one's own.

To ensure effective promotion and support, organizations offering leadership programs should periodically assess the alignment of the program with the mission of the institution. This can be done simply through a review of mission statements or through a meeting with senior administrators. The Rockefeller Center asks this question periodically: Is the mission of the Center aligned to the mission of Dartmouth College? For example, D-LAB's goal is to create self-awareness in first-year students about their values and leadership potential at the individual, team, and community levels, and to develop participants into mature, responsible, and authentic leaders. This aligns with the Rockefeller Center's mission to "educate, train, and inspire the next generation of public policy leaders." This mission also connects well to the overall mission of Dartmouth College, as it prepares students for a "lifetime of learning and of responsible leadership." The ability to highlight such an alignment is particularly helpful for fundraising efforts and for expanding or offering programs across an institution.

Another question that we ask ourselves is related to the long-term impact that participants report at two-year, five-year, and ten-year increments. To determine long-lasting impact, the Center conducts, in collaboration with Dartmouth's Office of Institutional Research, a baseline survey every five years to stay engaged with alumni and measure the influence of programs over time. Such information can also be collected through means such as focus groups or one-on-one meetings, and it enables the Center to think about immediate versus long-term (cumulative) program impacts on our alumni. Survey responses from alumni who are five years out indicate good recall of the individual leadership programs they have participated in. After that time period, however, they more generally recall the impact of the institution on their personal or professional growth as leaders rather than specific programs. We have also learned that, often, a personal relationship with an educator is one of the driving forces for alumni recollection of the program.

Surveys of alumni groups can also be done in collaboration with other departments, either within the institution or with an aligned program in another institution. Recently, the Rockefeller Center partnered with the McDonough Center on a joint survey of program alumni. The survey was administered by Dartmouth's Office of Institutional Research, which also assisted in the analysis of the data collected. There are many benefits to a collaborative project of this nature. It promotes shared learning between institutions with different experiences, contexts, cultures, structures, and programming styles. It also allows for a larger pool of insights that highlight what alumni consider to be the important outcomes and results of participating in a particular program. Finally, by reviewing each other's data, both the Rockefeller Center and the McDonough Center have deepened their understanding of how to improve their own programs.

The Rockefeller Center will be using this joint survey as a baseline for a follow-up survey in approximately five years. While it is important to be sensitive to the risk of "response fatigue" from the overuse of survey tools, the usefulness of this kind of data cannot be emphasized enough (Egleston et al., 2011). We have already begun to receive data in the form of responses from alumni, who speak about the impact programs have had on key competencies that have enabled them to excel in their careers. Below is an account from a 2010 Dartmouth graduate:

> In the Rockefeller Leadership [Fellows] Program, I was encouraged to have my own opinion challenged by others and through that experience with leaders from all parts of campus, I began to understand my leadership style and what that potentially means for how I develop communities and future organizations. I was pushed to think about managing a team, having difficult conversations, and inspiring others to work and follow a mission, and those practices prepared me for the rigors of working in the education sector in a low-performing, high-need school.

This type of feedback helps educators gauge the longer-term impact of programs for continuous improvement.

Stage Two: Set Assessment Indicators and Choose/Develop/Adjust Data Collection Tools and Processes

At this stage, the aim is to set indicators for the questions determined earlier and develop tools and processes for collecting data at the participant, department, and institutional levels. At the participant level, the Rockefeller Center measures knowledge, satisfaction, and competency in leadership. Information related to the three indicators is collected through the administration of surveys, focus groups, and group-reflection exercises through several tools and processes.

These are typically conducted immediately following a session; however, it is possible to get richer and more frequent participant-level data through the use of digital technology. We have noted the strengths and weaknesses of all these tools below and have found that relying on a set of tools at the participant, center, and institutional level gave us a broader and more nuanced understanding of how the programs were working. No single measurement provides the answers we seek, and each tool has advantages and disadvantages.

Data collection tools at the participant level

Mapping competencies All of the co-curricular programs at the Rockefeller Center use mapping tools to assess competencies. As described earlier, one tracking tool in use for this purpose is the simple spreadsheet illustrated in Table 8.1, which demonstrates the emphasis the Center places on selected competencies in the D-LAB Program. For each session, the presenter assesses the content to select appropriate competencies. These competencies first are selected by the speaker or educator leading the session and then are reviewed for consistency by a team of eight members at the Center. In addition to looking at competencies emphasized within a specific program, the Center measures the extent to which they are emphasized over multiple programs across the Center.

Competencies are first mapped by the program and then combined into one chart so program team members can assess how often we touch upon them during the continuum of programs we offer as well as gaps we need to address. As described earlier, Figure 8.2 illustrates the categories as well as the frequency with which competencies are addressed across the co-curricular program sessions offered by the Center.

The self-knowledge bar is higher compared to the other categories because of the Center's commitment to making learners self-aware as the first step which is vital to effective leadership. The chart reveals a lower emphasis on the principled action and intercultural mindset categories, which indicates a need to revisit programs to see whether there is indeed a gap or whether a previously recognized gap is being addressed. The co-curricular team took these two observations and examined to what extent programs were addressing principled action and intercultural mindset in session proposal forms developed for their respective program areas. They concluded that activities and the resulting reflections of students addressed principled action.

Further, they decided that each speaker should include a discussion on how development of an intercultural mindset should be incorporated across sessions within programs. The learning from this exercise is that, after review, the underlying data must be updated to ensure that they are reflected accurately in the reports and charts generated. Additionally, changes must be made in session design to address an identified gap. In either case, a review of this nature provides an opportunity to revisit programs and study their competency categories with a sharper focus.

As with any data collection method, there are limitations. To assure consistency in the way the competencies are interpreted, the competencies are first selected by the educator delivering the content. In addition, the Rockefeller Center staff review competencies selected for each session, which further adds consistency to the approach by which they are selected and interpreted across programs. The Rockefeller Center finds these measures to be valid on their face. There are additional validation measures that could be used to establish the distinctiveness of each of the categories as well as the internal validity of the competencies. Validity and reliability of such measures are important. Depending on availability of time and resources, these measures can be addressed even more systematically.

Pre- and post-test surveys   One survey used by the Center is the College Pulse, a student-centered mobile platform in which students engage in "Pulse Points" surveys in exchange for an incentive of their choice. The D-LAB Program used this tool[2] to conduct a pre-test (first session), post-test (last session), and final test (three months after the program) for 12 leadership questions. In the first session of D-LAB, a baseline measure for learners' attitudes and behaviors is established. In the last session, the 12 questions are administered again to see whether there are any observable changes. Three months after the program, the same questions are asked to determine if there are any further changes. The survey asks students to rate themselves on a scale of 1–4, ranging across seldom, sometimes, often, and almost always, on the following attitudes and behaviors:

1. I continually explore my values and views.
2. Other people understand how my values affect my position on important issues.
3. I aim to demonstrate congruence between my values and actions.
4. I am genuinely interested in hearing the ideas of those who disagree with my views.
5. I use effective listening skills.

6. I value the social identities of others.
7. I go out of my way to publicly recognize the contributions of others in our community.
8. I speak with conviction about the purpose or impact of important work in which I am engaged.
9. I encourage collaboration between those with different views when making decisions or solving problems.
10. I actively engage in opportunities to expand my worldview.
11. I listen to different voices when making decisions or taking action.
12. I prefer my "tried and true" ways when approaching new situations.

We will be reviewing the data collected and the usefulness of this tool. While we have provided College Pulse as an example, educators can use several survey formats. Regardless of which tool is used, it is in the educator's interest to collect baseline and follow-up data. Further, the format should be consistent and easy for participants to use. Finally, survey tools that assess student learning can help them to reflect on their growth and how a particular experience has helped them to do this. For examples, several programs at the Rockefeller Center ask students what they learned about a particular topic and how they will apply the learning to themselves or to the organizations they lead or participate in. This information can be gathered using a survey, or the educator can stop the session or class any time to process and reflect on an incident that has occurred. This enables the educator to reshape the activity or get the learners to internalize their observations.

Finally, while we acknowledge that the process of analyzing contrasts between genders, race, and ethnicity can be time-consuming, we encourage this wherever possible. By doing this, we can identify key impacts or needs which may not be evident from aggregated data.

Weekly online participant survey   This survey is administered immediately after each weekly session. It asks students a few reflective questions to provide a quick glimpse of student satisfaction with activities and discussions, the facilitator, and content, using a Likert scale of 1–5. The benefit of this tool is that it is easily recordable and effective for getting an initial, spontaneous reaction immediately after the session. The drawback, as with all survey instruments administered at the end of a session, is that the learners are rushed and do the bare minimum before moving on to their next scheduled activity. Another concern is that students have not had time to digest information or apply the skills learned and are therefore recording an immediate reaction to the session.

Facilitator weekly feedback meetings   Through weekly meetings before each session, educators have collaborative conversations with the D-LAB facilitators (upper-class peers of the participants) about how the students are receiving the content and how to tie the conversations together. The advantage of this tool is that it collects timely, detailed information from student facilitators, who work most closely with the participants. These meetings also create space for peer-to-peer learning. A potential drawback is that first-year participants may still be on their best behavior around the facilitators, especially if they plan to apply for the First-Year Fellowship, and student facilitators may feel that they are sharing confidential information about their group members by offering negative comments about them.

Also, data collected by this method can be spotty because class schedules or other commitments often prevent student facilitators from attending each meeting.

Data collection tools at the center level

Assessment indicators include student participation in the Rockefeller Center's programs by class year and give us the opportunity to see the breadth and the depth of the Center's program coverage. The Center also tracks participant enrollment, attrition, and completion in the program.

Tools include participation tracking, debriefs and analysis, session proposal forms, and partners' feedback.

1. Participation tracking Information regarding program participation is extracted annually from a simple database in which student participation is recorded by program and class year. For example, an estimated 30 percent of Dartmouth undergraduate students participated in programs offered by the Center in the last year, according to our internal data collection system using Batchbook. At each program level, target participation numbers are identified based on the quality of the student experience, the learning we want to create, the available budget, the reputation each program has developed over time, and the outreach strategy. For example, we have determined that the Rockefeller Leadership Fellows Program, which spans a year, needs to be capped at 25–26 students to ensure the quality of conversations, community learning, and personal in-depth reflection. In contrast, D-LAB has the capacity to engage 200 students in six sessions over a term.

The Rockefeller Center shares information on program participation in its annual report, and at the beginning of each budget cycle members of the senior management team review program efficiency and effectiveness based on available evidence. Then the team decides to begin, continue, expand, or discontinue programs. For example, before we began programming extensively on leadership, the Center had five discussion groups led by student leaders. As new programs with more clearly defined learning outcomes were added, attendance in the student discussion groups waned as interest and participation in the new programs grew. Continuing the student discussion groups with low attendance was no longer cost-effective and led to the discontinuation of three of these groups. Similarly, each one of the programs offered by the Center has added or discontinued sessions based on a review of efficiency and effectiveness.

2. Debriefs and analysis Every program at the Rockefeller Center conducts debriefs and a strengths, weaknesses, opportunities, challenges (SWOC) analysis. These tools serve to capture information immediately after a program. Changes that can be implemented in the following cycle are put into place within a fiscal year, or they are implemented during the following fiscal year's programming cycle. For example, at the end of a program, educators in D-LAB conduct a debrief session with small group facilitators. This debrief takes place only after they have reviewed participant and facilitator feedback. They provide their own observations and do a SWOC analysis. Sessions of this nature need to be well organized to accurately conceptualize and implement changes for the next iteration of the program.

3. Session proposal forms Assessment is also incorporated in the program design phase with session proposal forms. Using these forms as a guide, educators create learning outcomes in cooperation with a speaker for each session and choose three to five leadership competencies that will be addressed during that session. At the end of each session within a program, the educator responsible for the program verifies whether the learning objectives were satisfied or need to be adjusted. Any further adjustments that need to be made for a particular session that will be offered again are discussed with the speaker concerned. This process works well because all staff give speakers timely feedback and work together to ensure that student learning outcomes fit in with the Rockefeller Center's overall assessment framework and program planning. The constraint, as mentioned in Chapter 7, is that, owing to workload and stylistic differences, educators are not always consistent in updating changes to the session proposal forms. The Center is considering a peer review process that might spark fresh insights when peers work on this task together. This process might include pairing educators and getting them to informally assess all session proposal forms in their respective program areas.

4. Partners' feedback If leadership programs are implemented in partnership with other organizations on campus, it is important to get feedback from these partners in a timely manner. For example, the sixth session of D-LAB is designed to expose learners to other resources (academic advising, international experiences, or outdoor programming, etc.) that might match their personal interests on campus. Partners from various parts of campus give their time to be present at the session to discuss other opportunities on campus students can take advantage of. At the end of the program, these partners receive a survey, and a face-to-face debrief is organized to discuss the entire program and the results from the survey. This approach is helpful because it generates many ideas from experienced educators as they honestly express their opinions about the strengths and weaknesses of the sixth session.

The Rockefeller Center uses a database called Batchbook that allows it to create records on each student participating in the programs offered. The information generated through this database gives the Center a picture of who and how many students participated in the program during a given academic year through its curricular and co-curricular offerings.

Stage Three: Implement Assessment

With the key questions, tools, and processes in place at all levels, it is now time to put the tools in place to gather data while the program is being implemented. We recommend developing a systematic timeline first and then experiment with the best way to use these tools at the participant, center, and institutional level. For example, online participant surveys should be short and administered immediately at the end of a program's session for a high response rate. They may not yield deep reflection about lessons learned as a result of participating in the program, but short surveys might give insight into participant satisfaction for the particular session being evaluated. Use of multiple tools is advantageous, and comparing results from all the tools and processes in place has helped us identify strengths and areas that need improvement in our programs. We encourage educators to monitor programs to ensure repeated successful implementation. Note that assessment, program implementation, and monitoring inform each other as shown in Figure 8.1.

Stage Four: Analyze Data

The next step is to analyze data and organize the information to share with stakeholders. This step occurs when educators have opportunities to review the data and identify what went well and what needs to be improved. Several of the programs offered by the Center have changed significantly over time based on participant, educator, and speaker feedback. For example, based on participant feedback, the Global Leadership Program now offers a weekend learning immersion which deepens students' knowledge of working in cultures different from their own.

After analyzing the data, reports are produced for specific stakeholder needs and requests. This stage requires developing systems that provide information in a systematic manner. Interpreting data should be simple and accessible to educators to enable them to make program decisions. Working with peers allows educators to discover other perspectives on successes and challenges they are facing. It also helps to develop a support system and a culture of continuous quality improvement.

Lastly, this stage provides an opportunity to conduct conditional analysis to examine possible contrasts between different subgroups, such as men and women, diverse racial groups, etc. This kind of analysis can reveal disparities in impact between groups, which may not be immediately obvious through an analysis that only considers aggregate data.

Stage Five: Provide Information to Stakeholders

Stakeholders in a program typically consist of participants, the educators developing and managing the program, the directors, the partners, the board (if relevant), donors, prospects, and senior leadership of the institution. Information to all these stakeholders can be provided in person, on the website, in an annual report, or through other means. Here again, it is important not to flood the stakeholders with vast amounts of information. Educators designing an assessment plan should also find the best way to reach their stakeholders. This could include face-to-face meetings, phone conversations, written or digital communication, or formal and informal presentations. For example, relevant information about D-LAB is available in the Center's annual report. It also appears on the website for student, alumni, and community access. In another example, sharing of information about the Rockefeller Center's D-LAB Program with the Dean of the College has led to its expansion to the entire College through a new residential student housing system for which she is responsible.[3]

Strong information sharing enables senior leadership to articulate the institution's mission and objectives in a manner that is understandable for stakeholders. Data incorporated into stories often are the best way to illustrate a particular point. For example, Dartmouth College presidents have used the Center's Rockefeller Leadership Fellows Program and the Policy Research Shop as examples to illustrate the institution's commitment to leadership in their meetings with alumni and external stakeholders to build the College's reputation.

Stage Six: Revise Assessment Framework

Data gathering and analysis are vital for program revision and for improving the assessment plan itself. Program revisions are necessary and should be anticipated in the assessment framework. Unfortunately, they are often not effected in a timely manner. Once educators collect and analyze data to make recommendations for improvements, they should build in time to make program revisions to ensure that improvements occur in time to impact student learners. Depending on the complexity of the recommendations, educators could make changes either immediately or during the next academic cycle. For example, D-LAB expanded its sessions from an initial offering of three sessions to six sessions. Based on participant feedback, educators implemented the recommendation to expand the program to six sessions the following year to allow time for more in-depth discussion. In another example, the Rockefeller Global Leadership Program incorporated a journaling activity into the program as soon as it was recommended. By contrast, repeated recommendations about including an overnight trip for students to engage in deeper learning about cross-cultural communication and about one another were captured and could only be implemented the following year as a result of planning, scheduling, and budget considerations.

In addition to programmatic review, the assessment framework, and in particular the tools employed within it, should be assessed periodically. Sometimes, the questions we ask in the initial stage may not be the right questions. Tools we are using may not yield the information we seek to measure program effectiveness. Or some aspect of the program might be modified, leading to a change in the assessment framework. For example, the Rockefeller Center added new components to its assessment framework for D-LAB as a result of the program's expansion through the institution's newly established residential house system: an institutional-level pre- and post-survey through College Pulse was added; questions we would ask of participants at the end of each session were revised because we felt that the new set of questions would provide targeted information about student learning; and facilitation training for facilitators was revised based on participant feedback.

The revised assessment plan for 2016–2017 included the administration of an institutional level pre-program and post-program survey to participants. Previously, the Rockefeller Center administered a weekly five-point Likert scale, a survey focused on learning outcomes for participants. The Center then changed this process and began to allow participants to rate their student facilitators, and for student facilitators to register their satisfaction with the level of preparation and training they received for the program. During the winter term, the Center also asked facilitators to complete surveys each week to evaluate content, process, group cohesion, and the quality of discussion within their groups. Table 8.2 summarizes the Rockefeller Center's assessment framework and provides the reader with possible tools that can be used to make desired changes within a program.

Lastly, the director of the department should put into place a system for receiving feedback. One effective approach in this endeavor is to conduct a 360 review, in which the director receives feedback from multiple colleagues collaborating at all levels of the organization. Such a review, however, implies the existence of trust and open communication within an organization.

Table 8.2   *Summary of Rockefeller Center's assessment framework*

Stakeholders	Assessment tools	Tools used by	Type of measurement	When
Participants of leadership programs	Surveys; reflection papers; SWOC; one-to-one interviews; videos and PowerPoints developed by participant.	Team member responsible for leadership program and student program assistants.	Learning outcomes; satisfaction; attendance; retention.	During every session within a program, or after a program.
Donors	All information gathered at different levels of the program.	Center Director and staff communicating with donors and responsible for stewardship.	Effectiveness; efficiency; capacity; satisfaction; mission alignment to Center's mission.	As needed.
Alumni	Survey; focus groups; one-to-one meetings.	Educators collecting information.	Impact of programs.	Baseline and every five years.
Senior leadership at Dartmouth	Discussions with senior administration.	Department/ Center head and senior administration.	Alignment to mission.	As appropriate and as deemed necessary.
Rockefeller Center Director	Meetings and strategic planning sessions; senior management meeting.	Center head with curricular and co-curricular faculty and staff.	Departmental mission and alignment to institution's mission.	As appropriate and as deemed necessary; weekly.
Director and senior management	Meeting.	Manager/team member; senior management.	Effectiveness and efficiency monitoring.	Three times a year.
Educator	SWOC; one-to-one meeting; annual planning meeting; "Thinking Day"; performance appraisal form.	Manager/ team member responsible for the leadership program. This includes program and finance meetings.	Effectiveness; efficiency; capacity; satisfaction; mission alignment to Center's mission.	End of year, bi-weekly, and when issues arise; at the end of the academic year, before formal performance appraisal.

LESSONS LEARNED

1. *Develop a culture of assessment and continuous quality improvement*: Create an assessment framework, which involves educators in all stages. Assessment should not create a sense of resentment or fear. It should help educators and learners alike to celebrate successes and address areas for improvement. All the information points discussed in this chapter are things educators need to keep in mind when assessing a program: the levels, data, collection tools, analysis, communicating findings, and revising. Further, assessment and evaluation need to be timely and ongoing, and data collected should be easy to interpret and use in practice.

2. *Build in assessment early, and keep it simple*: Assessment should be considered during the program conceptualization and design phase. It is best to begin with simple measures. They can grow more complicated and robust over time as educators gain experience in assessing leadership programs. It is also important to select a limited number of measures for short-term outcomes and long-term impact and to set up efficient, effective systems for tracking and reporting on them accurately.

3. *Balance measures of satisfaction with measures of learning*: We caution educators not to focus only on measuring student satisfaction with the program or programs. Learners indicating satisfaction could mean they like the educator or the teaching methodology, but it doesn't necessarily mean they have learned anything from the session or achieved the desired proficiency level. For example, when 80 percent of the participants rate speaker X highly on his session on integrity and leadership, they could be saying they like the speaker's style or method, or they could be saying that they personally like the speaker. However, information about how participants define integrity and what it means to them must be captured in a way that demonstrates their learning about this topic.

4. *Promote ownership and accountability*: Educators in the co-curricular programs of the Rockefeller Center participated in developing the assessment and evaluation methods for assigned programs, which led to the overall development of the assessment and evaluation framework described in this chapter. The Center continues to refine this framework to meet its needs. Team members who have been fully involved in the process of program planning and implementation feel ownership and accountability for the quality of information being provided. We also recommend establishing peer reviews within an organization to build teamwork and a community of learning, and to look at successes and challenges through various lenses.

5. *Focus on mission alignment*: At the institutional level, educators and senior administrators from the departments and centers should be aware of how the institution presents leadership in its mission statement. If the statement clearly addresses leadership education, development, and training, then there are obvious opportunities to tie leadership programming to the specific organizational mission. If there is no mention of leadership in the mission statement of the institution, there is an opportunity to advocate for its incorporation, and to help with developing a collective vision for how leadership education can be offered. Additionally, it is always useful to make a connection to the mission of an institution to show the relevancy of the program to the broader goal of educating students. We strongly believe that institutional will and commitment are needed to create a culture that believes in leadership programming and its positive effects on students, the campus, and society at large.

6. *Invest in professional development*: While we measure learning outcomes for our students, we should also be investing in our educators. They carry a responsibility for ensuring they are developing future leaders, but also for developing their own personal and organizational skills to further improve the programs they have designed. At the Rockefeller Center, we create space and time for educators to reflect on how they will improve their own personal skills and abilities, as well as improve the programs for which they are responsible. For example, educators in the co-curricular programs are given a "Thinking Day." They take a full day to reflect on how they can improve aspects of programs they are responsible for (content, administration, management, and finance) and how they can improve their professional and leadership skills. At the end of this individual reflection, the supervisor receives a summary of their thoughts and arranges to discuss these reflections within a few weeks. The deep reflection done during "Thinking Day" also enables educators to report on achievements, crystallize program objectives for the coming year, and suggest professional development goals in the formal staff performance appraisal system of the institution. As a co-curricular team at the Center, we find this tool immensely useful for continuous quality improvement of programs and for personal and professional growth. Educators responsible for various programs feed information from this reflection tool into their formal performance appraisal form which is completed with their supervisor. The supervisor's performance, in turn, is conducted by the Director of the Center. Table 8.3 provides current sample questions for "Thinking Day."

7. *Internal versus external evaluation*: So far, we have discussed how we assess programs at the participant, center, and institutional levels.

Table 8.3   Sample "Thinking Day" questions

Performance evaluation goals/objectives questions
1. What professional goals or objectives did you have for the past year and what progress did you make in achieving them?
2. What accomplishment(s) are you most proud of?
3. Were there any work-related circumstance(s) or changed operational priorities that affected your ability to meet goals or objectives?
4. What would you like to accomplish in the year ahead?
5. What is your vision for success in your work and leadership?

Job satisfaction/role alignment
1. Which responsibilities/tasks do you enjoy most? Which do you least enjoy?
2. What motivates you to get your job done? What brings meaning to your work?
3. Are there areas in which you believe you could excel or contribute to your position, to the department, or to Dartmouth in a different way?
4. What do you appreciate most about our workplace? What could be better?
5. Which types of recognition are most meaningful to you? Which types are least meaningful?

Performance evaluation self-evaluation questions
1. What do you view as your strengths?
2. What areas do you want to develop? In which area(s) would you like to improve?
3. How do you work best?
4. What are your biggest obstacles to getting your work done (conflicting priorities, environment, communication, time management, etc.)?
5. Do you have the resources and tools you need to perform your job?
6. How do you like to receive feedback on your work?

Performance evaluation training and development
1. What are some resources (books, conferences, etc.) that you found useful during this past year?
2. What are one or two professional development goals you have and how do you plan to achieve them?
3. What type of career growth is most important to you (additional responsibility, leading a team/project, salary increase, promotion, etc.)?

Performance evaluation supervisory responsibilities
1. Describe any challenges and successes you have had in providing leadership, guidance, and support for your (students) staff.

This assessment framework is an example of an internal evaluation of programs which is done by educators to show results, improve programs, and share information with stakeholders. In contrast, grant-funded programs are externally funded and likely require evaluations by a third-party external evaluation. For instance, the Policy Research Shop, originally funded by a grant through the Fund for the Improvement of Postsecondary Education (FIPSE), required a third-party evaluation. The lessons about incorporating assessment and evaluation processes at the program start-up phase apply here as well, and we encourage educators to build these processes in when their grant-funded projects begin.

8. *Institutions as learning organizations*: Almost everything we have written so far is focused on the student learning outcome and the systems that support it. Peter Senge in his book *The Fifth Discipline* believes that "vision, purpose, reflectiveness, and systems thinking are essential if organizations are to realize their potential" (2006, p. 570). We have provided an opportunity to study how the Rockefeller Center is influenced by an iterative process and how embracing this approach has positively impacted not only educators but the Center in becoming a learning organization. Such a process can be frustrating at times but ultimately builds a sense of community tied together with addressing a common vision. We invite organizations to assess themselves and make changes where necessary to realize their potential as described by Senge.

REFLECTION QUESTIONS

1. In what ways have you framed a competency map that aligns with measurable learning outcomes?
2. What approaches might you take in your program to measure short-term and long-term impact?
3. At what levels (program, department, institution) have you implemented an assessment and evaluation process? What are the pros and cons of the processes at each level?
4. How have you put together information to share the results of your programs with your stakeholders? What impact has such information sharing had on your stakeholders? Which formats and methods (stories, graphs, charts, etc.) have been most effective and why?
5. Do you create space for "deep thinking" about the crucial aspects of your leadership program, including the program itself, and its administrative, management, and financial dimensions? How do you determine when to keep and when to let go of a program?

NOTES

1. D-LAB prepares first-year students to make thoughtful decisions about how they spend their time at Dartmouth. In small groups led by upper-class facilitators, participants explore their individual beliefs, values, and identity through discussions and interactive activities. Over the course of six weekly sessions, they examine how to act in line with their values and learn how to navigate these ideals within the greater community. D-LAB is co-sponsored by Dartmouth's Rockefeller Center and the Collis Center for Student Involvement. Since D-LAB is only in its fourth year of operation, the true level of its impact is yet to be determined. We need to wait until the next cycle (five years out) to get a more accurate picture of how alumni view this program's contribution to their personal and professional growth. We selected this program because it includes new features such as a pre- and a post-test, as well as a three-month recall.
2. The College Pulse is a student-centered mobile platform conceptualized by Terren Klein. It not only is statistically accurate but also puts the data right in the pockets of the students. Students are incentivized to take surveys through Pulse by "Pulse Points," which they can exchange for an incentive of their choice. This reliable outlet allows students to have their voices heard and quantified, leading to greater civic engagement on campus and a strong bridge of communication between the student body and the administration. Finally, because the Pulse team arranges for the incentives, the cost of running a survey is dramatically reduced for the administrators.
3. The College has designated the six new house communities that will provide permanent home bases for all Dartmouth undergraduates beginning in the fall of 2016. Website (https://news.dartmouth.edu/news/2015/11/college-unveils-six-house-communities-open-next-fall). Accessed May 20, 2017.

REFERENCES

Chavan, M. (2009). The Balanced Scorecard: A New Challenge. *Journal of Management Development*, 28 (5), 393–406.

Cruz, E. (2003). Bloom's Revised Taxonomy. In B. Hoffman (Ed.), *Encyclopedia of Educational Technology*. Website (http://coe.sdsu.edu/eet/Articles/bloomrev/start.htm). Accessed July 23, 2009.

Egleston, B.L., Miller, S.M., and Meropol, N.J. (2011). The Impact of Misclassification Due to Survey Response Fatigue on Estimation and Identifiability of Treatment Effects. *Statistics in Medicine*, 30 (30), 3560–72.

Komives, S.R., Dugan, J.P., Owen, J.E., Slack, C., and Wagner, W. (2011). *The Handbook for Student Leadership Development*. San Francisco, CA: Jossey-Bass.

National Institute for Learning Outcomes Assessment. (2016). *Transparency Framework: Student Learning Outcomes Statements*. Champaign, IL: National Institute for Learning Outcomes Assessment. Website (http://www.learningoutcomesassessment.org). Accessed March 21, 2017.

Schuh, J. and Upcraft, M. (2001). *Assessment Practice in Student Affairs: An Applications Manual*. San Francisco, CA: Jossey-Bass.

Senge, P.M. (2006). *The Fifth Discipline: The Art and Practice of the Learning Organization*. New York: Broadway Business.

Twersky, F., Nelson, J., and Ratcliffe, A. (2010). *A Guide to Actionable Measurement*. Seattle, WA: Bill and Melinda Gates Foundation. Website (https://docs.gates-

foundation.org/documents/guide-to-actionable-measurement.pdf).   Accessed May 2, 2017.
Upcraft, M.L. and Schuh, J.H. (1996). *Assessment in Student Affairs: A Guide for Practitioners*. San Francisco, CA: Jossey-Bass.

PART III

Growing as a leader

Rigorous curricular and co-curricular leadership programming, as discussed in the first two parts of this book, creates the foundation for leadership development. Part III delves into strategies to nurture and support a learner's personal and professional growth as a leader. While curricular and co-curricular programming helps learners to attain knowledge and leadership skills, educators are invited to consider incorporating mentorships and networking opportunities, which can help learners gain a deeper understanding of how leadership works in a variety of contexts.

Part III includes examples of programs implemented at Dartmouth's Rockefeller Center and Marietta's McDonough Center. We fully recognize that much of our programming is the product of distinct institutional contexts, so we invite educators to adopt, adapt, and adjust them to their own realities. The true test of the effectiveness of a leadership program not only lies in what the students learn while they are on campus but, more importantly, can be seen in how these students perform in later years, and how they continue to learn and grow as leaders. Our goal as educators should be to inspire a spirit of lifelong learning in our participants. It is this characteristic that will make them innovative and responsive to the complex challenges they will face as leaders.

9. Leadership development

So far, we have focused on the curricular and co-curricular sides of a leadership program. The combination of these two areas creates the foundation for leadership development (Owen, 2015; Guthrie and Osteen, 2016). Leadership development requires a long-term view, discipline, and hard work, and is deeply personal (Huber, 1998). Part of the leadership development experience is to realize that there is no easy way to become a successful leader, and that requires a certain level of humility (Campbell, 2013).[1] Through reflection and intentional introspection, educators can encourage learners to draw connections between what they are learning about individual, team, and organizational development in order to achieve societal good, in both the classroom and the outside world. Educators can spark the desire in students to be lifelong learners by enhancing their self-awareness and providing experiences to enrich this learning (Gallagher and Costal, 2012).

The process of leadership development can be deepened even further when educators build into their pedagogical approach an emphasis on the "right way to do the right thing," as described by Barry Schwartz and Kenneth Sharpe (2010) in their book *Practical Wisdom*. Drawing from Aristotelian roots, the authors suggest that our lives today require us to reflect and learn about "virtues" such as integrity, perseverance, thoroughness, open-mindedness, and kindness.[2] Educators can incorporate the idea of practical wisdom into their curricula to help participants understand the goal of their work and translate it into concrete action. Learners need to understand that performing tasks well is just one part of achieving a desired goal. Every goal should be viewed as larger than the sum of its tasks because it requires an understanding of how the actions affect others and connect to a larger mission – the desire to use and develop one's practical wisdom.

Practical wisdom is gained through experience, and learners need to be able to understand the choices they make and the consequences of their decisions. In achieving any goals they set for themselves, learners need first to consider how to treat other people. Treating others well requires empathy, perception, developing judgment, and deep reflection about choices that human beings constantly make. Leadership programs create the opportunity for students to reflect on their experiences, express what they learned from a good or bad experience, reflect on how it affected others, and decide what action steps they will take.[3] Ultimately, the hope is that our learners are well on their way toward practicing the right way to do the right thing at the right time – to be wise leaders and engaged citizens.

In this chapter, we provide examples of activities educators can use for creating an environment in which their learners can gain practical wisdom. Next, we suggest a few program strategies that develop leadership capacities in learners when working with others. We also examine the role of failure in gaining practical wisdom. Educators may already be aware of some of the information provided in this chapter, but different combinations, and different ways of presenting this information, yield different results. This chapter is a synopsis of our personal experiences and what has worked for us as well as our participants.

PERSONAL DEVELOPMENT

When our learners are asked about traits that they admire in a leader, they often list examples such as integrity, authenticity, dependability, accountability, good habits, compassion, or decisiveness.[4] These examples can have several meanings, and leadership curricula can create the space for deep exploration of what they mean and how they can be practiced (Crossan et al., 2016). In this section, we provide a few examples of how we can make these concepts applicable and practical for learners in their personal development as leaders or engaged citizens.

Developing Good Habits in Leadership

We begin with the premise that, when learners are given the opportunity to examine their own leadership traits in an intellectually supportive environment, they often identify the incongruence of their behavior to the values they embrace. We have chosen to discuss "integrity" as an example because our program participants most frequently cite it as a desired trait in leaders. We believe that integrity begins with the simple act of keeping your word to yourself and to others (Fisher, 2016). "Your word" can have many dimensions: what you or others will do or will not do in a particular situation; what you or others are expected to do; what you believe you stand for; or what you or others are expected to do within moral, ethical, and legal standards.[5]

A session that offers a discussion of integrity defines it for participants as a matter of their word – nothing more and nothing less. Using this definition, learners are invited to think about their actions during the past week and are asked whether they were able to fully keep their word to themselves and to others. Most students are quick to admit that they were "out of integrity." Others are slower to come to this realization and, when probed about their actions, they too realize that they were "out of integrity."

The educator's goal in this example is to help learners understand why it is important to keep one's word and discuss the implications of being seen as a person and a leader who keeps his or her word. Educators can take this one step further by asking learners what they will do to be "in integrity." We also have observed that this discussion can help learners establish the link between keeping one's word and other virtues such as being trustworthy, authentic, dependable, or accountable.

A related idea to keeping one's word is to explore with learners the practice of using words carefully and wisely (Mishra and Mishra, 2013). Words matter, and the choice of words often creates or destroys the conditions in which a conversation can take place. For instance, "I disagree" or "I want to push back" in a conversation can set the tone for possible defensiveness or can make the other person withdraw from a conversation. Activities designed to practice giving and receiving feedback help learners to discover the power of words in persuading others or coming to a compromise in situations where there are divergent points of view.

Discussions such as the one described above propel learners to think deeply about their vision of a great leader, and they recognize that they too can emulate these traits by practicing such actions until the actions become a habit and a "way of being" (Duhigg, 2012).

Educators can support learners' efforts to practice habits they identify to be crucial in their development as leaders and to establish a system that makes them accountable to observe their progress (George, 2015). An example of an activity is the use of accountability partners. In this exercise, students work in pairs to develop goals, such as keeping their word, reading for an hour every day, exercising for 30 minutes a day, or completing assignments two days before they are due. Students then meet in person or talk on the phone once a week on a mutually agreed-upon day and time and share how well they were able to achieve the stated goals.

An Excel sheet is used to record the progress a person is making weekly. Analysis of these goals reveals how well people have been able to accomplish them and helps students to come up with strategies to become consistent and successful. This requires learners to work hard at staying consistent and being honest with themselves and their accountability partners as well. It helps them to develop good habits because they are constantly evaluating and reflecting on their actions. Developing good habits enable learners to become more efficient and effective with their physical, mental, and emotional approach to daily, monthly, and long-term tasks. When more tasks start feeling like a routine, it creates the energy and space for creativity and innovation – competencies required of our contemporary leaders.

Our students often complain about information overload and multiple demands on their time, which can result in anxiety, stress, depression, or lack of productivity. The practice of "mindfulness" can help learners to recognize and become aware of their patterns of behavior and habits (Marturano, 2015). This awareness, in turn, can promote clarity about actions they need to take to manage themselves. Mindfulness has been defined in several ways. In this book, we have settled on Jon Kabat-Zinn's definition of mindfulness as the "awareness that surfaces when an individual pays attention to purpose, is in the present moment, and is non-judgmental."[6] All of the concepts in his definition apply to leadership development in higher education. Helping students to connect to a cause larger than themselves gives them purpose and helps them to attach meaning to their lives. Being in the present moment encourages them to develop the power of observation, concentration, and focus. Finally, introducing the concept of being non-judgmental in the practice of mindfulness is important. The human brain is wired to "automatically judge things as good or bad, right or wrong, fair or unfair, important or unimportant, urgent or non-urgent, and so on."[7] Helping students to understand this idea and be intentionally aware of how their judgments might be affecting choices they make enables them to look at their experiences with a different perspective or lens. Doing this also helps them to develop emotional intelligence (as discussed in Chapter 2) and connect more effectively with those around them and those they lead.

Incorporating mindfulness practices in leadership curricula also creates the space for students to be better prepared for a world in which organizations have increasingly begun to incorporate such programs for their employees. "Mindfulness helps improve strategizing, the decision-making process and the resulting decisions because the brain is able to be present and focused on what is actually on the table, and therefore the leader is able to listen more fully and respond more appropriately."[8] While these attributes of mindfulness may be immediately related to the development of leaders in the business world, learners in our leadership programs also stand to benefit from improved decision-making. Leadership development takes place over the length of a lifetime (Ruderman and Ohlott, 2000); however, having the ability to think strategically and critically is essential for students as they consider preparing for their exit from college and entrance into the workplace.

Oftentimes people believe that mindfulness is about doing "nothing." Mindfulness isn't doing "nothing." Research has shown that it helps people to achieve concentration and focus.[9] Furthermore, practicing mindfulness becomes an active decision to refocus when distracted. It is important to recognize that, while this book focuses on leadership development in higher education, the benefits reaped from mindfulness in the workplace (e.g., increased productivity, efficiency, effectiveness, focus, better attitude) are the same benefits educators can expect students to reap in a higher education context. For example, in order to be better learners and leaders, students must develop concentration and focus. This helps them to be better prepared to complete the myriad tasks associated with being student leaders and balance these with their academic workloads.

In concluding this discussion about mindfulness, we provide a few ideas of how it can be incorporated into leadership programming. Several programs at the Rockefeller Center have begun offering mindfulness sessions or sometimes short exercises within a session. For example, a full session is devoted to the importance of the practice of mindfulness in leadership in the Rockefeller Leadership Fellows Program and the Rockefeller Professional Preparation Program. In other programs, we have observed that even a few minutes devoted to breathing as an exercise can help to center learners and thus help them to focus on the content being covered during a session. Finally, educators can use YouTube sessions on mindfulness or apps such as Headspace, Smiling Mind, iMindfulness, or mindful. org to develop sessions on mindfulness.

Developing a Leadership Mindset

In her book *Mindset*, Carol Dweck (2012) draws a distinction between a "fixed" mindset and a "growth" mindset. When educators place these two variables as the extremes of a continuum, they can study learners' psychological disposition, ranging between an assumption of innate intelligence (fixed mindset) and an openness to development (growth mindset).

At one end of the spectrum, students with a "fixed mindset" believe that they have an innate level of intelligence or talent that cannot be changed. In contrast, an openness to development of leadership skills through hard work and commitment implies a "growth mindset." In a "growth mindset," individuals do not make assumptions about innate intelligence and seek to develop themselves as leaders through hard work. We believe that a leadership mindset requires a "growth mindset" and is guided by students developing their own philosophy of leadership, as well as a resulting definition that informs actions taken by them. In our experience, students begin their exploration of leadership by starting a discussion on character traits such as loyalty, courage, integrity, or open-mindedness. By asking them to develop a philosophy of leadership, learners are invited to dig deeper and examine how their behavior as leaders reflects their personal values. That exercise requires reflection on leadership theories students are learning and the experience they are gaining during their years in a college setting.[10] We now provide a couple of examples of how students are facilitated to examine their philosophy of leadership in our respective institutions.

At the McDonough Center, students are encouraged to articulate their philosophy of leadership during their second year in the program. That is an intentional step. It takes at least a year of leadership classes and the implementation of a few projects before the students begin to frame their view of how leadership works. This philosophy of leadership is developed in the "Theories and models" course, after the students have taken the "Foundations of leadership" and "Organizational leadership" courses in their first and second semesters respectively. During their junior year, the McDonough Scholars have an opportunity to "test" how this philosophy of leadership fares in the real world through an experiential component (e.g., internship, study abroad, service project). For the students in the leadership major, they debrief this experience in the capstone course during the senior year.

In another example, the Rockefeller Leadership Fellows Program at the Rockefeller Center has introduced the same exercise of developing a philosophy for its participants. Participants provide their philosophy of leadership in writing at the beginning of the program. They then add insights gained as well as the applicability of these insights to personal and professional growth at the end of each session in the program. Reflection is based not only on content covered during the session, but also on insights gained from personal experiences. Learners share their reflections with their "accountability partner" (discussed earlier in this chapter) at the next session offered during the program. At the end of the program, students are ready to share their philosophy of leadership with each other in small groups and are requested to distill it down to 300 words. Finally, educators compile these summaries into one document and distribute this as a parting gift during an informal gathering of incoming and outgoing students in the program.

These examples have a few things in common. Educators recognize that experience and reflection are key to gaining practical wisdom. Students begin with articulating their personal philosophies of leadership and, through reflective exercises in either a curricular or a co-curricular setting, gain further insights about their own understanding of leadership. We believe that this exercise helps them not only to clarify who they are as leaders but also to articulate what they believe to be effective leadership through experiences they have gained.

PROGRAM STRATEGIES TO BUILD LEADERSHIP CAPACITY

In the previous section, we explored the relationship between personal development and practical wisdom. We now turn to program strategies educators can consider for preparing students to gain such wisdom. The examples included in this chapter not only help students to gain self-awareness as individuals, but also provide opportunities to learn about their own leadership style in teams, thus including important considerations for effective teamwork. When this is done well, learners are able to reflect on self, team, community, and organizational behaviors, and how all these concepts work together to achieve a common goal or societal good. There are no doubt other strategies that are not discussed in this chapter, and we invite educators to experiment with these as well.

Curricular Programs and Experiential Learning

Two curricular courses at the Rockefeller Center, "Introduction to public policy research" and the "Practicum in global policy leadership," incorporate experiential learning and have unique elements that lend themselves to being adopted or adapted by other institutions. Leadership development may not be the main goal, as in other programs at the Center designed expressly for this purpose, but we observe that these courses offer an excellent avenue for such development. For example, the "Introduction to public policy research" culminates in the Policy Research Shop, in which students work in small groups to conduct non-partisan research for state policy-makers in the states of Vermont and New Hampshire in the US, delivered in a non-advocacy manner.

The student teams present their analysis to legislative committees, statewide commissions, or executive agencies on critical issues related to a public policy topic facing state policy-makers. Policy Research Shop faculty mentors solicit research topics from legislators or their staff and, since 2006, the Policy Research Shop has produced over 150 policy briefs. Small group work under the skillful guidance of a faculty mentor is rigorous, and students wrestle with a wide range of public policy topics such as homelessness, assessment of the state of art education in Vermont, and a comprehensive review of social impact bonds.

This is just the beginning, however. In addition to the knowledge they gain about a particular public policy topic, students often remark on their deeper understanding of personal work styles and how these can complement each other, as well as the successes and challenges of working on a team aiming to achieve a common goal. Through the extensive research undertaken for the preparation of a multi-authored policy brief that culminates in formal testimony before a state legislative committee or state-wide commission, the students develop critical, analytical, communication, and problem-solving skills. They also learn about how to address the needs of their "clients," a skill that serves them well after they graduate.

The "practicum in global policy leadership" is another curricular offering in which a select group of students gain in-depth knowledge about the history and context of a public policy challenge in a particular country or region through a term-long curricular course. At the end of that term, students visit the country or region to interview local policy leaders including politicians, academics, civil-society leaders, business leaders, diplomats, and community members. This combination of theory and practice enables them to define and assess the challenge from different perspectives, which can often present conflicting points of view. They then develop solutions.

As a final project, students complete and disseminate a memo consisting of specific recommendations, which enables them to synthesize the knowledge they have gained in and out of the classroom, and on and off campus. The unique part of this memo is that students work together to write a single memo. This provides them with an opportunity to practice leadership and teamwork within the group. The process by which they organize themselves to produce a single coherent work product is an important part of the learning experience.

As we observe from these descriptions, students learn how to interpret the policy challenge from different perspectives. Committed faculty offering these courses open the door for students to practice doing the right thing, the right way, and at the right time. This includes active listening, the art of conducting interviews, empathy, project development, and working in teams. Students are thus assisted to develop these policies required for domestic and global leadership.

Outdoor Experiential Learning Exercises

Experiential learning exercises that use the principle of "learning by doing" are effective in inspiring participants to examine leadership principles and practice competencies. When teams and their leaders have the opportunity to experience working together toward a common goal and subsequently reflect on that experience through structured debriefing or analysis, they learn about the challenges and opportunities of leading themselves and others in real time. For example, the Dartmouth Athletics Department uses an exercise in its Dartmouth Peak Performance Program. Called the "Olympics of the mind," this exercise is designed to help participants to learn about their personal strengths as well as weaknesses as a team.

In "Olympics of the mind," participants are divided into smaller teams of 12 members each. Their task as a team is to complete six challenges within a specific time period, ranging from three to 15 minutes in six different locations in an athletic facility. The exercises in the six locations can be completed in any order. All teams have unlimited attempts at each challenge in a given location. However, before moving on to the next location after completing the challenge at a particular location, regardless of success or failure, each team must run one full lap around the facility and do 15 synchronized weighted squats. If a team is unable to complete a given challenge within the specified time-limit, it has failed that attempt. A failed attempt requires all members of a team to climb to the top of a climbing rope and then complete 15 synchronized squats and one lap around the track. Each team member must first attempt to climb the rope; those with a limiting injury are exempted. Even if a team succeeds at a challenge in a location, team members are required to do 15 synchronized squats and run one lap around the track before proceeding to the next challenge. At the end of the exercise, each team completes self-reflections individually and together as a team before they can leave for the day.

Questions they consider for reflection include but are not limited to:

- What were your first impressions of the exercise, honestly? Describe it in terms of your attitude. Did your attitude change over the exercise? If so, how?
- Which of your character strengths and weaknesses were on display today?
- Did any leaders emerge on the team (including yourself)? At what moments and why?
- Would you say you were an asset to the team? Why or why not?

In the self-reflection exercises, educators facilitating this exercise observe that team members often conclude that effective communication, hard work, and clear use of team members' strengths and weaknesses are essential to success. Steven Spaulding, director of the program, explains:

> Exercises like these have immediate as well as long-term effects on teams because team members learn to trust each other in a non-typical context as well as identifying how they can function better long-term. Further, adversity builds cohesive teams and gives an opportunity for a team to fail or succeed.

Another example of experiential activities includes ropes courses that lend themselves to reflective practices. Dartmouth College's Outdoor Program runs courses for the College's professional institutions such as the Geisel School of Medicine and the Tuck School of Business. In a typical ropes course, participants work in teams to solve a problem and come up with solutions collectively as a group. In an activity called "Rock rescue," participants in small groups with assigned activities are given the challenge to "rescue" a person and lower that person down a steep cliff. The safety of this person and the rescue effort require all groups to work together as a team to develop a strategy and a plan, practice skills such as tying knots and securing a person in a harness, and lowering him or her down a steep cliff.

The teams spend time practicing tasks assigned to them and discussing the plan. It is obvious that all members are anxious about wanting to ensure that the harness is balanced and that the act of lowering the person in the harness is smooth. All of this is done under the watchful eyes of trained educators who facilitate this exercise. The successful "rescue" of the person and freeing the person from the straps that have him or her secured to the harness are the end of the activity. Participants breathe a sigh of relief, as does the person who has been rescued! After the excited chatter that results from this exercise fades, deep reflection begins.

The facilitators now run a discussion with participants that includes but is not limited to such questions as:

- What did you observe?
- In what ways did you make the person being "rescued" feel comfortable?
- What was your role and the role of others? What went well and what issues did you encounter?
- What did you learn about yourself? Your team?
- What were some assumptions you made when you started this exercise and when you were executing the rescue?
- What were you thinking about when the person you were "rescuing" was being lowered down the cliff?
- What are some key takeaways from this exercise?

Educators also pose questions to the person "rescued" in the exercise: What were you feeling when you were being secured in the harness? Did you feel confident with the team tasked with "rescuing" you? What did team members say or do to make you feel comfortable and safe? What could they have done better?

The deputy director of Dartmouth's Outdoor Program, Brian Kunz, encourages educators to incorporate such exercises in their curriculum. He says these courses help students to learn about themselves, and how they interact with each other, understand others, develop skills and confidence, and gain an experience they would have otherwise not had. They get to a level of learning much faster as a result of such experiences. Additionally, students gain respect for each other and learn how to work with each other. An educator's role then becomes tying learning to leadership and always asking "why" a student or students choose to pursue a particular course of action to come to an informed conclusion. Students can reflect on what motivates or drives them to become leaders and understand the conditions (leadership for small groups or large groups) under which they can do this successfully.

In both examples, educators facilitate the exercises by dividing participants into teams either through self-selection or through assigning members into teams, providing training to ensure safety, and giving clear instructions. They also ensure participants follow the "rules" and guide them through the reflection questions after exercise completion.

Peer-to-Peer Learning

Peer-to-peer learning is another strategy educators employ for leadership development. Students can learn a great deal from each other by articulating their thoughts, ideas, successes, and challenges (Boud et al., 2001). They can also practice working in groups and learning about team dynamics and management. Our personal experiences with establishing programs that foster peer learning require that students are clear about their roles and expectations with these programs. Educators also need to be clear that their role is principally to support and not to direct the activities in such programs. Students gain experience and competencies by learning from each other and by implementing these programs. Care should be taken to see that the peer-to-peer learning is organized well. We now turn to examples of programs that foster peer-to-peer learning from our respective institutions.

McDonough Center's Experience Civic Engagement and Leadership (EXCEL) Workshop

Since 1987, when the first group of McDonough Scholars at Marietta College participated in this annual orientation event, the McDonough Center has offered incoming first-year students with the opportunity to develop relationships with upper-class students, faculty, and staff in preparation for their new academic year. The EXCEL Workshop takes place during the week before the fall semester begins. A group of upper-class leadership students puts together and implements this event.

A student EXCEL coordinator, guided by a faculty adviser, serves as the leader of the EXCEL leaders. The overall goals of the workshop are: to build a strong camaraderie among the new scholars; to establish mentoring relationships with EXCEL leaders who help guide students; to inspire students to act in ways which promote the well-being of their community; and to introduce incoming first-year students to the study and application of leadership through fun and impactful activities. Each day has a theme, and brief descriptions for each are provided below:

- *Day one*: Beginning the adventure. This day provides opportunities for students to begin to build positive and encouraging relationships among the cohort members.
- *Day two*: Discovering support from within. This day enables students to experience the power within themselves to move outside of their comfort zone and take risks for personal development within the context of an outdoor high- and low-ropes challenge course.
- *Day three*: Investing in public service. On this day, students are introduced to concepts related to civic engagement. During this day, incoming first-year students participate in service activities and learn about challenges facing the local community as well as the world.
- *Day four*: Breaking boundaries. This day emphasizes the similarities and differences that exist within a community and the necessity of breaking boundaries in order to work successfully and ethically.
- *Day five*: Becoming a McDonough Scholar. This day provides participants with an opportunity to celebrate the week's accomplishments, and to begin their academic journey as McDonough Scholars. Through selected leadership texts, leadership instructors lead discussions and introduce the scholars to the academic and intellectual expectations of the program.

Reflections on the EXCEL Workshop experience   Here are three reflections from students who participated in the workshop when they arrived as first-year students, and who later became EXCEL leaders and mentors to subsequent cohorts:

EXCEL is more than a student orientation; it is the place where I first started to feel comfortable about being myself, and this is where I met many of my current friends. Going into EXCEL, I viewed the world in a very structured way; but at every turn my opinions were challenged. I had to start thinking more carefully about why I held certain opinions, and how I could communicate those reasons to the people around me. EXCEL helped me to see that I had strengths and understand that I was going to fail at some point, and that as long as I got back up, it was going to be okay. I went through EXCEL once as a student, and chose to return three times as a leader, because I know the impact the workshop had on me, and I wanted to help ensure that incoming classes could have their own experiences. Being a leader in the EXCEL workshop was my way of giving back to the program that gave so much to me, and a way for me to support the freshmen during an overwhelming transition in their lives. (Eric Wilken, Class of 2018)

EXCEL is a unique and special experience for both the freshmen and upperclassmen who participate in it. As a freshman, I was warmly embraced by both the student leaders and other members of my cohort and provided an environment, for the first time, that welcomed genuine collaboration and discussion with people of varying backgrounds and beliefs. The Workshop made me excited to start college, eager to continue to develop my personal perspective on leadership and my multi-dimensional community and global outlooks that I'd begun to explore throughout the week of EXCEL. Getting to serve as an EXCEL Leader for all three years that I was eligible to has been my most rewarding on-campus experience. Countless hours are invested by the leader team to improve the Workshop each year. Throughout all those hours, the leader team always develops into a close-knit group of not just peers but friends, eager to harness each other's strengths to make the best Workshop possible. Going through the Workshop as a leader offers its own sense of transformation and growth. Leaders learn and develop insights from the new cohort and the other Leaders every day of the Workshop. We, as leaders, strengthen the bonds of friendships we have with members of the leader team and cherish the new ones we're able to now develop with the incoming cohort. (Mandee Young, Class of 2018)

Aside from the obvious "giving back the gift" through serving the program that has so positively influenced me and the opportunity for my personal leadership development, I've received unexpected benefits from my involvement with the EXCEL Workshop that have transitioned into one of my main motivators. My role as a student leader, and eventually student workshop coordinator, has caused me to be very conscious when reflecting on my own experiences as a freshman entering the program. I am constantly reminded of the rewarding relationships that were built with upper and underclassmen each year. By committing to the structure of a student leader team, the program creates an intimate environment where mentorship roles form organically. These bonds later proved to be crucial to my collegiate success, especially in my formative underclassman years. (Evan Hensel, Class of 2018)

Rockefeller Peer Mentoring Program

The goal of this program is to provide mentoring opportunities to students seeking guidance from peers, faculty, and staff with shared interests in public policy and leadership. The program provides a resource for students seeking experience in public policy while also expanding students' awareness of additional resources at the Rockefeller Center and throughout campus. It helps students develop networking and mentorship skills that will be valuable in the professional world and provides a mechanism through which upper-class students can give back to the community.

The Rockefeller Peer Mentoring Program was first established in

2012. Based on their mutual fields of interest, seniors participating in the Rockefeller Leadership Fellows Program were matched with one or two students participating in the First-Year Fellows Program (first-year students). The mentoring relationship included a kick-off session and monthly meetings over the course of one year.

In the years since the program was originally introduced, educators have tried many approaches to implementing this "facilitated" (Murray, 2001) mentoring program. The year-long engagement between mentor and mentee provided mixed results and was a challenge because of Dartmouth College's unique academic schedule. Mentors and mentees did not stay in touch with each other when they were participating in foreign study programs or were off campus doing an internship.

In the program's current incarnation, Student Staff Program assistants pair first-year students interested in leadership and public policy with sophomores, juniors, or seniors active in programs at the Rockefeller Center. The program has been shortened to a six-week spring-term engagement consisting of weekly "mentoring hour" meetings. The Center settled on the spring term because students at this stage of their first year in college are more established with their new routine in college and are ready to think about future directions.

The weekly meetings between mentor and mentee are a hallmark of the program, giving students a regular time and place for discussing various topics of interest. Each session includes a short informational segment that covers such topics as the role of students in internships, the importance of creating a LinkedIn profile, and the basics of networking. These introductory segments create a framework for discussion between mentors and mentees. In addition to the weekly meetings, two networking receptions with faculty and alumni are included in the program schedule. These provide opportunities for students to utilize and hone the skills developed during their weekly sessions with a new cohort, faculty, and staff. While the program tries to keep meeting times consistent for the students, flexibility around students' academic schedules is also beneficial to the program. In particular, during the weeks of mid-terms, pairs meet on their own based on their availability.

Over time, students have taken a greater role in designing and facilitating sessions and making program development suggestions. Student Staff Program assistants now facilitate sessions, handle communications, and are the face of the program. They use their knowledge of the student community and their peers to help match mentors with the mentees and are also responsible for the logistics of the program. Not only does this help the program make better matches between mentors and mentees, but it also gives the program assistants a unique opportunity to practice their own management and leadership capabilities. As a result, the educator has taken on more of a supporting role, but still oversees the overall design of the program. Below are short descriptions of each session:

- *Session one*: Kick-off. Students are introduced to each other, are matched by policy area of interest, and learn about networking best practices.
- *Session two*: Identifying resources and mentoring hours. Students meet in pairs or in small groups while learning about resources for internship opportunities. They also discuss professionalism and the ability to manage oneself and manage others.
- *Session three*: Networking and mentoring hours. Students informally meet in pairs or in small groups while learning about best practices for growing their professional network through academic and personal connections as well as social media.
- *Session four*: Academic plan strategies and mentoring hours. Students meet in pairs or in small groups while discussing tips for developing a plan to meet their academic and career goals.
- *Session five*: Group mentoring event. Students meet in larger groups to learn about other mentors' and mentees' experiences on campus and in the professional realm.
- *Session six*: Closing event. Students are able to use this event as a way to practice their networking skills developed during the program and to reflect with their partner on what they learned during the term.

We conclude our discussion of peer-to-peer learning programs by suggesting that working with students to develop and implement such programs is an effective strategy. Many students who work in partnership with educators to design and implement these programs take ownership of the program and are invested in its success. This partnership also gives them the opportunity to build their competencies as managers and leaders; through this exercise, they not only learn to conceptualize, plan, and implement a program, but also develop skills in organizing and evaluating activities. Participants of the program, on the other hand, learn from the experiences of others, learn how to articulate their ideas clearly, and become aware of resources they can access.

The Student Role in Defining Programs

Leadership programs provide the perfect environment to empower students to develop programs and ideas for leadership development. By integrating them into the development process, as with peer-to-peer programs, students come to feel like stakeholders in the success of a program. We provide three examples of how students can be engaged in this process.

Example 1: McDonough Scholars' core values

We begin with an example from the McDonough Center at Marietta College.[11] A few years ago, the McDonough Center educators invited a group of students, under the leadership of Ryan Turnewitsch from the Class of 2015, to develop the core values that McDonough Scholars should exhibit as a result of participating in the four-year leadership curriculum. This exercise turned out to be an incredibly rewarding process of "value checking" and empowerment for these students. In the end, they came up with four core themes, which inform curriculum development and refinement each year. These themes are now used to orient incoming McDonough Scholars. We have provided a brief description of each theme:

- *Engagement.* First-year theme: Building community and finding your place in it. "Actively seeking a role both on campus and in the community during your first year will empower you to develop your initial perceptions about leadership. Meaningful involvement within the classroom and beyond will equip you to fully participate in your learning experience, thus allowing you to gain the most from your collegiate career. Engagement is a commitment to entirely investing yourself into the relationships, opportunities, and experiences lying before you in order to establish the foundation for your future endeavors."
- *Enlightenment.* Second-year theme: Creating your leadership model through self-discovery. "After engaging in the first year, you are now prepared to mature your personal leadership goals. By synthesizing course material, hands-on-learning experiences, campus and community roles, and new leadership lessons attained over your two years, you will see the world through a larger lens. Your broadened perspectives and deepening knowledge will strengthen your growth as a leader and enable you to create your personal leadership vision."
- *Resilience.* Third-year theme: Testing your leadership model. "Leadership is not easy. Setbacks inevitably challenge the greatest of leaders, and during your third year, the theories and practices of leadership you have refined for two years will be tested. These trials will teach you that self-confidence, patience, and resilience are integral to your ability to be both a capable follower and an effective leader. Celebrating all of the experiences that have brought you this

far, you will learn to appreciate the value of failure because only through overcoming it will you become a stronger leader."

• *Direction.* Fourth-year theme: Answering the question: Leadership for what? "Upon your final year, you will gain a sense of direction. At this point, you have taken the classes, you have acquired the skills, and you have made an impact within your community. Now, you must ask yourself: Where do I want to go with all that I have learned? As you reflect on your future beyond Marietta College, you will have the chance to decide how, where, and to whom you wish to 'give back the gift.' This is your opportunity to make an impact in the world; now all you must do is to go take that initial step."

The student group intentionally framed the four themes based on key developmental stages: finding community (developing a sense of belonging); developing one's own philosophy of leadership through knowledge; testing that philosophy in the "real world" (through action); and finding a calling that will transcend the college years.

Each year, McDonough Center students build on their leadership knowledge about themselves, others, and organizations. By the end of their four years, they can see how these components work together to achieve a team goal or mission. Starting with asking students to examine why they are in a leadership program, as well as the values that drive them, the program progresses with helping students to empower others. It then ends with challenging students to articulate their vision for the future.

Example 2: Rockefeller Leadership Fellows Program participant selection
The Rockefeller Leadership Fellows Program participants play a significant role in selecting their successors at the end of the year-long program. Aspiring Fellows apply to the program, gather peer and faculty recommendations, and undergo individual and group interviews. Current Fellows form a marketing and outreach group, an application review group, and an interview group. Each group reviews and finalizes roles and responsibilities and develops a Gantt chart outlining timelines and who within each group is responsible for each task. Finally, the group develops criteria and a process for selecting its successors. All Fellows attend the final selection process to determine the new cohort.

The Rockefeller Center has used this process since 2006 and has learned many lessons. It is undoubtedly a process that reviews concepts discussed earlier in the year. The process brings the participants together and, sometimes, the practice of working together in a group can create tensions about unequal participation. This requires the educator to be mindful and vigilant at all times, because the goal is that participants leave the program as friends and bear no animosities toward each other. It is an extremely time-consuming and labor-intensive exercise – both for participants and for the educator. That said, with each successive year, the Center has witnessed a stronger cohort than the last, and the credit for this goes to all the participants in the program who are single-minded in their effort to leave the program stronger than they found it.

Example 3: Training for Rockefeller Student Staff Program assistants

If they have not already done so, institutions should consider creating positions for students to work together with educators in planning, implementing, and monitoring programs. In this subsection, we discuss the Rockefeller Center's Student Staff Program, which provides Dartmouth students with the opportunity to experience a workplace environment where they can witness, practice, and reflect upon leadership and management skills. The experience is intentional because it helps them to develop competencies, which sets the stage to learn about excelling in a professional work environment. It also is one of the steps they take toward becoming lifelong learners. This program was conceptualized by the Center's Senior Assistant Director, Elizabeth Celtrick. Individual sessions were designed and implemented by the Center's co-curricular staff. The program is designed to address the following competencies: collaboration, effective communication, effective reasoning, management, self-knowledge, principled action, and an intercultural mindset.

The Rockefeller Center educators overseeing the co-curricular programs commit to modeling professionalism, which strengthens their ability to coach and mentor Student Staff Program assistants. This creates a work experience for students in which taking on the risks associated with new initiatives and responsibilities is encouraged and supported. The program description and related components are provided below:

- *Student staff performance reviews*. Performance reviews are a natural part of communicating ongoing expectations, setting short-term objectives, and providing a framework for continual mentoring and guidance. Constructive dialogue between a student assistant and his or her supervisor about performance and growth expectations should consist of three elements:
    - articulated professional purpose and vision for success in one's work;
    - SMART professional performance objectives tied to measurable results;
    - professional development goal(s) and a plan for goal achievement.

- *Group learning sessions.* Student Staff Program assistants are required to participate in group learning sessions that take place twice a term during the fall, winter, and spring terms. The sessions focus on the following themes:
  - performance management;
  - giving and receiving feedback;
  - goal setting;
  - initiative and accountability;
  - reflection and assessment.
- *Mini-Grant Committee.* Student Staff Program assistants serve on the Rockefeller Mini-Grant Committee, which meets every two weeks to review small grants submitted by other students from all over campus for implementing events or to cover registration fees for conferences. Serving on this committee helps students to learn about protocols and procedures that are part of an organization, how to make decisions as a group, and how to allocate money fairly and ethically.

The Role of Failure in Leadership Development

We would be remiss if we did not highlight the role that failure can play in leadership development. In Western culture, many of our learners grow up being sheltered from failure, and it is often viewed as a setback. In reality, however, failure can have a very positive role in leadership development.

In the leadership literature, moments of failure are described as "crucible" experiences that define the development of great leaders. Warren Bennis and Robert J. Thomas, in a 2002 *Harvard Business Review* article entitled "The Crucible of Leadership," suggest that "our recent research has led us to conclude that one of the most reliable indicators and predictors of true leadership is an individual's ability to find meaning in negative events and to learn from even the most trying circumstances."[12] We find this to be true in our experience as educators. A key lesson is not to protect students from failure. In fact, the goal should be to develop a culture of constant learning that draws leadership lessons from both successes and failures. Incorporating exercises that help students to analyze mistakes and failures and to learn from them is powerful. For this reason, the Rockefeller Center leadership programs intentionally include activities in which participants receive feedback. Such activities introduce to students the practice of being humble, accepting mistakes and learning from them, and gaining new insights about themselves. It sets them on the path of developing resilience, courage, and strength to deal with the adversities life will offer.

We approach the end of this section with an uplifting thought from Sydney Latimore from the Class of 2018:

> The only thing more certain in life than death and taxes is that we, particularly as young adults, will fail. The only redeeming truth about the inevitability of failure is that, when approached as a learning opportunity, it can create a moment for growth that exceeds our wildest expectations. I firmly believe that through failure we learn to be better people, students, friends, and mentors.

In this chapter, we discussed personal and program strategies that educators can use to facilitate their learners to think about the "right way to do the right thing." We now share our concluding thoughts about how educators can think about the overall purpose of their leadership programs. Effective leadership programs are less about credentialing and more about competency-building and inculcating "a way of being" in our learners.

We believe educators can consider their programs successful if learners walk away with the understanding that leadership is not just positional and that one person in a leadership capacity does not and should not in any way inhibit others from exhibiting leadership. Leadership programs provide the avenues for learners to describe in their own words who they are, what they stand for, what they believe in, and why. In the end, students will be able to articulate how they are connected to a mission that is larger than themselves. Nelson Rockefeller (Rockefeller Brothers Fund, 1958), the 41st Vice President of the United States said: "It is essential that we enable young people to see themselves as participants in one of the most exciting eras in history and to have a sense of purpose in relation to it." When students are able to understand this idea, in practical terms, they become ethically engaged and compassionate leaders and citizens who make our world a better place.

REFLECTION QUESTIONS

1. In this chapter we defined leadership development as the acquisition of a mindset that opens a person to the possibility of self-evaluation, learning, and in the process guided changes in outlook and behaviors. How often do you encourage your learners to practice this mindset?
2. If you were to ask your students to develop the core values of your leadership program, which values would they list? Why?
3. What is your philosophy of leadership?
4. How do you encourage peer-to-peer learning through your leadership programming?
5. How do your students approach failure? What role can failure have in your leadership programming?

NOTES

1. In recent years, the topic of humility has grown in the leadership literature. Aside from a chapter on humility, Crossan et al. (2016) devote other chapters to critical traits such as drive, collaboration, humanity, integrity, temperance, justice, accountability, courage, transcendence, and judgment. Spaulding (2015) lists humility, vulnerability, transparency, empathy, and love.
2. Aristotle listed other "virtues" such as loyalty, self-control, courage, fairness, generosity, gentleness, friendliness, and truthfulness, as described by Schwartz and Sharpe (2010).
3. Conger (1992) provides a comprehensive study of popular leadership development programs. In his *Learning to Lead*, he suggests four categories of learning processes found in those programs: 1) personal growth ("finding my true self" – learning associated with self-exploration and higher levels of self-awareness); 2) understanding conceptual approaches (learning through the formal acquisition of theoretical knowledge); 3) feedback ("looking through the mirror" – the use of assessment instruments that leaders can use to gain knowledge of how their leading is viewed by others); and 4) skill-building ("mastering the Zen of leadership" – helping leaders master certain desirable skills through training and practice).
4. Kraemer (2011) offers four principles of value-based leadership: self-reflection; balance and perspective; true self-confidence; and genuine humility.
5. Dean's leadership training at Dartmouth College, held on June 20–27, 2012.
6. As quoted in Jeanne Meister (2015), Future of Work: Mindfulness as a Leadership Practice, *Forbes*, April 27. Website (https://www.forbes.com/sites/jeannemeister/2015/04/27/future-of-work-mindfulness-as-a-leadership-practice/#69a369883e1c). Accessed October 25, 2017. See also Kabat-Zinn (1994).
7. Elisha Goldstein. Website (http://www.huffingtonpost.com/elisha-goldstein-phd/non-judgmental-awareness_b_3204748.html). Accessed September 29, 2017.
8. C. Cassica (2013), Mindfulness in Leadership, December 3. Website (http://rady.ecsd.edu/blog/p). Accessed September 30, 2017.
9. Michael Carroll (2012), Lead by Achieving Nothing. Seriously, *Forbes Leadership Forum*, November 16. Website (https://www.forbes.com/sites/forbesleadershipforum/2012/11/16/lead-by-achieving-nothing-seriously). Accessed September 30, 2017.
10. Many successful leaders in a wide variety of fields have published their philosophies of leadership; see, for instance, Walsh (2010).
11. This example is taken from the McDonough website (https://webapps.marietta.edu/~lead/?q=Mission). Accessed September 30, 2017.
12. As quoted in https://hbr.org/2002/09/crucibles-of-leadership. Accessed May 25, 2017.

REFERENCES

Boud, D., Cohen, R., and Sampson, J. (Eds.). (2001). *Peer Learning in Higher Education: Learning from and with Each Other*. London: Kogan Page.

Campbell, D. (2013). *The Leader's Code: Mission, Character, Service, and Getting the Job Done*. New York: Random House.

Conger, J. (1992). *Learning to Lead*. San Francisco, CA: Jossey-Bass.

Crossan, M., Seijts, G., and Gandz, J. (2016). *Developing Leadership Character*. New York: Routledge.

Duhigg, C. (2012). *The Power of Habit: Why We Do What We Do in Life and Business*. New York: Random House.

Dweck, C. (2012). *Mindset: How You Can Fulfil Your Potential*. London: Robinson.

Fisher, J. (2016). *The Thoughtful Leader: A Model of Integrative Leadership*. Toronto: University of Toronto Press.

Gallagher, D. and Costal, J. (2012). *The Self-Aware Leader*. Alexandria, VA: ASTD Press.

George, B. (2015). *Discover Your True North*. Hoboken, NJ: Wiley.

Guthrie, K. and Osteen, L. (Eds.). (2016). *Reclaiming Higher Education's Purpose in Leadership Development*. San Francisco, CA: Jossey-Bass.

Huber, N. (1998). *Leading from Within: Developing Personal Direction*. Malabar, FL: Krieger Publishing Co.

Kabat-Zinn, J. (1994). *Wherever You Go, There You Are: Mindfulness Meditation in Everyday Life*. New York: Hyperion.

Kraemer, H. (2011). *From Values to Action: The Four Principles of Values-Based Leadership*. San Francisco, CA: Jossey-Bass.

Marturano, J. (2015). *Finding the Space to Lead: A Practical Guide to Mindful Leadership*. New York: Bloomsbury Press.

Mishra, A. and Mishra, K. (2013). *Becoming a Trustworthy Leader: Psychology and Practice*. New York: Routledge.

Murray, M. (2001). *Beyond the Myths and Magic of Mentoring: How to Facilitate an Effective Mentoring Process*. San Francisco, CA: Jossey-Bass.

Owen, J. (Ed.). (2015). *Innovative Learning for Leadership Development*. San Francisco, CA: Jossey-Bass.

Rockefeller Brothers Fund. (1958). *The pursuit of excellence: Education and the future of America*, 5, Doubleday, p. 46.

Ruderman, M. and Ohlott, P. (2000). *Learning from Life: Turning Life's Lessons into Leadership Experience*. Greensboro, NC: Center for Creative Leadership.

Schwartz, B. and Sharpe, K. (2010). *Practical Wisdom: The Right Way to Do the Right Thing*. New York: Riverhead Books.

Spaulding, T. (2015). *The Heart-Led Leader: How Living and Leading from the Heart Will Change Your Organization and Your Life*. New York: Crown Business.

Walsh, B. (2010). *The Score Takes Care of Itself: My Philosophy of Leadership*. New York: Portfolio Penguin.

10. Supporting personal and professional growth

Leadership development does not end when our learners complete our programs. Just as they needed our support while striving to balance their academic and personal lives as students, they also need our help to learn how to identify mentors and develop networks as they move beyond campus (D'Abate et al., 2003; Bland et al., 2012). We use "mentors" as a broad term that encompasses educators, peers, friends, and family, as well as role models from the communities in which our learners live (Mertz, 2004).

Students often remark that leadership is a lonely proposition. They suggest that leaders should not appear weak to their followers and not show signs of vulnerability. Further, they comment that, while leaders can get input from others, they are ultimately responsible for both good and bad decisions and are to be held accountable for them. For this reason, we believe it is important to prepare our students to develop vibrant networks of mentors from whom they can seek input for problems they face or decisions they must make. By leaning on both their support networks and their mentors, our young leaders are best placed to make good decisions based on the information they have at that time.

In this chapter, we describe the many different ways an educator can approach student growth and guidance and how mentorship and networks can play a role. First, through a review of the current literature, we examine how mentorship is defined. We examine the benefits of mentorship to mentors and mentees alike, present examples of mentoring programs that our students have found useful, and outline lessons we have learned as a result of implementing these programs. We conclude this chapter with an examination of the concept of networking and how it can support personal and professional growth.

MENTORSHIP IN LEADERSHIP PROGRAMS

There are many ways to define mentorship (Dominguez and Hager, 2013). Zachary (2000), for instance, defines mentoring in terms of a reciprocal learning relationship that involves partnership, collaboration, and mutually defined goals. While this view suggests a shared approach to mentoring, Ragins and McFarlin (1990) define mentoring as a relationship that involves hierarchy between a mentor with advanced knowledge and a mentee interested in upward support and mobility. Crisp and Cruz (2009) contend that academia looks at mentorship in one of two ways: it is seen as a specific set of activities conducted by a "mentor" (such as in the afore-mentioned definition) or as a concept or process. In this book, we reframe mentoring as a type of developmental relationship characterized by reciprocal learning and focused on goal attainment and personal growth.

A mentoring relationship can take many forms (Eby et al., 2006). Most mentorship experts suggest that mentoring can be both formal and infor-mal (Allen and Eby, 2008). Informal mentoring relationships may occur spontaneously throughout an individual's life and without an explicit request. Both peer and supervisory relationships often develop in this manner. Formal mentoring relationships, on the other hand, are marked by intentionality. In a formal relationship, both partners agree to the terms of the relationship and make agreements about its nature. "Facilitated" mentoring programs have become increasingly common on college cam-puses. The Rockefeller and McDonough Center programs described in the section on peer-to-peer learning in Chapter 9 can be classified as "facilitated" mentoring programs (Murray, 2001).

Mentoring is a complex process and is marked by certain characteristics and stages (Karcher et al., 2006). The literature on mentoring suggests that not all mentoring relationships will lead to equally positive outcomes. Campbell et al. (2012), for instance, emphasize the importance of process and position in developing a student's socially responsible leadership capacity. They suggest that the type of mentor influences leadership outcomes (Ragins and Scandura, 1999). Our experience indicates that both student-affairs practitioners and faculty have tremendous influence on learners, but their roles are different. Most faculty are extremely skillful in helping students choose their professional paths, while student-affairs practitioners often place the emphasis on life skills and leadership capacity-building. The important point is that these two types of mentor-ships should coexist, with faculty and staff working together to support the personal and professional growth of a learner.

A successful relationship takes time and effort to develop (Kram, 1983). Zachary (2000) lists the behaviors necessary to progress through the mentoring relationship, including preparation, negotiation, enabling, and closing. During the preparation stage, the tone for the relationship is set and roles defined for the mentor and mentee. Both the mentor and the mentee must recognize their own motivations for entering the relationship, and their readiness to commit to it. Zachary sees this stage as "critical to building and maintaining the relationship and forging the connections that sustain the relationship over time" (2000, p. 65). During the negotiating stage, partners create a shared understanding of expectations, goals, and needs. They can establish a timeline, set a meeting schedule, and discuss boundaries or underlying assumptions about the relationship. In the enabling stage, growth and development become central to the relationship. The mentor can nurture this by establishing an open and affirming learning climate, providing candid and constructive feedback, and reflecting on the learning progress continuously.

The closing stage is not always necessary, because there may be signals that the relationship is no longer effective, or that the goals have been met. For programs that have a set schedule, this last stage may be a good time to evaluate personal learning and celebrate progress. The outcome for this stage will often be dictated by the type and strength of the relationship formed at the beginning.

Ensuring that both individuals have reached a certain level of self-awareness and have established agreed-upon expectations, goals, and needs increases the likelihood for success. Trust and rapport are not built overnight, and each individual and pair are likely to vary in how they progress, but recognizing the continuum of these behaviors is critical to the development of productive mentoring relationships.

As with any relationship, the experiences, skills, and personalities of the individuals involved strongly affect the outcomes. In addition to carefully aligning the interests and personalities of mentor and mentees, mentors are often encouraged to foster certain competencies. Linda Phillips-Jones (2001), author of *The New Mentors and Protégés: How to Succeed with the New Mentoring Partnerships*, identifies four key mentoring skills that result in the most successful mentoring relationships: 1) listening actively; 2) building trust; 3) determining goals and building capacity; and 4) encouraging and inspiring. In addition, mentors need to demonstrate empathy, understand issues from another person's point of view, and dedicate time for this relationship. Through adequate training of mentors and recruitment of positive role models, mentoring programs can create more positive experiences for all parties involved.

During their college years and throughout their lives, individuals are likely to have many different mentors. Ideally, learners should surround themselves with a variety of mentors who can speak to their different needs, ranging from both professional and formal to casual and informal relationships. Jessica Hagy suggests cultivating relationships for a learner's diverse needs that include: someone who will challenge a student (instigator); someone who will motivate and cheer on the student (cheerleader);

someone who plays the devil's advocate (doubter); someone who will push for accomplishment (taskmaster); and someone who facilitates connections to resources (connector).[1]

Although no individual can realistically take on all of these roles, there are certain personality traits and attributes that have been linked with successful and satisfying mentor–mentee relationships. Matching a suitable mentor purposefully to a mentee is crucial to the mentoring process (Bell and Treleaven, 2011), but there is still conflicting evidence on how best to support the pairing process in organizational mentoring programs. Ehrich et al. (2004) found that "professional expertise and/or personality mismatch" was one of the two most frequently cited problems with mentoring relationships. In several studies, mentor pairs formed by a program coordinator achieved satisfactory relationships (Ragins et al., 2000; D'Abate and Eddy, 2008), while other studies demonstrate that participant input into the pairing process was preferable (Allen et al., 2006; Bell and Treleaven, 2011). Participant input is not always feasible and can be a time-consuming process, but, regardless of the way in which the pairing process takes place, educators should put time and effort into ensuring the best possible matches for mentors and mentees.

Educators who engage in planning the implementation of mentorship programs should give adequate attention to the context in which mentoring will take place. The dynamics of culture as well as the student's personal background affect implementation, regardless of the scope of the mentoring program. Given the various challenges and demands each student may face, it becomes important for educators to consider learners' backgrounds and communities to provide the individualized support they need (Zachary, 2000). Educators should be aware of research suggesting that strong mentorship programs have especially positive impacts on vulnerable or underprivileged populations. Mentors in such programs need to demonstrate intercultural competency and be skilled at assessing how a learner's particular background may dictate the support he or she needs. The importance of considering context involves the comparison between the mentor's and mentee's perspectives. Both mentors and educators should develop a "flexible cultural lens" (Zachary, 2000, p. 42), and pay careful attention to assumptions made in cross-cultural situations.

Colleges play an increasingly important role in helping students become authentic, productive, socially responsible, and resilient citizens, and we believe that mentorship and personalized attention are crucial to the personal and professional development of these young adults. Decades of literature have demonstrated a relationship between mentorship and positive student, career, and leadership outcomes (Jacobi, 1991; Kezar and Moriarty, 2000; Dugan and Komives, 2007, 2010; Campbell et al., 2012).

Mutual Benefits to Mentors and Mentees

While the literature on mentorship most often highlights benefits for the mentee, we suggest that the mentor is also likely to gain from the relationship. Mentors may experience enhanced self-awareness, empathy, and listening skills, an increase in self-confidence, clarity of thought, and even potential changes in attitude (Rekha and Ganesh, 2012). The relationship between a mentor and his or her mentee is not typically one-sided. Mentors have an opportunity to reflect on their experiences and improve their own interpersonal skills.

As mentoring programs become increasingly common in universities and organizations, many educators are likely to find themselves in a mentoring role. In designing programs to facilitate mentoring relationships, educators should consider the potential benefits and why mentors choose to be involved (Cho et al., 2011). Through their work, Philip and Hendry (2000) have identified four general explanations for why adults may choose to mentor a youth: 1) to make sense of their own past experiences; 2) to gain insights into another person's life; 3) to establish a different type of relationship; and 4) to build skills in providing a helping relationship.

Thus, by considering what motivates a mentor, educators can make programs more appealing to younger alumni by highlighting mentoring as an opportunity to build leadership competencies. They should also acknowledge when the role might not be a good fit; educators and mentors should not be pressured or reluctantly recruited into these programs, as this can lead to considerable variation in commitment to the mentee and the program itself (Eby and Lockwood, 2005).

For the learners, feeling supported and having deep learning experiences during college become helpful in preparing them for life after graduation. Research over the last few decades has shown that students with a mentor feel more anchored to their school, feel more connected to a larger educational context, perform better academically, are aware of more resources, and have increased agency over their experience (Campbell and Campbell, 2007; Snowden and Hardy, 2013).

Even after several years in college, students are likely to be uncertain about their priorities and goals. During a focus group conducted by the Rockefeller Center with graduating seniors, students discussed the successes and challenges they faced during their college career.[2] All were excited to discuss their entry into college life, and many openly shared how stressful they found the first year in college. They identified major sources of stress, which included anxiety about academic performance, mental health, and financial pressures.

Students also cited a reluctance to seek help or lack of knowledge about where to find it. The stress did not end in their senior year and took on a different meaning. Understandably, as seniors, they were concerned about how prepared they were for life beyond college. Most interestingly, although they were excited about transitioning into the workplace, many were also uncertain about whether the path they had chosen would be meaningful. Such stressors are common among young adults (Park, 2005). We are suggesting that strong mentorship relationships in this example would have been useful in helping to reduce stress and would have also helped the learners to find meaning and purpose.

We share a final observation on the mutual benefits of mentorship to mentors and mentees. Many researchers are finding that students' involvement in mentoring relationships emerges as a powerful predictor of improvement in leadership capacity (Kezar and Moriarty, 2000; Thompson, 2006; Dugan and Komives, 2010). This underscores the importance of incorporating mentorship in leadership programming so that learners receive the support they need to develop personally and professionally.

Examples of Alumni Mentoring Programs

As described above, many factors influence the success of any mentoring program. In this subsection, we describe mentoring programs developed at the McDonough Center and the Rockefeller Center, and the lessons we have learned for successful program implementation.

Example 1: The Rockefeller Alumni Mentoring Program

The Rockefeller Alumni Mentoring Program at Dartmouth was created in 2012 in an effort to connect seniors with recently graduated alumni who have three to five years of work experience in their area of interest. The program selects such alumni specifically as mentors because they are closer in age and experience to seniors. The idea grew from discussions with alumni and seniors about a gap in helping students grow personally and professionally as they move beyond the campus setting.

Alumni discussed the difficulties they faced in adjusting to their first professional challenge after graduation and suggested that the Rockefeller Center create a program that would allow them to share lessons learned with seniors. For their part, seniors welcomed the idea of connecting with young alumni. As a result, this program was designed to help seniors connect with young alumni as mentors for transitioning from an academic environment to a professional one. It also aims to create an ongoing relationship between students and their mentors throughout the students' senior years. The design of this program was unique because a Dartmouth alumna from the Class of 2012 worked with an educator from the Rockefeller Center to implement it. In the initial years, the Dartmouth alumna did all the matching of the mentor and mentee pairs. Now, matching of students to alumni is done by student program assistants. The alumni coordinator for this program, Caitlan Keenan, from the Class of 2012 shared this reflection:

> My opinion of the program is that it fills an important gap in the resources typically available for preparing students to be successful after graduation. While I was in school, I wish that the difficulty of transitioning from school to work was acknowledged or discussed more. Most of my peers dealt with similar feelings of confusion, frustration or inadequacy, but we were all afraid to talk about it! I would have loved to have a venue for discussing that as a senior or as a young graduate, let alone someone to help me identify my growth areas and/ or an action plan to improve them. I feel lucky to have had a really great mentor at work who helped me understand that skills for being successful professionally take time to develop and were often very different from skills needed to succeed at Dartmouth. I hope this program provides other students with a similar venue.

With four cycles of mentorship pairs to date, the program has been able to build a strong, diverse alumni mentor pool and, along with it, a robust library of resources for mentors and mentees. Mentees now have multiple mentors available to them in various topic areas, and the program is able to match pairs based on niche interests. With this growing network, the Rockefeller Alumni Mentoring Program is better able to support students in a wide range of career directions.

In this program, mentors and mentees are required to complete a short application to match mentors to mentees. Once mentors and mentees are matched and accepted into the program, mentors are expected to view a 30-minute mandatory training video in September before being introduced to their mentees. Training for mentors includes an overview of the program, expectations, logistics, and key mentoring techniques. Mentors and mentees are asked to commit to four months of active participation (September through December), but the exact times and methods of communication are determined by individual mentorship pairs. Mentors and mentees are able to meet in person, or through Skype or phone calls at least two times a month. Four newsletters are emailed to mentors and mentees containing conversation starters and articles to build skills in networking and mentoring. Mentors and mentees are requested to complete online surveys and a program evaluation at the end of the program in the fall term.

Like every leadership program offered by the Rockefeller Center, this program undergoes review and subsequent changes every year to make it more responsive to participants. Since the program's establishment, the scope of the program curriculum has extended beyond strictly professional workplace skills. Today, the Rockefeller Alumni Mentoring Program seeks to provide an experience that emphasizes emotional intelligence skills – including authentic listening and effective conversation – and provides opportunities to extend the mentorship beyond the formal program.

The Rockefeller Alumni Mentoring Program now has two different tracks: 1) for students who have already secured a job for after graduation; and 2) for students who do not have a job and are currently applying for jobs, internships, or graduate school. Mentors will be expected to provide guidance according to the needs of their mentee. A website (https://www.dartmouthramp.com/) featuring additional resources for mentors and mentees has been created, and we invite educators to use it for their programming purposes.

Feedback about the value of the Rockefeller Alumni Mentoring Program has been consistent from both mentors and mentees. Surveyed students report growing "comfortable talking to alums and actually enjoy-ing it," while mentors have reported "feeling much less shy about seeking mentorship" for themselves within their own careers. Many alumni report benefiting from their participation in the program, while the students draw information as well as lasting friendships from it. An alumnus, Lee Cooper, from the graduating Class of 2009 provided some reflections on his participation as a mentor:

> Just a few years after graduating from Dartmouth, I was contacted by the Rockefeller Center, in which I had been involved as a student, about a new Rockefeller Alumni Mentoring Program. I gladly offered to participate, both because I thought it would be rewarding to mentor a graduating student, and because my own young career had been aided by so many generous alumni who took an interest in me and my decisions.

These are the kinds of relationships the Rockefeller Center seeks to promote with its mentoring programs, and the Rockefeller Alumni Mentoring Program will continue to seek participant feedback for grow-ing its network and building an even larger database of tools available to alumni. Not all relationships will be as productive and rewarding as the one described above; however, incoming mentors and mentees can learn from both successful and unsuccessful mentoring relationships, as can those educators who plan to develop similar programs in their institutions. In such programs, it is critical to demonstrate the benefit for mentors and create a compelling case for why mentors may want to volunteer time and energy toward the development of someone else. Being clear about "what's in it for mentors" helps to ensure commitment, quality, and engagement.

Example 2: The McDonough Mentorship Program

In another example of engaging alumni as mentors, the McDonough Center offers leadership development opportunities for students from all fields of study at Marietta College. A McDonough Scholar, while going through the four-year Leadership Program, can engage with a McDonough graduate whose career aligns with the student's professional plans. Established in 2007, the purpose of the McDonough Mentorship Program is to provide current leadership students with the opportunity to exchange ideas, seek advice, and expand their knowledge of leadership by engaging with alumni. Mentees may also ask their mentors to review resumes, talk about graduate school, and provide advice about the transition to the world of work. Participants initially communicate with each other primarily through email exchanges. This program is offered through a collaboration between the McDonough Center and Marietta College's Career Center and Alumni Office.

Participation in the McDonough Mentorship Program is optional. At the beginning of each academic year, a call is sent out to the McDonough student body seeking those interested in participating in the program. Students who respond to the call are asked three questions: 1) what major, minor, or certificate they are pursuing; 2) what their career interests are; and 3) what their thoughts are about an "ideal" mentor. We ask the third question, in particular, because the aspiring mentee may have different expectations of the relationship. For instance, a student in the Engineering Leadership Certificate may be interested in having a mentor who started his or her own business involving engineering. A history student, on the other hand, in the minor in Leadership Studies may be interested in a mentor who is working in a museum.

The applications are submitted to the McDonough Dean's Office, which then has the task to find a graduate who matches this expectation. With close to 1000 graduates since its inception in 1987, the office is bound to find a good match. However, if a match is not readily available, the Dean's Office may "negotiate" with the student applicant to find the closest match possible. Every effort is made to find a combination that meets both the student's and the graduate's professional interests.

The program carefully matches students with graduates from the Leadership Program. This prerequisite enables participating alumni to have a clear sense of the student's educational background. However, there have been occasions when the McDonough Center has matched a leadership student with a graduate of the College who did not participate in the program. This usually occurs with alumni who graduated from the College before 1987, when the first McDonough cohort started in the Leadership Program.

Once the match is made, the McDonough Scholars are invited to make the first contact. Beyond that initial contact, the program requests the mentor to take the initiative to keep the relationship going. Mentors make a commitment to a full academic year. That gives an "out" to either participant. However, in some cases, the relationship has continued and even resulted in internships and employment offers. That is not the expectation, though.

For the past decade since the establishment of this program, the Center has learned that alumni are eager to contribute to the mentees' leadership development. The mentors take their commitment very seriously. The "giving back the gift" culture, which is established from the beginning through the EXCEL Workshop (discussed in Chapter 9), continues beyond graduation. The graduates want to contribute to the program in meaningful ways. They relish the fact that the Center is able to engage them in a relationship with students who can update them on the latest curricular and co-curricular activities. This becomes a valuable way to keep the alumni engaged in the life of the Center.

Lessons Learned in Developing Mentoring Programs

As discussed previously, mentoring programs present a dynamic learning opportunity for both mentors and mentees. The Center has observed that most mentors appreciate the opportunity to guide their mentee, and many continue to maintain their relationships long after the formal program has ended. Many mentees also are grateful for the guidance they receive. In mentoring programs, however, there are many challenges and pitfalls that can occur. Key issues our centers have discovered include the struggle to find a suitable mentor–mentee match, the difficulties in establishing robust communication between the pairs, and the attrition of mentors or mentees in the program. In reviewing the causes of attrition, for instance, the Rockefeller Center identified opportunities to train mentors and mentees and added a training component to its program. There are many ways in which the skills of students and alumni can be strengthened. For instance, mentors can be trained: to know the difference between mentoring, coaching, and counseling; to recognize when their mentee needs specialized assistance; and to encourage their mentees to access various resources on campus. Coaching is focused on a certain activity or outcome that a mentor wants to achieve with a mentee. Counseling, on the other hand, is helping students with a particular problem (social, academic, psychological, or personal). Mentors can also be provided with training on emotional intelligence, which can have mutual benefits.

Mentees, on the other hand, can be guided to initiate a mentoring relationship and trained to ask the right questions, move the process forward, and maintain the relationship if they so desire after the formal duration of the program has ended. During this training for mentees, expectations can be established regarding who should reach out to whom and the roles in the relationship. Finally, as mentioned earlier, mentors should ideally be chosen from pools of people who are closer to the mentee's age and stage in life. This said, older and more experienced alumni should also be considered as valuable resources for additional advice and guidance. One way to do this is to invite older alumni to participate in a LinkedIn program, which is then made accessible to current students and younger alumni.

To address the issue of attrition, the most successful strategy has been to establish a program with a fixed time period, a set location, and a congenial environment. Such an environment supports mentoring in small groups or in pairs. In selecting a venue, educators should ensure that conversations can take place in confidence, and that the noise level is not so loud that it drowns out conversations when several groups are meeting in the same location at the same time.

As with any college program, commitment issues arise on both the mentor and the mentee side of the relationship. Mentees and younger college students often have a hard time balancing their schedules, leading to dropouts from the program. Mentors, whether alumni or students, also demonstrate considerable variation in commitment. Such issues appear to be common across similar programs in other institutions. Eby and Lockwood report that unmet expectations and mentor neglect, which both seem to stem from lack of mentor commitment, are two of the most commonly reported problems in mentoring programs (Eby and Lockwood, 2005).

The Rockefeller Center recognizes that students participating in these programs are endowed with a broad range of experiences, personalities, and skills, and that some are more confident than others. The Center's mentoring programs aim to develop students' confidence and facilitate their personal and professional growth. The long-term expectation is that they will develop the skills to reach out to mentors on their own and broaden their networks for personal and professional growth as leaders and engaged citizens.

NETWORKING IN LEADERSHIP PROGRAMS

Students in our leadership programs express discomfort with the concept of networking and feel that it is a process that takes advantage of people. In fact, when asked about networking, students often describe it as "sleazy." We believe that networking is not taking advantage of people for personal benefit, but rather it is the act of finding people who inspire you. Educators should facilitate a discussion about the importance of developing networks as a resource for personal and professional growth and help learners to recognize that developing networks is as tangible and useful as technical skills. In a *Forbes* article, Jessica Hagy makes a compelling case for the idea that an individual needs to help others and be helped by others because "nothing incredible is accomplished alone."[3] Hagy suggests that one needs to find people who can inspire, motivate, or ask difficult questions. There are others who can help our learners to stay on track, and to find allies, new ideas, and mentors.

Investing in "Weak Ties"

Back in the 1970s, sociologist Mark Granovetter developed a pioneering argument that networks can have strong ties (relatives, friends) and weak ties (acquaintances). He argued that "weak ties" actually matter (Granovetter, 1973). After all, acquaintances can provide a valuable connection between social groups. By investing time in "weak ties," our learners can gain access to new groups, which is a critical step into the world of work. There is nothing "sleazy" about networking; it is a strategic move that helps learners make a successful transition out of college. Granovetter called this strategic consideration the "strength of weak ties."

Robert Putnam (2000) has expressed concern that rampant individualism in our society today is weakening the social fabric. He has argued that societies build "social capital" through the networking, collaboration, and interdependence of their members. In particular, he identified two types of social capital – bonding and bridging. Putnam's argument mirrors Granovetter in the sense that bonding social capital deals with the "strong ties" and bridging social capital reflects the importance of "weak ties." Quite often, our learners invest time and energy in developing bonding social capital, but neglect to nurture bridging social capital.[4]

Since the 1990s, there has been an explosion in "how-to" books on networking skill development (e.g., Fisher and Vilas, 1991; Lowstuter and Robertson, 1995; Misner and Donovan, 2008). Networking is presented as a "smart" strategy for personal and organizational success (Baker, 1994; DeNucci, 2011). New technologies, such as LinkedIn, are expanding the concept of networking to include online relationship-building as well. We may even consider adding a third category to Granovetter's network theory – "virtual ties," which will include relationships with people we may never meet. "Social networking" is now an essential part of career development (Salpeter, 2011) and strengthens leadership development.

Strategies for Developing Networks

More recent studies have connected networking to intentional leadership development (Runde, 2016). Building networks can be fun for aspiring leaders. Educators can encourage learners to think of people with whom they share strong or weak ties and intentionally reach out to them. This is an effective way to learn about career paths, professions, or fields of interest to learners. Our experience in helping students to develop networks suggests that they need support to be prepared and intentional, and to gain confidence in approaching others for advice and help.

Students are often reluctant to reach out for help because they think they will be wasting other people's time or they do not know how to initiate conversations. In such instances, students need to be encouraged to go out of their comfort zone and develop questions to start a conversation with people who are accomplished and inspire them. Strategies to help learners develop their networks are provided below. There may be others as well, and we invite educators to experiment with them.

A systematic approach is helpful for developing networks, and educators can help learners in many ways to develop their personal and professional networks. Some of these strategies are listed below:

- Learners can begin by conducting research on the individual or employer with whom they would like to connect. Once they have identified the person, they can begin a conversation based on what they know about the person or organization and talk about common interests. People value sharing their experience, and learners can cultivate such relationships by asking for their knowledge or assistance.

- A rich pool of people with connections includes friends, family members, and alumni. It is surprising how often learners do not think of this group as part of their network for personal and professional growth. While many of them have initiated conversations, follow-up with leads and suggested contacts does not always take place. Learners can be helped with bringing intentionality of purpose to conversations with their personal connections. Students can also help connect other students to their personal connections. This approach might be particularly helpful to first-generation students or students from low-income backgrounds. Oftentimes, these students may not receive the advice they need from their existing personal networks.

- Attending conferences and meetings or formal networking events is another way to develop networks. Educators can help students identify others at such events who have common goals or interests.

The McDonough Center, for instance, hosts a leadership networking lunch once a month. An accomplished leader is invited to have a meal with a small group of seven to ten leadership students. The dress code is "business casual." When introducing themselves, students are asked to provide four items: name; home city and state; major, minor, or certificate; and career plans. These items are selected deliberately to allow students to articulate their plans. Even if these plans change, and they often do, the very exercise of verbalizing them has its own merits.

- Learners often describe the discomfort they feel in approaching strangers. The key is to encourage them to meet others and not just experience these events with other people they already know. If learners are unsure about their networking skills, encourage them to accompany a great networker to an event. Students then have an opportunity to learn a lot by observing and listening. At such events, suggest to the learners that they observe what the person did well and what approaches the learner can adopt. At all times, learners should be encouraged not to imitate an approach with which they are not comfortable.

- Social media platforms such as LinkedIn can be an intentional way to help students establish wider networks with others who have similar interests. Educators can help students establish LinkedIn accounts and demonstrate how they can be of help.

- A chance meeting with an influential and accomplished person can offer learners an opportunity to build their networks. In such an event, educators can encourage learners to be genuine, authentic, and proactive. Being proactive requires the action of asking for contact information or a business card. It includes a follow-up with the new contact within 24–48 hours. If the contact person connects learners to a valuable resource, educators should discuss the need for the learner to let that person know what happened as a result of this connection.

Maintaining Relationships in Personal and Professional Networks

All connections can become part of a learner's personal and professional network, but connections also require an investment of time to develop relationships and friendships. Further, learners should seek to find ways to reciprocate and become a resource for those in their network, and not just seek to have others as resources. Educators can work with learners to identify ways in which students will incorporate this habit in their lives. Students also frequently worry about how to maintain a relationship with people in their network and often feel they will be wasting someone's time or have nothing to offer – particularly if the person in their network is older and more experienced. Educators can reassure students by emphasizing that networking is about building relationships and friendships and that, one day, they will also have the opportunity to "give back" to younger people. Further, older and more experienced people in their network appreciate opportunities to help or share their personal experiences. Educators can then discuss the following approaches to maintaining relationships with personal and professional networks:

- Learners can reach out to their contacts when something reminds them of a contact. They can also ask contacts to share their thoughts and opinions on an article or current event.
- They can send along occasional updates or interesting and relevant information about themselves via email or a phone call to stay in touch. At all times, learners should be aware of the preferred way to communicate.
- Learners can reach out to their contacts in advance of job searches. For example, they can send their resume and the job descriptions of jobs to which they are applying and get feedback to prepare them well for the application or interview process. Learners should follow up with their contacts to let the contacts know about the outcome of the process. It is also an opportunity to reflect on what went well and what could be improved for future searches if a particular search proves to be unsuccessful.
- It is important for educators to discuss with learners ways to remember the information discussed with contacts. Not only does this give the impression that a learner is serious about the advice a contact person has given, but also it is a chance for the learner to build credibility. A good way to remember conversations is to write quick notes either on business cards or electronically. Learners can also keep a simple spreadsheet about conversations they have had.[5]

As a final point, identifying mentors and developing networks are powerful strategies for personal and professional growth. Educators should consider incorporating those activities in their leadership programs. These activities help learners build their communication skills and gain knowledge from several sources and resources. Ultimately, they also create a support system for learners to further develop as individuals and as leaders.

REFLECTION QUESTIONS

1. In what way can you consider the diversity and background of the student to assure a robust mentor–mentee relationship?
2. What considerations are you putting into place to ensure that the position of the mentee is optimal for the relationship and development of the student? What kind of process would you need to put into place to ensure this?
3. How have you crafted a compelling reason for mentors to stay committed and engaged? What is the value for them in mentoring a student, and how might they gain useful knowledge and tools for their own personal and professional development?
4. How is technology changing our concept of "networking"? How can we put it to use based on generational preference and ease of use?
5. What role can you play to help learners further develop their personal and professional networks?

NOTES

1. Jessica Hagy (2012), The 6 People You Need in Your Corner, *Forbes*, July 17. Website (https://www.forbes.com/forbes/welcome/?toURL=https://www.forbes.com/sites/jessicah agy/012/07/17/the-6-people-you-need-in-your-corner/&refURL=&referrer=). Accessed June 15, 2017.
2. This focus-group exercise was conducted in the winter of 2014 with seniors participating in the Rockefeller Leadership Fellows Program. The purpose of the focus group was to understand how students perceived the term "resilience" and to recommend strategies to help students build resilience.
3. Jessica Hagy (2012), The 6 People You Need in Your Corner, *Forbes*, July 17. Website (https://www.forbes.com/forbes/welcome/?toURL=https://www.forbes.com/sites/jessicah agy/012/07/17/the-6-people-you-need-in-your-corner/&refURL=&referrer=). Accessed June 15, 2017.
4. Putnam's concern dealt with the perceived decline of both bonding and bringing social capital. He worried that the decline in membership of social organizations (e.g., bowling leagues) constituted an indication that the forces bringing people together were disappearing in American society. For examples of communities successfully building social capital, see Putnam and Feldstein (2004).
5. Mini-MOOCs developed for the Young African Leaders Initiative in 2014 by Sadhana Hall. Website (https://yali.state.gov/course-855/#/lesson/networking-to-get-ahead-yali?_ k=yy0mr7). Accessed October 25, 2017.

REFERENCES

Allen, T.D. and Eby, L.T. (2008). Mentor Commitment in Formal Mentoring Relationships. *Journal of Vocational Behavior*, 72 (3), 309–16.
Allen, T.D., Eby, L.T., and Lentz, E. (2006). Mentorship Behaviors and Mentorship

Quality Associated with Formal Mentoring Programs: Closing the Gap between Research and Practice. *Journal of Applied Psychology*, 91 (3), 567–78.

Baker, W. (1994). *Networking Smart: How to Build Relationships for Personal and Organizational Success*. New York: McGraw-Hill.

Bell, A. and Treleaven, L. (2011). Looking for Professor Right: Mentee Selection of Mentors in a Formal Mentoring Program. *Higher Education*, 61 (5), 545–61.

Bland, H.W., Melton, B.F., Welle, P., and Bigham, L. (2012). Stress Tolerance: New Challenges for Millennial College Students. *College Student Journal*, 46 (2), 362–76.

Campbell, C.M., Smith, M., Dugan, J.P., and Komives, S.R. (2012). Mentors and College Student Leadership Outcomes: The Importance of Position and Process. *Review of Higher Education*, 35 (4), 595–625.

Campbell, T.A. and Campbell, D.E. (2007). Outcomes of Mentoring At-Risk College Students: Gender and Ethnic Matching Effects. *Mentoring and Tutoring*, 15 (2), 135–48.

Cho, C.S., Ramanan, R.A., and Feldman, M.D. (2011). Defining the Ideal Qualities of Mentorship: A Qualitative Analysis of the Characteristics of Outstanding Mentors. *American Journal of Medicine*, 124 (5), 453–8.

Crisp, G. and Cruz, I. (2009). Mentoring College Students: A Critical Review of the Literature between 1990 and 2007. *Research in Higher Education*, 50 (6), 525–45.

D'Abate, C.P. and Eddy, E.R. (2008). Mentoring as a Learning Tool: Enhancing the Effectiveness of an Undergraduate Business Mentoring Program. *Mentoring and Tutoring: Partnership in Learning*, 16 (4), 363–78.

D'Abate, C.P., Eddy, E.R., and Tannenbaum, S.I. (2003). What's in a Name? A Literature-Based Approach to Understanding Mentoring, Coaching, and Other Constructs That Describe Developmental Interactions. *Human Resource Development Review*, 2 (4), 360–84.

DeNucci, P. (2011). *The Intentional Networker: Attracting Powerful Relationships, Referrals, and Results in Business*. Austin, TX: Rosewall Press.

Dominguez, N. and Hager, M. (2013). Mentoring Frameworks: Synthesis and Critique. *International Journal of Mentoring and Coaching in Education*, 2 (3), 171–88.

Dugan, J.P. and Komives, S.R. (2007). *Developing Leadership Capacity in College Students*. College Park, MD: National Clearinghouse for Leadership Programs.

Dugan, J.P. and Komives, S.R. (2010). Influences on College Students' Capacities for Socially Responsible Leadership. *Journal of College Student Development*, 51 (5), 525–49.

Eby, L.T. and Lockwood, A. (2005). Protégés' and Mentors' Reactions to Participating in Formal Mentoring Programs: A Qualitative Investigation. *Journal of Vocational Behavior*, 67 (3), 441–58.

Eby, L.T., Durley, J.R., Evans, S.C., and Ragins, B.R. (2006). The Relationship between Short-Term Mentoring Benefits and Long-Term Mentor Outcomes. *Journal of Vocational Behavior*, 69 (3), 424–44.

Ehrich, L.C., Hansford, B., and Tennent, L. (2004). Formal Mentoring Programs in Education and Other Professions: A Review of the Literature. *Educational Administration Quarterly*, 40 (4), 518–40.

Fisher, D. and Vilas, S. (1991). *Power Networking: 55 Secrets to Success and Self Promotion*. Houston, TX: DUKE Publishing.

Granovetter, M. (1973). The Strength of Weak Ties. *American Journal of Sociology*, 78 (6), 1360–80.

Jacobi, M. (1991). Mentoring and Undergraduate Academic Success: A Literature Review. *Review of Educational Research*, 61 (4), 505–32.

Karcher, M.J., Kuperminc, G.P., Portwood, S.G., Sipe, C.L., and Taylor, A.S. (2006). Mentoring Programs: A Framework to Inform Program Development, Research, and Evaluation. *Journal of Community Psychology*, 34 (6), 709–25.

Kezar, A. and Moriarty, D. (2000). Expanding Our Understanding of Student Leadership Development: A Study Exploring Gender and Ethnic Identity. *Journal of College Student Development*, 41 (1), 55–69.

Kram, K.E. (1983). Phases of the Mentor Relationship. *Academy of Management Journal*, 26 (4), 608–25.

Lowstuter, C. and Robertson, D. (1995). *Network Your Way to Your Next Job – Fast*. New York: McGraw-Hill.

Mertz, N.T. (2004). What's a Mentor, Anyway? *Educational Administration Quarterly*, 40 (4), 541–60.

Misner, I. and Donovan, M. (2008). *The 29% Solution: 52 Weekly Networking Success Strategies*. Austin, TX: Greenleaf Book Group Press.

Murray, M. (2001). *Beyond the Myths and Magic of Mentoring: How to Facilitate an Effective Mentoring Process*, Revised Edition. San Francisco, CA: Jossey-Bass.

Park, C.L. (2005). Religion as a Meaning-Making Framework in Coping with Life Stress. *Journal of Social Issues*, 61 (4), 707–29.

Philip, K. and Hendry, L.B. (2000). Making Sense of Mentoring or Mentoring Making Sense? Reflections on the Mentoring Process by Adult Mentors with Young People. *Journal of Community and Applied Social Psychology*, 10 (3), 211–23.

Phillips-Jones, L. (2001). *The New Mentors and Protégés: How to Succeed with the New Mentoring Partnerships*. Grass Valley, CA: Coalition of Counseling Centers.

Putnam, R. (2000). *Bowling Alone: The Collapse and Revival of American Community*. New York: Simon & Schuster.

Putnam, R. and Feldstein, L. (2004). *Better Together: Restoring the American Community*. New York: Simon & Schuster.

Ragins, B.R. and McFarlin, D.B. (1990). Perceptions of Mentor Roles in Cross-gender Mentoring Relationships. *Journal of Vocational Behavior*, 37 (3), 321–39.

Ragins, B.R. and Scandura, T.A. (1999). Burden or Blessing? Expected Costs and Benefits of Being a Mentor. *Journal of Organizational Behavior*, 20 (4), 493–509.

Ragins, B.R., Cotton, J.L., and Miller, J.S. (2000). Marginal Mentoring: The Effects of Type of Mentor, Quality of Relationship, and Program Design on Work and Career Attitudes. *Academy of Management Journal*, 43 (6), 1177–94.

Rekha, K.N. and Ganesh, M.P. (2012). Do Mentors Learn by Mentoring Others? *International Journal of Mentoring and Coaching in Education*, 1 (3), 205–17.

Runde, J. (2016). *Unequaled: Tips for Building a Successful Career through Emotional Intelligence*. Hoboken, NJ: Wiley.

Salpeter, M. (2011). *Social Networking for Career Success: Using Online Tools to Create a Personal Brand*. New York: LearningExpress.

Snowden, M. and Hardy, T. (2013). Peer Mentorship and Positive Effects on Student Mentor and Mentee Retention and Academic Success. *Widening Participation and Lifelong Learning*, 14 (1), 76–92.

Thompson, D. (2006). Informal Faculty Mentoring as a Component of Learning to Teach Online: An Exploratory Study. *Online Journal of Distance Learning Administration*, 9 (3), n3.

Zachary, L.J. (2000). *The Mentor's Guide: Facilitating Effective Learning Relationships*. San Francisco, CA: Jossey-Bass.

11. Leadership programming for personal growth

Leadership development does not take place accidentally. It is the product of intentional programming that allows students to expand their knowledge of how leadership works in different contexts. Programming also helps learners acquire critical leadership competencies through practice. Ultimately, educators should want learners to reflect on those experiences, connect them to theories, and grow as thoughtful leaders in the process. A "learning leader" is able to bridge theory and practice in order to gain practical wisdom.

In this chapter, we offer brief descriptions of programs from our respective institutions. Beginning with the goal or the "why" of what we intend our learners to walk away with, we continue by providing a description of how we address an intended goal. Our intention is to share our experiences and provide a space for reflection on how these activities may translate into other educators' own institutional reality. We fully recognize that much of our programming is the product of distinct institutional contexts and hope these programs will create an opportunity for our colleagues in different environments to adopt, adapt, and adjust program ideas to their own realities.

EXAMPLES FROM THE ROCKEFELLER CENTER

Create Your Path (CYP)

Goal: To help students develop a robust process for reflection that leads to actionable steps to achieve personal and professional goals based on identified strengths, interests, and values.

Description: Open to undergraduates of all majors, CYP affords students the opportunity to develop a strategic plan for their future through a process of structured exercises that incorporate self-reflection and practical next-steps planning. The program consists of three sessions: hindsight, insight, and foresight. These three stages build on each other and use a variety of structured activities to guide students through a reflection on defining moments in their lives and identification of strengths, interests, and values before helping them to develop a strategic plan for their continued progress through Dartmouth.

Session 1: Reflecting on your past
Learning objective: Students will practice a reflection process. *Activity*: Students create a list of experiences that have shaped them and begin to prioritize interests.

Session 2: Analyzing your present
Learning objective: Students will be able to articulate a personal statement based on visualized priorities, interests, and abilities. *Activity*: Students create several mind maps to aid them in visualizing any overlap or disconnect between their interests and abilities.

Session 3: Plotting your future
Learning objective: Students will evaluate their lists of priorities, abilities, and interests within a single chart after scanning their environment for resources and mentors. *Activity*: Using Venn diagrams, along with lists of mentors and resources, students then develop a SMART goal and a plan for their future.

First-Year Fellows Program (Civic Skills Training)

Goal: To help students develop and practice communication, management, and leadership skills, gain professional experience, and live and work independently with their peers in Washington, DC.
Description: Open to all first-year students who have completed: Public Policy 5: Introduction to Public Policy; a social science statistical methods course; and the Dartmouth Leadership Attitudes and Behaviors (D-LAB) Program. The First-Year Fellows Program places competitively selected students into summer public policy fellowships in Washington, DC, with Dartmouth alumni living in the area providing mentoring. Students attend four on-campus civic skills training sessions during the spring term and an additional five days of training in Washington, DC before their fellowships begin. Training sessions include topics such as public speaking, networking, professional communication strategies, team-building, advocacy writing, project management, and professionalism.

Writing a constituent letter
(With Ron Shaiko, Senior Fellow and Associate Director for Curricular and Research Programs, Nelson A. Rockefeller Center for Public Policy and the Social Sciences, Dartmouth College)

Learning objective: Students will be able to describe key components of a constituent letter and how to present content effectively as an engaged and informed constituent. *Activity*: Students craft a constituent letter addressed to their member of Congress on a topic of interest to them, researched with relatable examples and a call to action. The letters are then hand-delivered by the students to the members' offices on Capitol Hill.

Shine while you dine
(With Robert Shutt, Etiquette Educator and Author, Public Speaking Professor, Binghamton University)
Learning objective: Students will be able to demonstrate appropriate behavior in professional meal settings and learn to appreciate why courtesy and manners matter. *Activity*: Students participate in a networking and full-course dining experience while listening to a step-by-step etiquette presentation.

Business communications
(With Diane Andreas, Business Communications Consultant)
Learning objective: Students will be able to demonstrate how to clearly and concisely create and respond to various types of business communications. *Activity*: Students review and edit some of their own correspondence created thus far in the program and practice various communications they may encounter during their summer internships.

Teamwork: laying the groundwork for successful group living
(With Elizabeth J. Winslow, Adjunct Assistant Professor of Business Administration Associate Director, M.B.A. Program, Tuck School of Business)
Learning objective: Students will be able to describe the stages of a group's life, identify their own living styles, and discuss possible pitfalls of group living, solutions to potential problems, and how to craft effective living agreements. *Activity*: Students design an agreement that accommodates the various styles of group members.

Thinking and speaking with precision
(With Susan Miller, Ph.D., Principal and Founder of Voicetrainer, LLC)
Learning objective: Students will practice how to use effective body language, project their voices easily, speak clearly and distinctly, introduce themselves and their ideas eloquently, remain poised when challenged, and present succinct, meaningful, and inspirational messages. *Activity*: Students participate in multiple interactive exercises designed to practice and perfect their public-speaking skills and to give and receive feedback.

Advocacy writing with precision
(With Matthew Davis, Health Scientist at the EPA)
Learning objective: Students will learn about various types of advocacy writing and be able to demonstrate a clear, simple, and persuasive message for an identified target audience. *Activity*: Students practice putting together three different types of advocacy writing and share the products and lessons learned with the group.

What to expect on the Hill
(With Ruth Hupart, M.B.A. Candidate at Georgetown's McDonough School of Business)
Learning objective: Students will be able to explain the structure of Congress and how a bill does or does not become a law. *Activity*: Students are led through an interactive exercise mimicking the process of introducing and stewarding a bill through the legislative process.

Networking: the art of give and take
(With Sean Garren, Northeast Regional Manager at Vote Solar)
Learning objective: Students will be able to identify strategies to effectively tap into and grow their network. *Activity*: The group discusses and enacts scenarios that cover everything from chitchat and navigating a room to mapping a network both in person and online in order to help themselves and others.

Fundamentals of project management
(With Sadhana Warty Hall, Deputy Director, Nelson A. Rockefeller Center for Public Policy and the Social Sciences, Dartmouth College)
Learning objective: Students will be able to write SMART goals, list at least seven skills of effective project managers, describe key principles related to project management, and practice developing a project plan. *Activity*: Students participate in a field exercise and group presentation to practice key principles, techniques, and processes, and receive feedback on their experience.

Young alumni experiences in the civic sphere
(With four to five recent Dartmouth alumni)
Learning objective: Students will be able to learn from recent graduates who are currently working in the civic sphere about the various career paths and opportunities taken, lessons learned, and experience gained since graduation. *Activity*: Students and alumni participate in a "world café"-style round-table discussion, which allows for an in-depth Q&A exchange between Fellows and alumni.

Dartmouth Leadership Attitudes and Behaviors (D-LAB)

Goal: To help first-year students discover the relationship between leadership and personal values.

Description: Open to all first-year students. D-LAB provides a time and place for first-year students to discuss their values, explore the correlation between perception, intent, and impact, and seek opportunities for continued leadership growth. D-LAB is a student-facilitated, small group discussion-based program designed for first-year students. The six sessions build progressively from reflection about self, to others, to community. First, students explore their individual beliefs and values and how these relate to their individual identities. They then analyze the relationship between their values and others' values, along with perception, intent, and impact. Finally, they explore how their core values relate to those of the greater Dartmouth community and identify ways to uphold the "principle of community" at Dartmouth College. D-LAB is co-sponsored by the Rockefeller Center and the Collis Center for Student Involvement.

Session one: Leadership from within (character) part I

Learning objective: Students will engage in reflective thinking about the identities and experiences that shape their values and practice of leadership. *Activity*: Through the use of the "Where I Am From" poem template, students complete their own model of multiple dimensions of identity, which enables them to identify at least three attributes of their core identity and three attributes of their social identity.

Session two: Leadership from within (individual values) part II

Learning objective: Students will: assess how values can be lived through actions, behaviors, and experiences; define integrity; and discover what "keeping one's word" means to them. *Activity*: Students identify their top three values and then write out their entire schedule from the previous weekend and look for evidence that their values are reflected in how they spend their time.

Session three: Leadership with others (friends)

Learning objective: Students will analyze and apply the relationship between intent and impact and examine the role of perception in influencing actions and reactions. Students will reflect on the impact of core values on interactions with others and how these interactions result in either positive or negative outcomes. *Activity*: Students analyze real-world scenarios in which values come into conflict and reflect on the dissonance that lies at the core of ethical dilemmas.

Session four: Leadership for others (community) part I

Learning objective: Students will discuss how community values and individual values interrelate and influence one another. *Activity*: Students are tasked with individually listing Dartmouth's top ten values, and then as a group they decide how to rank or visually display everyone's input.

Session five: Leadership for others (community) part II

Learning objective: Students will analyze how their perceived concerns relate to their identities and experiences and explore how to negotiate when their priorities differ from others'. *Activity*: From a pre-existing list (to which they can add) students are asked to rank (with consensus if possible) ten identified community concerns at Dartmouth from least important to most important.

Session six: Leadership in practice (next steps)

Learning objective: Students will reflect on their SMART goals and then gain insight into how to intentionally engage in the Dartmouth community by speaking with representatives from various campus centers and departments about the opportunities available to students. *Activity*: This session invites representatives from departments and centers from all over campus, including first-year deans and the Center for Professional Development. Using a "world café" format, students have the opportunity to explore their interests and their potential involvement with different programs on campus.

Management and Leadership Development Program (MLDP)

Goal: To develop practical competencies and capacities that students can apply in real time within their leadership and management roles on campus, during leave-term internships, and in their careers beyond Dartmouth.

Description: Open to all sophomores, juniors, and seniors. MLDP offers theory and practical instruction on management and leadership skills that students can apply within their leadership and management roles on campus, during leave-term internships, and in their careers beyond Dartmouth. MLDP is a one-term program developed around the skills employers seek. Expert guest speakers facilitate the nine sessions with a blend of theory and hands-on learning exercises of core management and leadership skills. An off-campus visit also takes place during the term to provide students with the opportunity to explore management and leadership practices at a local business or nonprofit organization. Participants work individually and in small groups throughout the program to develop practical skills that they can apply immediately to their leadership roles on campus, during leave-term internships, and in their careers after Dartmouth.

Session 1: Taking ownership of your leadership development
(With Sadhana Warty Hall, Deputy Director, Nelson A. Rockefeller Center for Public Policy and the Social Sciences, Dartmouth College)
Learning objective: Students will learn to take ownership of their own leadership development and understand the purpose of the personal leadership challenge and how to craft SMART goals in addressing their challenge. *Activity*: Casual Thursdays, an on-campus improv group, helps to set the tone for challenging assumptions and cultivating a growth mindset.

Session 2: Using your strengths for effective professional communication
(With Jennifer Sargent, Visiting Associate Professor of Writing, Institute for Writing and Rhetoric, Dartmouth College)
Learning objective: Students will review the characteristics of all 16 combinations of the Myers–Briggs communication types and be able to analyze their strengths and those of their teammates to work most effectively in a workplace. *Activity*: After analyzing their Myers–Briggs test results, students compose a list of existing strengths and a list of things they would like to build on, or into, their oral communication style.

Session 3: Understanding your strengths in the context of management and leadership
(With Gama Perruci, Dean of the McDonough Leadership Center and McCoy Professor of Leadership Studies, Marietta College)
Learning objective: Students will analyze similarities and differences between management and leadership, examine how strengths – defined as a preferred way of thinking, feeling, and behaving – may be categorized into the areas of management, leadership, or a combination of both. *Activity*: Having completed a strengths test, each student then identifies his or her top three strengths related to management or leadership, and potential areas of improvement. In small groups, students then categorize all identified strengths into either management or leadership and discuss as a group their determinations.

Session 4: Presenting yourself professionally
(With Dave Uejio, Strategy Program Manager at the Consumer Financial Protection Bureau)
Learning objective: Students will become comfortable responding to the common interview or professional request to "Tell me about yourself." *Activity*: While being recorded, students present to their peers and provide

support and feedback to each other. Recordings optimize critique and reflection.

Session 5: Being an effective team player

(With Steven Spaulding, Assistant Athletic Director for Leadership, Dartmouth College)

Learning objective: Students will describe and discuss how to engage team members and ensure that all members of a team contribute to a chosen goal. Students will learn how to identify and draw upon the strengths of individual team members, understand and value the concept of a "growth mindset," and learn that any challenge can be addressed through appropriate leadership. *Activity*: In small groups, students participate in a competitive activity where only effective teamwork will allow them to reach their end goal.

Session 6: Building relationships

(With Kate Hilton, Director, ReThink Health, Faculty and Strategic Advisor, Institute for Healthcare Improvement, Principal in Practice, Leading Change Project at Harvard University)

Learning objective: Students will explain why structure matters within and between teams and how to establish the essential conditions that enable teams to function effectively. *Activity*: Students evaluate a team they belong to using a diagnostic checklist. They use their own experiences as mini-case studies for the group at large to discuss and brainstorm solutions in real time together.

Session 7: Problem-solving, decision-making, and negotiation

(With John Burwell Garvey, Professor and Director, Daniel Webster Scholar Honors Program at the University of New Hampshire School of Law)

Learning objective: Students will develop an understanding of how to iden-tify and analyze problems, the process involved in constructive decision-making, and the basic tools and processes used in negotiation. *Activity*: In small groups, students work on a negotiation and decision-making simulation deciding two crucial elements of a life-or-death situation. Two small groups join together and must renegotiate the elements, but in a competitive manner.

Session 8: Communication in the workplace

(With Jennifer Sargent, Visiting Associate Professor of Writing, Institute for Writing and Rhetoric, Dartmouth College)

Learning objective: Students will learn best practices to apply to their workplace writing. They will be able to identify what language makes the best impression and what language is appropriate and inappropriate, professional and unprofessional, and accurate and inaccurate. They will be able to identify their audience and learn how to target their message. *Activity*: Each student assesses an assigned workplace situation, identifies the key audience(s), and demonstrates how to use a communication technique to effect a positive outcome.

Session 9: Connecting the parts
(With Robin Frye, Program Officer, Nelson A. Rockefeller Center for Public Policy and the Social Sciences, Dartmouth College)
Learning objective: Students reflect upon the connections between each session's key takeaways. *Activity*: Beginning individually, and then progressing into small and then large group discussions, students participate in a "gallery walk" exercise that facilitates drawing connections between their and other participants' key takeaways.

Off-campus session
(With community businesses and organizations)
Learning objective: Students will analyze management and leadership challenges faced by an organization. *Activity*: Students choose between visiting a nonprofit and for-profit organization, take part in a brief tour, and then work through some case studies with employees.

Rockefeller Global Leadership Program (RGLP)

Goal: To prepare students for leadership roles in a culturally diverse yet interdependent world.
Description: Open to sophomores, juniors, and seniors. RGLP, a one-term program, prepares students with cultural understanding, flexibility, communication skills, and an ability to utilize technology that brings people together who share similar goals but not necessarily culture, worldview, or communication style. Weekly sessions are led by a variety of facilitators, who employ experiential learning techniques that encourage students to practice intercultural competencies both in a classroom setting and during a weekend learning experience in Montreal, New York City, or Boston.

Session 1: Introduction to the Rockefeller Center Global Leadership Program and program overview
(With Sadhana Warty Hall, Deputy Director, Nelson A. Rockefeller Center for Public Policy and the Social Sciences, Dartmouth College)
Learning objective: Students will be able to discuss their expectations of

the program, introduce themselves to one another, and review details related to program sessions. Each student will know at the end of this session the names of his or her peers and one anecdote about that person's unique background. *Activity*: Students participate in group exercises to get to know each other, share their expectations, and learn about program sessions.

Session 2: Intercultural developmental inventory (IDI): assessing cultural proficiency
(With Amy Newcomb, Senior Programs Officer, and Casey Aldrich, Students Program Manager, Dickey Center for International Understanding, Dartmouth College)
Learning objective: After completing the IDI assessment, students will be able to analyze their own progression, as well as the group's, along the continuum of cross-cultural competence based upon a compilation of their group scores as described in the IDI. *Activity*: Students take part in a "pacing activity" that illuminates communication styles: pauses, turn-takers, and overlappers.

Session 3: Framing global leadership and developing a global consciousness
(With Gama Perruci, Dean of the McDonough Leadership Center and McCoy Professor of Leadership Studies, Marietta College)
Learning objectives: Students will be able to: define four key terms associated with globalization ("global awareness," "global attentiveness," "global consciousness," and "global citizenship"); examine some of their own cultural assumptions; and draw conclusions about different leadership strategies to develop global consciousness. *Activity*: Students are asked to self-assess where they are and to place themselves around the room respectively; afterwards, they participate in a "share-out" to explain why they placed themselves where they did. Through the Albatros simulation, students explore how the concept of global consciousness relates to their own leadership development in the context of a global environment.

Session 4: Cultural fluency: understanding the other by developing self
(With Dottie Morris, Ph.D., Chief Officer of Diversity and Multiculturalism, Keene State College)
Learning objective: Students will be able to: demonstrate understanding of personal culture; describe the importance of racial, ethnic, and cultural privilege; reflect on the impact of racial, ethnic, and cultural privilege for shaping attitudes and beliefs; and work with other students to define culture, privilege, and ethnocentrism. *Activity*: By use of the scattered chair exercise, student learn the basics of "being comfortable being

uncomfortable" and explore the accuracy of assumptions they make of others through small group discussion.

Session 5: Capoeira
(With Fábio Nascimento, Capoeira Instructor, Lecturer at the University of Vermont)
Learning objective: Students will be introduced to a new cultural framework and art form – capoeira, a Brazilian style of dance. This activity takes students outside their comfort zone and allows them to reflect on the implications of working in a culture different from their own. *Activity*: Students participate in capoeira. They examine their reactions and application to situations outside their comfort zone.

Session 6: Action and participation in intercultural communication
(With Uju Anya, Ph.D., Assistant Professor of Second Language Learning, Research Affiliate, Center for the Study of Higher Education, Pennsylvania State University, College of Education)
Learning objective: Students will be able to analyze how language, both oral and written, shapes thought, discourse, and interaction. Students will learn how to critically analyze the roles power, dominance, and inequity play in intercultural communication. *Activity*: Reflection exercises, using intercultural praxis activity and group discussion, guide participants to understand and deconstruct an individual's many selves, which may exist across linguistic and cultural boundaries.

Session 7: Refugees: stories of oppression, resilience, and hope
(With Courtney Perron, Community Outreach Coordinator, Lutheran Social Services: Services for New Americans)
Learning objective: Students will gain familiarity with the refugee resettlement process as it pertains to the United States and New Hampshire. Students will explore concepts including economic stability, mentorship (as enabling versus empowering), and the role of the United Nations High Commissioner for Refugees. *Activity*: Participants talk with several individuals who have personally experienced the resettlement process and conclude the session with a collective, reflective activity.

Session 8: Montreal field immersion
Learning objective: Participants will have the opportunity to reflect upon lessons learned so far while in a different geographical location and within several different cultural contexts. *Activity*: Students take part in a self-guided, data collection activity throughout the city of Montreal, Quebec, which includes suggested questions to ask locals, prompts to learn about

the metropolitan city, and tasks to facilitate interactive observations. They participate in a D/deaf culture workshop led by Seeing Voices Montreal, a nonprofit that raises awareness of the D/deaf community through educa-tion. Students also experience a guided meal at restaurant O'Noir, which operates in the dark and is served by visually impaired staff. Reflection about these activities as well as the program is key. Similar programs are offered in New York City and Boston.

Session 9: Translating theory to practice

(With Sadhana Warty Hall, Deputy Director, Nelson A. Rockefeller Center for Public Policy and the Social Sciences, Dartmouth College)
Learning objective: Students will connect at least three of the previous sessions' learning objectives to interpret their Montreal experiential field excursion. *Activity*: Participants give small group presentations about their experiences in Montreal and lessons learned from previous sessions. Debriefs following New York City or Boston are designed in a similar fashion.

Rockefeller Peer Mentoring Program (RPMP)

Goal: To provide networking opportunities and resources to students seek-ing guidance from peers, faculty, and staff with shared interests in public policy.
Description: Open to all first-year students, juniors, and seniors. RPMP pairs first-year students interested in leadership and public policy with juniors or seniors active in programs at the Rockefeller Center. The pro-gram provides a resource for students seeking experience in public policy, expands awareness of resources at the Rockefeller Center and throughout campus, develops networking and mentorship skills that will be vital in the professional world, and provides a mechanism through which seniors can give back to the Rockefeller Center and the Dartmouth community.

Kick-off session

Students are introduced to each other, are matched by policy area of inter-est, and learn some networking best practices.

Identifying resources and mentoring hours

Students are given the opportunity to informally socialize in pairs or in small groups while learning about resources for internship opportunities.

Campus connections gathering

Open to all undergraduates, this event gives students the opportunity to chat with experienced faculty and staff about career choices, resources on and off campus, and the pros and cons of pursuing various paths to reach their academic and professional goals.

Social media networking and mentoring hours
Students are given another opportunity to informally socialize in pairs or in small groups while learning about best practices for utilizing social media to grow their professional network.

D-Plan strategies and mentoring hours
Students are given another opportunity to informally socialize in pairs or in small groups while discussing tips for developing their D-Plan to meet their academic and career goals.

Closing event
Students are able to use this event, which is held during the Rockefeller Center's senior appreciation barbeque, as a way to practice their networking skills and to reflect with their partner on what they learned during the term.

Rockefeller Leadership Fellows Program (RLF)

Goal: To motivate seniors to deeply reflect upon their leadership skills and experiences as well as those of their peers and mentors in preparation for leadership challenges after graduation.

Description: Open to all seniors. The RLF Program provides Fellows with resources in leadership theories and practical skills. As they take part in the workshops, dinner discussions, and team-building exercises, students gain a better understanding of the qualities and responsibilities expected of leaders and how to adapt their own leadership styles to different situations. Throughout the program, Fellows learn from the insights and experiences of distinguished guests, as well as from each other. During the spring term, Fellows participate in selecting their successors in the program.

Leadership, establishing credibility, and building power
(With David Ager, Director of Undergraduate Studies and Lecturer on Sociology, Department of Sociology, Harvard University)

Learning objective: Students will recognize how the performance appraisal process can support larger organizational goals and provide opportunities for employees to become involved in the career development process.

Activity: Using a case study and role-play, students practice conducting sensitive performance evaluations and coaching techniques.

How to frame three hard cases
(With Sonu Bedi, Associate Professor, Department of Government, Dartmouth College)
Learning objective: Students will have a greater sensitivity to the role language plays in framing debate and be able to craft language in a way that invites dialogue rather than discord. *Activity*: Through the use of three case studies, students encounter situations where the language of rights often generates disputes and stalemate rather than genuine engagement.

Facilitative leadership: blending individual styles to achieve common goals
(With Jay Davis, Program Officer, Department of Education, Tucker Foundation, Director, First-Year Summer Enrichment Program – FYSEP)
Learning objective: Students will be able to identify their own and others' individual styles and voices and come to appreciate that the ability to recognize team members' individual styles is a necessary skill to move the group toward a collective goal. *Activity*: The leadership compass activity is based on a Native American-based practice called "the medicine wheel" or "the four-fold way." Students reflect on their styles and work through an exercise which highlights various strategies for successful facilitative leadership.

In the arena: translating thought into action as a young leader
(With Nathaniel C. Fick, Chief Executive Officer, Endgame, Inc., Author of *One Bullet Away: The Making of a Marine Officer*, and Dartmouth Trustee)
Learning objective: Students will be able to distinguish between formal and informal authority, recognize that authority can be delegated but responsibility cannot, and be able to appreciate that duty runs both upward and downward in an organization. *Activity*: Using real-life scenarios, students examine the realities of leadership and its dangers and rewards.

Don't go it alone: effective delegation and empowerment for leaders
(With Alison Fragale, Professor of Organizational Behavior, Kenan-Flagler Business School, University of North Carolina at Chapel Hill, Nelson A. Rockefeller Center Board of Visitors)
Learning objective: Students will be able to: assess their current level of delegation within their leadership role; identify what else could be delegated to others; determine how it should be delegated (using the E–P–O model); and decide to whom it should be delegated. *Activity*: Using a classic puzzle game, the tanagram, students experience first-hand the consequences of practicing, or ignoring, various levels of delegation.

Emergent leadership for life

(With Kate Hilton, Director, ReThink Health, Faculty and Strategic Advisor, Institute for Healthcare Improvement, Principal in Practice, Leading Change Project at Harvard University)

Learning objective: Students will be able to visualize their first steps as leaders after leaving Dartmouth and be able to describe why distributed leadership is essential to generating the power needed to effect change. *Activity*: In small groups, students discuss the essential conditions that enable leadership teams to function effectively and reflect on their hopes for their own leadership legacies.

Letting others have it your way: the art and science of negotiation

(With Brian Mandell, Senior Lecturer in Public Policy and Director, Kennedy School Negotiation Project)

Learning objective: Students will examine both the analytical and the interpersonal dimensions of negotiation and be able to identify which negotiation strategies work best in certain situations. *Activity*: Using multi-party simulations, students practice the ability of leaders to negotiate successfully and discover how good negotiation rests on a combination of analytical and interpersonal skills.

Systems thinking and leadership

(With Steve Peterson, Independent Consultant and Senior Lecturer, Thayer School of Engineering, Dartmouth College)

Learning objective: Students will gain a first-level fluency in using "stocks and flows" to represent system structure and in understanding the role of feedbacks, delays, and nonlinearities in system behavior, and they will learn how to apply systems thinking in a leadership context. *Activity*: By use of the production–distribution game (also known as "the beer game") students experience in real time the dynamics of system structure and how they personally react in various roles.

Making your ideas stick

(With Peter Robbie, Professor, Thayer School of Engineering, Dartmouth College)

Learning objective: Students will be able to identify and implement several brainstorming methods and gain insight into how playful, safe, and focused creative collaboration can provide solutions to long-standing community problems. *Activity*: By use of several brainstorming tools, such as provocative operation statements (or "po statements"), students ideate on some Dartmouth-specific areas for improvement.

Leadership and the curse of natural resources
(With Andrew Samwick, Director, Nelson A. Rockefeller Center for Public
Policy and the Social Sciences, Sandra L. and Arthur L. Irving Professor
of Economics, Dartmouth College)
Learning objective: Students will become aware of what is meant by the
"natural resource curse" and how leaders can avoid falling victim to it.
Activity: Using lecture and discussion, students discuss examples of the
"natural resource curse" from economics and other fields.

Leadership in civil society
(With Ron Shaiko, Senior Fellow and Associate Director for Curricular
and Research Programs, Nelson A. Rockefeller Center for Public Policy
and the Social Sciences, Dartmouth College)
Learning objective: Students will be able to identify qualities that best serve
civil-society leaders in achieving and maintaining social networks and
utilizing such networks for the common good. *Activity*: Using lecture and
discussion, students will analyze the Dartmouth community as a test case
for civil society.

Contemporary leadership competencies
(With Harry Sheehy, Director of Athletics and Recreation, Dartmouth
College)
Learning objective: Students will analyze the different character qualities
of followers and be able to identify energy-taking traits and energy-giving
traits, both in themselves and in others. They will be able to construct a
clear vision and identify how to foster a group's motivation by repeating
this vision. *Activity*: Several small group and individual reflection activities
allow students to assess their own strengths and weaknesses as leaders.

Filter bubbles: how we process data and make decisions
(With Curt Welling, M.B.A., J.D., Senior Fellow, Tuck School of Business,
Dartmouth College)
Learning objective: Students will learn how individuals process and internalize information and how that process leads to an individual's perspective and,
in turn, informs decisions. *Activity*: Using lectures and discussions, students
draw from their own experiences and share how they made certain decisions.

The art of telling people what they don't want to hear
(With Charles Wheelan, Senior Lecturer and Public Policy Fellow, Nelson
A. Rockefeller Center for Public Policy and the Social Sciences, Dartmouth
College)
Learning objective: Students will be able to identify the gap between the

intellectual understanding of policies and the public perception of the same policies and to understand how people process policies and political messages. *Activity*: Using lecture and discussion, students draw upon their understanding of current events to examine various examples of policies and political messaging.

Leadership, personal development, and the feedback cycle
(With Betsy Winslow, Adjunct Assistant Professor of Business Administration, Tuck School of Business, Dartmouth College)
Learning objective: Students will gain an understanding of the following four leadership areas: personal excellence, situational control, managing relationships, and achieving results. *Activity*: Using case studies and role-play, students practice giving and receiving feedback, which is essential in all four areas.

Rockefeller Alumni Mentoring Program (RAMP)

Goal: To foster a community of support amongst Dartmouth alumni pursuing careers in public policy.
Description: Open to graduating seniors and young alumni three to five years post-graduation. RAMP pairs graduating seniors with recent Dartmouth graduates. The entire program takes place off campus within the first four months after graduation to facilitate the recent graduate's transition into the professional world. Mentees are given the chance to benefit from a powerful resource and strong network of alumni matched to their field of interest, while mentors practice leadership and mentoring skills that can boost their professional careers. A successful mentorship results in an ongoing go-to relationship, strengthened confidence, and plans to achieve personal and continuing career goals.

Matching and training
Following the application process, program coordinator and alumni volunteer Caitlin Keenan matches mentors and recent graduates through a combination of policy area of interest, experience, and geographic location. Alumni mentors are asked to watch the following training video: https://youtu.be/0FcQ9mkkb0I.

Kick-off
The mentorship officially kicks off via an introductory email. This email introduces the pair and briefly explains how they were matched before explaining best practices of connection, such as connecting face to face for at least the first time (either in person or by means of video chat).

Newsletters

Four newsletters are sent out, in July, August, September, and October, with opportunities offered to match additional or alternative mentors as needed.

Closing survey

The program officially concludes in October, and participants are asked to complete a closing survey. Pairs are encouraged to stay in communication on their own.

EXAMPLES FROM THE MCDONOUGH CENTER

The McDonough Leadership Program (McDLP)

Goal: McDLP helps students gain a deeper understanding of leadership, practice their leadership skills, and in the process grow as engaged leaders on campus, in the local community, and beyond.

Description: The McDonough Leadership Program (also referred to as the Scholars Program) is open to undergraduate students from all majors, who are accepted into the program through a separate selection process. The program offers five academic tracks: International Leadership Studies major (a comprehensive four-year program); minor in Leadership Studies (a four-year program, which can be combined with any major on campus); Certificate in Leadership Studies (a two-year program, which goes well with majors with a heavy course load); Teacher Leadership Certificate (especially designed for students in the Education major); and Engineering Leadership Certificate (especially designed for students in the engineering field). Students apply to the Scholars Program when they are seniors in high school. Once they are accepted to Marietta College, students with high academic credentials are invited to apply to the Scholars Program. The McDonough Selection Committee reviews all applications and makes decisions based on three criteria: academic achievement; a strong record of leadership involvement in both high school and the community; and thoughtful application answers. For the 2018–2019 academic year, 75 students were selected from the incoming freshman class to participate in the Scholars Program.

Leadership Consultants Projects

Goal: To provide McDonough Scholars with opportunities to practice their leadership skills and in the process gain a deeper understanding of their own leadership styles.

Description: Open to all McDonough Scholars. McDonough provides short-term consulting projects that allow the McDonough Scholars to work in teams and experience the different stages of project development, implementation, and evaluation. Students are provided with opportunities, including local, national, and global projects. For instance, a team of McDonough Scholars recently organized and ran a candidates' debate for the municipal court judge elections. Another team worked as a research satellite for the America's Best Leaders Project, a collaboration between Harvard Kennedy School's Center for Public Leadership and *U.S. News & World Report*. In our final example, a team prepared a youth leadership development program that a Peace Corps volunteer (also a McDonough graduate) implemented in Paraguay. McDonough faculty and staff served as project advisers and engaged the team in "pre-flection" and reflection.

NextGen Program

Goal: To create an understanding about the inner workings of nonprofit boards through an intentional leadership immersion experience with a nonprofit.

Description: Open to all Marietta College students, regardless of class and major. The McDonough Center's Office of Civic Engagement (OCE) oversees the NextGen Program through its grant-funded Nonprofits LEAD initiative. The mission of Nonprofits LEAD is to build a strong, sustainable nonprofit community in the Mid-Ohio Valley in which every organization is able to effectively and efficiently achieve its mission. NextGen places each participating student on a local nonprofit board of directors. The students act as full board members, attending meetings, participating on a committee, and in most cases having voting rights. At the same time, they meet as a group each week to discuss their experiences, reflect, and gain support from their peers and faculty. The program spans three semesters. In the first semester, students learn about board governance and work toward conducting an organizational-capacity assessment for the group they are working with. The Center helps them use the information they have learned to analyze the organization's strengths, weaknesses, opportunities, and threats. In the second semester, students use information learned to identify a capacity need or opportunity, and then work with the organization to design a project to meet that need. During the semester, the students receive training on grant writing in class. They also evaluate each other's applications and make decisions about which grants will be awarded, which gives them experience as philanthropists or investors. In the final semester, students are given the freedom to design and implement a service-learning project that connects their academic interests and skills with their organization's mission. In small groups, students in the past have created employee-appreciation programs, promotional films, marketing campaigns, board retreats, and more. The program can be taken as a class for academic credit, or it can be done as a co-curricular or volunteer project. The Center builds the meeting times for the group around their class schedules.

Alternative Break Program

Goal: To give students an opportunity to develop critical-thinking skills in the context of social-justice issues.

Description: Open to all students on campus. An "alternative break" is a general term for a student-led trip that includes education, service, and reflection. Alternative breaks at Marietta College involve students in meaningful service while providing them with opportunities to learn about and experience diverse cultures. Additionally, they engage in reflection, analysis, and discussion about important social issues. The McDonough Center's Office of Civic Engagement (OCE), in partnership with the Student Life's Office of Campus Involvement and the Office of Diversity and Inclusion, organizes two types of alternative break programs: an international service trip during the winter break and a domestic program during spring break. These programs help OCE fulfill its mission "to empower students to be active leaders in their communities, promote critical thinking about social-justice issues, and develop citizens committed to a lifetime of public service."

McDonough Leadership Study Abroad Program

Goal: To foster in our students an appreciation for cultural diversity, cross-cultural leadership challenges, and the foundation for understanding global leadership issues.

Description: Open to all students on campus. The McDonough Center's Leadership Study Abroad Program provides opportunities for students to travel abroad and learn more about leadership. Through these experiences, students are asked to expand their thinking about global leadership issues and to consider a more significant immersion, such as a semester or a year-long program abroad. The Leadership Study Abroad Program offers four main types of trips: 1) travel to international conferences; 2) exchange visits; 3) international experience for students in the International Leadership Studies major; and 4) a for-credit undergraduate course. Every spring after graduation, the McDonough Center organizes a study trip under LEAD 350 (leadership study abroad). This for-credit trip allows a faculty member to take a group of students to study a country or countries experiencing significant changes. Countries explored under these faculty-led trips have included Peru, Costa Rica, Belize, Thailand, Cambodia, Hungary, Brazil, and China. Trips to international conferences have taken students to countries such as Belgium, Spain, Canada, the Czech Republic, and the U.K.

McDonough Bloggers Program

Goal: To help McDonough Scholars reflect on their cross-cultural experiences while studying abroad.

Description: Open to all McDonough Scholars who have completed the core courses in the McDonough curriculum, including global leadership (LEAD 203). During their junior year, many McDonough Scholars choose to study abroad as part of the experiential requirement for the major in International Leadership Studies and the minor in Leadership Studies. While abroad, they participate in the McDonough Bloggers Program, which encourages leadership students to reflect on their study-abroad experiences through blogging. For students who are studying abroad in the spring semester, blogging also becomes an opportunity to exchange ideas with students taking the sophomore-level LEAD 203 class (global leadership). LEAD 203 students are required to follow at least one of the blogs and write comments during the spring semester. Through their study-abroad experiences, McDonough Scholars are able to expand the LEAD 203 students' global perspective while developing their own critical-thinking skills. Recently, McDonough Scholars have blogged from a wide variety of countries, including China, Germany, Italy, Spain, France, Finland, and Ireland.

"In-Residence" Programs

Goal: To give students an opportunity to interact with accomplished leaders in an environment that allows the latter to share their leadership wisdom with the program participants.

Description: Open to all students on campus. The McDonough Center offers three types of "in-residence" programs. The Visiting Executive Program provides short-term interaction between accomplished leaders and students – normally lasting a day or two. The visiting executives serve as guest lecturers, have meals with a small group of students, and meet one on one with participants for interactive coaching sessions. The Fitzgerald Executive-in-Residence (EIR) Program allows an accomplished executive to work collaboratively with a group of students to develop and implement a year-long project that involves a culminating experience. For instance, a senior executive worked with a group of students to study the feasibility of using drones in the delivery of packages. The students were divided into three teams (business, government regulations, and engineering). The group presented their findings to executives at FedEx Ground. The Schwartz Leader-in-Residence (LIR) Program rotates among different academic departments. Through an endowment established for the purpose of supporting the infusion of leadership education across campus, the McDonough Center works collaboratively with faculty from a wide variety of fields to bring to their department a leader-in-residence who implements a year-long project with a group of students from the hosting department. For instance, the Music Department recently hosted the Executive Director of the Ohio Arts Council, who worked with music students to develop greater knowledge and skills in the advocacy of music and the arts. The culminating experience for the LIR Program involved a highly successful festival – the Brick Street Bash – in downtown Marietta, featuring music, visual art exhibitions, performances, speakers, and other presentations.

Leadership Experiential Education Fund (LEEF)

Goal: To support the experiential learning of the McDonough Scholars as they seek to expand their knowledge of leadership, enhance their leadership competencies, and grow as thoughtful leaders.

Description: All McDonough Scholars are eligible to apply to receive a LEEF grant during their college career at Marietta. LEEF grant applications are reviewed on a rolling basis, unless specific deadlines are announced in a separate email message to the McDonough Scholars. The action pillar of the McDonough Leadership Program is based on the idea that students develop new insights about leadership by taking their knowledge and applying it to the "real world" in a guided experiential education setting. At McDonough, this experiential education focus involves five types of activities: internships, study abroad, service-project trips, conference participation, and undergraduate research (e.g., honors thesis). LEEF supports participation in these five areas by giving grants to leadership students to use for their experiential education activities. LEEF grants provide powerful eye-opening experiences that shape the students' professional paths beyond college. While the McDonough Center offers intellectually stimulating seminars that expose our students to the latest concepts and models of leadership, experiential education provides a bridge from the classroom to the world at large. Students are then able to see how the concepts and models work in the "real world."

McDonough Leadership Conference

Goal: To promote undergraduate research in the field of leadership studies and to develop the project management skills of McDonough Scholars by providing them with the opportunity to organize and implement a national leadership conference.

Description: This national event brings together undergraduate leadership students from many different institutions. The conference was established in the spring of 2010, following the death of a beloved political-science faculty member at Marietta College. Melissa Varga (McDonough Cohort 20) came up with the idea of a conference focusing on women and political leadership, which was the main research topic of the political-science faculty member. Varga took on the leadership role of organizing the conference with the support of the McDonough Center. The success of the first event prompted the Center to build the conference as a national gathering, focusing on undergraduate research in the area of leadership studies. The conference also gives the McDonough Scholars a valuable opportunity to gain practical leadership skills. The conference chair and assistant conference chair are always upper-class McDonough Scholars. The leadership rotation system is similar to that of the EXCEL Workshop, using an apprenticeship model. The assistant chair serves as an apprentice being mentored by the conference chair. In the subsequent year, the assistant chair becomes the conference chair and selects an assistant to serve as his or her apprentice. The dean serves as the faculty adviser for this conference, and the chair selects a group of McDonough Scholars to serve as conference guides entrusted with the responsibility of providing logistical support during the event. The conference chair and assistant chair meet regularly with the faculty adviser as they develop the plans for the conference.

Great Decisions Series (Foreign Policy Association Program)

Goal: To give local community members an opportunity to discuss critical issues involving American foreign policy; and to allow McDonough Scholars to practice their facilitation skills.

Description: McDonough Scholars who are either going through or have completed McDonough's facilitation-skills training are eligible to participate in the program. The series is part of an annual national project organized by the Foreign Policy Association (FPA), with headquarters in New York City. The program is held all over the United States, and McDonough serves as one of the host communities. The McDonough program is offered on Sunday afternoons for six weeks beginning in January.

An upper-class McDonough Scholar serves as the program coordinator. The weekly sessions are divided into two parts: 1) a guest speaker reviews the topic as an expert in the field; and 2) subsequent discussion of the topic is facilitated by the leadership students. The McDonough Scholars are trained in facilitation and use this discussion as an opportunity to practice their leadership skills. Before adjourning, each participant completes an opinion ballot. The ballot information then is sent to the FPA, which drafts a report showing public opinion on pertinent topics involving U.S. foreign policy.

CONCLUDING REMARKS

The examples provided in this chapter give educators a wide variety of activities that can be generated through careful consideration of students' maturity and developmental stages. In some cases, we have purposefully targeted our programming to first-year students alone. Such programs help our students transition to a higher level of learning beyond high school. In others, we focus on seniors as they prepare to make the transition out of college.

Educators also may have noticed that we connect theory to practice through reflection. Reflection and debriefing are critical components of the learning process. The activities listed above always include a reflection component, which enables participants to draw insights that lead to personal and professional growth. We invite educators to build their programming by keeping the goal, or the "why" of their program, in mind first. The "how" is next. This sequence ("why," then "how") is important, because it provides the linkage between theory and practice.

REFLECTION QUESTIONS

1. What programs or ideas may be relevant to your institutional context?
2. How might you adopt, adapt, or adjust ideas presented in this chapter?
3. What resources (faculty, staff, or alumni) can you tap into for ideas presented here that are not in your current program offerings and that you might be interested in incorporating?

12. Concluding thoughts on teaching leadership

We began this book with a simple question: "Can we teach leadership?" We hope that the answer ("Yes, we can") is now evident. This book, however, took you beyond the "yes," by suggesting the "how" – *how* our programs teach leadership. In this concluding chapter, we share our reflections on how to move forward as educators and pave the path for continued learning about leadership. We broke down the field of leadership studies into three branches – leadership education, leadership training (competency-building), and leadership development. Teaching leadership takes on different characteristics depending on which branch you are pursuing. In reality, the three cannot be neatly separated as discrete objects. As our examples demonstrated, when teaching leadership, educators are constantly stitching all three into a single fabric.

An academic course on "foundations of leadership" can introduce the learner to the basic concepts of leadership, but it can also include a service project that builds teamwork and planning skills. When reflecting on the leadership competencies gained in the project, and making connections to the concepts explored in class, the learners grow and gain leadership insights that translate into "practical wisdom."

The last chapter of this book is designed to emphasize key takeaways from the previous chapter. We recognize that readers will find different aspects of the book more valuable depending on their individual needs. There are a wide variety of leadership programs which focus on different developmental stages of learners' and organizational priorities. In this chapter, we seek to emphasize the priorities that we believe should be common to all educators when teaching leadership.

Commit to the Ongoing Development of Faculty and Staff as Educators

Chapter 5 discussed the need for educators to be self-aware and work to align personal values with behavior. When learners feel confident that this alignment exists, it sets a strong foundation for integrity, authenticity, and transparency. It also opens up a space in which educators can dare to be innovative and can make the changes they see as appropriate in their leadership programming. Learners will support these changes and will trust that the changes are being made to achieve good program outcomes.

In addition to this alignment of behavior, it is important that educators make a profound personal investment in the professional growth and well-being of their learners. Participants observe words and actions, as demonstrated in this quote from a conversation with a graduating student from the Dartmouth Class of 2017:

> It is important for educators to recognize their visibility to students and the attentiveness of learners to their teachers. This may seem obvious when considering a formal educator relationship within a typical classroom but it extends much further. The educator role is constant and permanent. Learners observe how you [educators] interact with your fellow educators and others in your life, the time you dedicate to other learners, the commitments you keep in your work and personal life.

The field of leadership studies is constantly changing and progressing. With regard to leadership education, educators must stay abreast of contemporary research and practice and develop professional development plans to fill gaps in their expertise. This can be addressed by taking advantage of the numerous resources available through leadership associations and conferences. Where budget constraints prevent this type of participation, educators have many more options for continuing their education. One strategy involves forming teams within and across institutions for formal or informal educator development programs. They can be delivered as workshops, webinars, or on-campus meetings. Whatever the format, the programs should be designed and implemented with the same rigor as those developed for students. Technology can also be incorporated as a tool for connecting educators domestically and globally in competency-building around shared interest areas.

Develop and Share Best Practices in Leadership Studies

Higher education is a unique professional arena. Given the stage of development of this field in which we find ourselves, educators should always look for ways to develop new ideas, share those ideas, assist others in problem-solving, and make connections beyond their campuses. They should look to building a spirit of collaboration that transcends intellectual property rights.

Teaching leadership falls under this collaborative spirit. Educators should continually look for best practices and be willing to share innovative ideas that advance the study and practice of leadership. We encourage our colleagues to put this spirit into practice whenever possible. As you develop innovative leadership courses, share your syllabi with the leadership academic community. As you master a particular leadership competency-building workshop, make the program and logistical details available to other institutions. Support your graduates who are working at other institutions and developing their own leadership programs.

As the old saying goes, "What goes around, comes around." As we strive to develop leadership studies as an academic field (explored in Part I of the book) and deepen our offerings of co-curricular activities for a wider audience (Part II), we should get all the help we can find. Ultimately, we are all in the same business of developing the next generation of leaders (Part III) who will tackle the complex challenges that everyone faces in an increasingly interconnected world. In sharing our best practices, we will develop, in Verna Allee's (2003) words, "value networks." In the end, we will all benefit from a little more sharing.

Expand the Learning Environment to Life after Graduation

Programs begin with an understanding of participants' needs and backgrounds. A key consideration is the importance of discussions about intergenerational communication, both in the context of the relationship between educator and learner and as a leadership competency for development. It is important to continuously look for opportunities that allow participants to apply new leadership competencies to situations that draw on concepts of social justice, social responsibility, intercultural competence, and ethics, all of which are areas of emphasis students will face when they step into personal and professional roles beyond campus life.

Ultimately, teaching leadership does not deal simply with the immediate academic requirements of our leadership studies programs, for example fulfillment of credit hours and course requirements. It involves a lifelong commitment to leadership development. In our classrooms, we have the awesome responsibility to spark in our learners a yearning for more knowledge, experience, and wisdom, beyond graduation.

Teaching leadership involves the development of certain habits – what Robert Bellah and his colleagues (2008) called "habits of the heart." Through our leadership programs, we have a rare opportunity to engage our graduates in continuous learning. As James Kouzes and Barry Posner argue, "learning leadership must be a daily habit" (2016, p. 191). In this book, we made several suggestions of ways to engage our alumni. Engagement goes beyond networking events and speaking appearances. We must continue to challenge our alumni to reflect on their professional experiences and create opportunities through which they can mentor someone with less experience and be mentored by those with more experience.

They must derive lessons from their career path that will provide valuable lessons for themselves – and for others. As they seek to grow as leaders, they will also participate in the development of other leaders (the "hidden leaders") within their organizations, and even society in general (Edinger and Sain, 2015).

Create More Rigorous Systems for Assessment and Evaluation

Developing leadership programs is hard work, and educators should build continuous quality-improvement measures into their program, administrative, management, and financial systems and make desired changes in a timely way, as we discussed in Chapter 8. It is essential that educators become proficient in designing and implementing experiential activities which help learners build competencies at the individual, team, and organizational levels to become prepared for the workplace.

With the ever-changing domestic and global landscape, educators need to be "situationally" aware about programs that no longer fit the needs of their learners. This often presents a dilemma. The hardest decision educators will sometimes need to make is to discontinue programs in which they have a personal investment; sometimes less is more. The Inter-association Leadership Education Collaborative recommends that "Innovative research and practice should inform each other. Thus, the goal of our research and practice is not only to clarify, but also question current trends in leadership theory, human development, workplace effectiveness, and educational practices to expand educators' access to resources."[1]

It is the responsibility of scholars and practitioners in leadership education to evolve the field and establish collaborations that are grounded in rigorous research and practice. These create the backdrop for sound leadership programming. Scholars must work with practitioners to document best practices and find ways to share this knowledge. Such partnerships will help to develop more rigorous methods for data collection and the production of evidence-based information. As is often emphasized in leadership education itself, presenting this information in clear and simple language for others should be embraced as a guiding principle. When complex concepts are communicated in unpretentious language, it ensures that information is accessible to all, and particularly to funders.

Consider Institutional Linkages

Educators should look for opportunities to collaborate on leadership programming with colleagues in various parts within the institution. This strategy builds connections between professionals working in the field, it adds to the body of knowledge, and it also extends the reach of programs. Collaborative programs will be most effective if there is a shared set of guidelines that include an agreed-upon goal, a clear definition of the target population for participation, and a clear definition of roles and responsibilities (Kezar and Lester, 2009). Budgetary responsibility and oversight should also be identified early and formalized once the program is conceptualized and ready for implementation. Finally, honest, regular, and timely discussions about strengths and areas of concern are critical in any programming partnership.

Educators in supervisory positions must also develop recognition programs for their direct reports (Fisher, 2015). Formal recognition programs have been shown to build community, make employees feel valued, improve organizational communication, reduce turnover, promote engagement, and lower frustration and stress in the workplace.

Some best practices for incorporating recognition programs include: recognizing people in an individualized manner based on specific results and behaviors; implementing peer-to-peer recognition in addition to top-down recognition; sharing recognition stories; making recognition easy and frequent; tying recognition to your organization's values or goals; and rewarding employees with basic praise and the chance to contribute to decision-making processes. Such practices go a long way in positively impacting employee morale, productivity, and effectiveness.[2] Supervisors of educators must also find ways to lift constraints on their direct reports by setting up flexible systems, procedures, and norms. These types of support structures free educators to be creative and innovative, and to learn from mistakes without fear of reprisal.

Final Reflections

Teaching leadership requires courage, intellectual curiosity, and a sense of mission. On the courage side, educators soon realize when teaching in a leadership program that the field is still in its infancy. It lacks a certain level of legitimacy on many campuses; therefore, it requires courage to embrace this intellectual enterprise as a new "home." We always admire educators who leave established disciplines in order to teach leadership full-time. We suspect that over time these cases will diminish, as our graduate programs will produce the next generation of educators in the field of leadership studies.

The professionalization and institutionalization of the field should not take away the intellectual curiosity that drives leadership studies. The empirical study of leadership may be a century old, but the thirst for knowledge about leadership goes back millennia. What keeps us moving forward is the sense of mission that we all have as leadership educators – the urgency of gaining a deeper understanding of how leadership works, not just for intellectual curiosity, but also for the desperate need that we currently have for more thoughtful leaders.

As educators, we are responsible for advancing the area of teaching leadership. In acknowledging people who helped her when she wrote *Radical Candor*, Kim Scott (2017) suggests that "no book is the work of just one person." She goes on to say: "I'm honestly not sure why we've come to insist on the myth of 'the author.'" Nothing has been truer for us in writing this book and in developing leadership programs. A good idea becomes a great idea with the input and help of many.

In this spirit of sharing ideas and experiences, we close this book with a collection of quotes from our McDonough and Rockefeller graduates.[3] In a way, these quotes reflect the themes of the book: learning about leadership, developing leadership competencies through carefully designed curricular and co-curricular programs, and continuously learning and growing after graduation. These statements capture the impact that we are all making in preparing and developing thoughtful and engaged leaders:

Leadership is learned. I had always thought that leadership was something people were born with – they either have it or do not. Being taught that leadership can be learned transformed the way I thought about my leadership skills and made me want to continually strive to be a better leader throughout my life. It also taught me that all other skills in life can be learned if I am committed. This has greatly expanded the way I view opportunities in my personal and professional life. (Tendai Masangomai)

This is a life-long learning process, but the information that you are gaining now will be a substantial foundation to this process. You will not only be better leaders, but you will be better people. And that will inform your leadership and management choices for the better. And you will make mistakes. Acknowledge them, learn from them, grow from them. (Valerie Byers)

When hearing someone's opinions on cultural issues or courses of action, I take a second to suspend my judgment and think critically as to avoid unfairly judging someone's ideas based on my own cultural and social upbringing. I take note of people's style of communication whether they interrupt or wait and exchange when brainstorming in a group. (George Sy)

[The program] encouraged me to think for myself when presented with many different theories, and I appreciate that now – being able to consume different opinions but ultimately having one myself. I find many people lack the confidence or the capability to do this, and it is one of the biggest advantages gained from the dialogues and debates held in leadership classes. (Lindsay Shuba)

I continue to strive to listen to and understand my coworkers in a way that makes them feel individually valued. This, in turn, has contributed to [the] best office chemistry. I strive to be passionate and driven each and every day, while also staying positive in a competitive, adversarial environment. In addition, because I am a law clerk for a federal judge, I am required to work as a servant-leader. This means that while I must at all times follow my boss's directives (unless they are immoral or unethical, which they never are), I also need to demonstrate leadership amongst my coworkers. This means everything from standing up for what I think is right or, in specific circumstances, the proper application of the law. (Evan Nogay)

As a manager of cross-functional teams in my current work, I was well-prepared in my studies at [the program] to understand my own personal leadership strategy and how to effectively implement and execute to achieve our team's common goals. It has also helped me identify others' leadership and management strategies and enabled me to work well with and under others that may employ practices and strategies that differ from my own management preferences. (Jacqueline Hartle)

I think [the program] prepared me to be an adaptive leader, and to appreciate that different leadership styles are necessary in different situations. In this way, I have better insight into when I am an effective leader to mobilize a group, and when I need to step back and let someone else lead. (Patrick Campbell)

I am currently leading the marketing content team in my company, which is a global leader in claims and productivity management. Leadership training helped prepare me to be able to delegate and coach appropriately as we interact with departments and experts across the company, large and small clients, and those impacted by our business here in the US and across global cultures. (Amy Sagle)

[The program] made me think hard about the nature of leadership and the differing contexts in which leadership can take place. There are some immutable laws of good leadership but much of good leadership depends on the situation around you, be it your team, organization, field, or some wider environmental context. (Welton Chang)

I have found that self-reflection has been the best tool for individual leadership development after leaving college. By taking the time to connect with myself, understand how I am doing as a leader, and determining areas of improvement, I have been able to grow as a person. (Ellen Schott)

As the quotes above make clear, leadership is personal. We thank you for reading this book and hope that it will be useful to you both personally and professionally. Our hope is that it will help you become proficient in teaching leadership and in continuing to evolve your own philosophy of leadership. We live in a century in which leadership development should not be viewed as the luxury of an elite. Rather, global challenges demand (yes, demand) the development of effective leaders and followers. We do not mean to overstate this, but to us teaching leadership is the most critical human need of this century! We wish you all the best!

NOTES

1. Website (https://acui.org/docs/default-source/default-document-library/ilec_final.pdf?sfvr sn=b49a885f_2). Accessed June 1, 2017.
2. Sadhana Hall (2016), Creating Employee Recognition Programs: Rationale, Best Practices, and Recommendations. Report prepared for Dartmouth College.
3. These statements were retrieved from the 2016 alumni survey that the two institutions jointly undertook. Through the survey instrument, the graduates gave us permission to use their names.

REFERENCES

Allee, V. (2003). *The Future of Knowledge: Increasing Prosperity through Value Networks*. Boston, MA: Butterworth-Heinemann.
Bellah, R., Madsen, R., Sullivan, W., Swidler, A., and Tipton, S. (2008). *Habits of the Heart: Individualism and Commitment in American Life*. Berkeley: University of California Press.
Edinger, S. and Sain, L. (2015). *The Hidden Leader: Discover and Develop Greatness within Your Company*. New York: AMACOM.
Fisher, J. (2015). *Strategic Reward and Recognition: Improving Employee Performance through Non-monetary Incentives*. Philadelphia, PA: Kogan Page.
Kezar, A. and Lester, J. (2009). *Organizing Higher Education for Collaboration: A Guide for Campus Leaders*. San Francisco, CA: Jossey-Bass.
Kouzes, J. and Posner, B. (2016). *Learning Leadership*. Hoboken, NJ: Wiley.
Scott, K. (2017). *Radical Candor: Be a Kickass Boss without Losing Your Humanity*. New York: St. Martin's Press.

Index